T0305782

PLATFORM STRATEGIES

Over the past decade, platforms have spread through many industries and generated an increasing share of the global economy. Many of the world's most valuable companies have adopted a platform-based business model and today, we find that platforms pervade our everyday lives. So far, however, the existing management literature has failed to provide professionals and students with appropriate tools to understand the business models that make those platforms successful. This book offers rigorous analysis of the complexity of platforms, as well as practical strategic guidance and tools to help you deal with this complexity.

Written in an accessible style and based on a comprehensive approach, Platform Strategies is self-contained and does not require the reader to have specific prior knowledge. The book is both academically rigorous and a pragmatic and efficient guide, incorporating path-breaking insights from academic research on platforms with real-world applications of concepts and tools. The book engages with case studies and highlights important take-aways that can be implemented in practice. You'll learn how to use new tools of strategic management and how to adapt well-established ones.

This book is an invaluable resource for entrepreneurs (experienced or aspiring), managers of existing platforms and businesses, professionals, and students in business, management, and economics.

Paul Belleflamme is professor of economics at UCLouvain. He is the author, with Martin Peitz, of Industrial Organization: Markets and Strategies (2015) and The Economics of Platforms: Concepts and Strategy (2021).

Nicolas Neysen is lecturer in strategy at HEC Liège (University of Liège), where he also leads the Digital Lab. He holds a PhD in Management Sciences and worked for seven years as a consultant for Accenture.

"This is THE book for anyone interested in founding, growing, or transforming a business into a platform."

Chiara Farronato, *Assistant Professor of Business Administration, Harvard Business School*

"This book is a comprehensive take on the strategies for building platform businesses. It adapts the well-known business theory to the age of platforms and explains the unique characteristics of these businesses using a combination of a theoretical framework and a large set of case examples. Recommended reading for anyone building a platform business."

Juho Makkonen, *Co-founder and CEO, Sharetribe*

"As a co-founder and CEO of a platform, I have found this book very helpful to better understand my business and challenges, even after more than 10 years running a platform.

The book suggests in its introduction that entrepreneurs actually (and maybe regularly) read strategy books to better run their business. I might be an exception, but I'm not sure this is often the case. It certainly isn't my case. Why? Probably for multiple reasons like lack of time or interest or even because entrepreneurs don't even think about it, but I believe that it is mostly because entrepreneurs believe that there is a gap between their reality and what academics think they know about it, too big a gap to get anything useful out of such a book.

Well, I think this book might be the exception! The concepts are laid out in simple terms and the book takes a very practical approach. A must-read for platform entrepreneurs (to be) or for 'traditional' entrepreneurs willing to analyze the opportunity to move towards a platform model!"

Charles-Albert de Radzitzky, *Co-founder and CEO, Spreds*

"A tour-de-force combination of academic insights and practical relevance, *Platform Strategies* is a timely and masterful guidebook on value generation through platform business models."

Michael Zhang, *Irwin and Joan Jacobs Chair Professor, School of Economics and Management, Tsinghua University*

"Belleflamme and Neysen's book uses sharp economic reasoning, sound managerial intuition and evocative examples to create a unique offering in the crowded space of books on the platform economy. Structuring the book around the building blocks of Value Proposition, Value Creation and Value Capture, the authors take the reader through the intricacies of digital platforms and how entrepreneurs can navigate on and around platforms. This book is rigorous, entertaining and it leaves the reader with a host of useful prescriptions on how to thrive in the platform economy."

Tobias Kretschmer, *Professor of Management and Director, Institute of Strategy, Technology and Organization, LMU Munich*

"A fabulous book. Belleflamme and Neysen translate their deep economic expertise into a concise, complete and highly accessible roadmap for launching and growing a platform business. A must-read for any entrepreneur, executive or business student looking to succeed and thrive in the rapidly evolving platform economy."

Arun Sundararajan, *Harold Price Professor of Entrepreneurship, New York University; author,* The Sharing Economy

"Finally! An easy-to-read, pragmatic, and no-nonsense toolbox for entrepreneurs who want to be successful in the booming platform business world!"

Bart De Ridder, *Intelligent Platform Services Lead France & BeNeLux, Accenture*

"With *Platform Strategies*, Belleflamme and Neysen offer us a valuable addition to the ideal library for platform entrepreneurs anywhere. This guidebook is a thorough yet reader-friendly volume, full of actionable principles and examples."

Annabelle Gawer, *Chaired Professor in Digital Economy, University of Surrey; co-author of* The Business of Platforms: Strategy in the Age of Digital Competition, Innovation, and Power

PLATFORM STRATEGIES

A Guidebook for Entrepreneurs in the Platform Economy

Paul Belleflamme and Nicolas Neysen

Routledge
Taylor & Francis Group

LONDON AND NEW YORK

Designed cover image: Getty Images / akindo

First published 2023
by Routledge
4 Park Square, Milton Park, Abingdon, Oxon OX14 4RN

and by Routledge
605 Third Avenue, New York, NY 10158

Routledge is an imprint of the Taylor & Francis Group, an informa business

British Library Cataloguing-in-Publication Data
A catalogue record for this book is available from the British Library

Library of Congress Cataloging-in-Publication Data
Names: Belleflamme, Paul, author. | Neysen, Nicolas, author.
Title: Platform strategies : a guidebook for entrepreneurs in the platform economy / Paul Belleflamme and Nicolas Neysen.
Description: Abingdon, Oxon ; New York, NY : Routledge, 2023. |
Includes bibliographical references and index. |
Identifiers: LCCN 2022048554 (print) | LCCN 2022048555 (ebook)
Subjects: LCSH: Multi-sided platform businesses. |
Strategic alliances (Business) | Strategic planning.
Classification: LCC HD9999.M782 B453 2023 (print) |
LCC HD9999.M782 (ebook) | DDC 338.7—dc23/eng/20221020
LC record available at https://lccn.loc.gov/2022048554
LC ebook record available at https://lccn.loc.gov/2022048555

ISBN: 978-1-138-59070-0 (hbk)
ISBN: 978-1-032-46169-4 (pbk)
ISBN: 978-0-429-49087-3 (ebk)

DOI: 10.4324/9780429490873

Typeset in Joanna
by codeMantra

For my sons, Charles and Marcel, my inexhaustible source of love.

Nicolas Neysen

CONTENTS

ILLUSTRATIONS

Figures

Tables

CASES

PREFACE

The idea of writing this book originated in June 2017, on the heels of a master's thesis defense at the Louvain School of Management. Two students had just presented their project of a digital platform that would connect hockey players and clubs from all over the world, with the idea to organize camps mixing hockey training with language education. As evaluators of the thesis, we were torn between two conflicting opinions. On the plus side, the students came up with an original idea and laid out a comprehensive roadmap for how to design their platform, touching on marketing, operational, and financial issues. On the minus side, although they apprehended the web of interdependences between the users of their platform, they failed to untangle this web in a clear and articulated way. Nevertheless, we could not decently blame them for this shortcoming because they had not been given the right keys: The conventional strategic management toolbox that they used was simply inadequate.

After leaving the two students (with our congratulations and a good mark), we sat ruminating about ways to improve the situation. Those were not the first students – or entrepreneurs, as we realized – who got lost in the intricacies of platforms. And, quite frustratingly, we could not find the appropriate tools to guide them, despite the plethora of books, articles, and blog posts extolling the virtues of platforms.

As Hanif Kureishi wrote, "It's frustration which makes creativity possible." The next day, we began to mull over the outline of a new book. Judging by the number and length of the emails that we exchanged, our frustration must have run deep. It was only matched by our enthusiasm to start working on a common project. Two weeks later, we met for a few days in Aix-en-Provence (where Paul was working at the time). Inspired by the beauties of Provence, we drafted the pitch for our book project. We sent it to Routledge a couple of weeks later.

To be frank, our initial plan for the book was chaotic (maybe, the Rosé wine from Côteaux d'Aix-en-Provence was a bit too inspirational). We wanted to organize our framework around the acronym "P.L.A.T.F.O.R.M.S.". Each letter corresponded to a building block of the framework and was associated with two keywords (like Purpose and Proposition, Linkage and Leverage, or Actors and Affiliation). Fortunately for us, four anonymous reviewers, whom Routledge invited to evaluate our first pages, unanimously told us that a mnemonic with nine letters and 18 words was not likely to assist anyone in remembering anything! Yet, they liked the project very much and encouraged us to go forward. We are extremely grateful for their help. Without their constructive advice, the letters of 'platforms' would have been rearranged into 'smart flop' (yes, we also thought of using anagrams to indicate how to navigate our impossible framework…).

We then decided to follow Thomas Mann's wise words: "Order and simplification are the first steps toward the mastery of a subject." *Order*: The book is now divided into six chapters, organized in a straightforward sequence – value proposition (Chapters 1 and 2), value creation (Chapters 3 and 4), and value capture (Chapters 5 and 6). *Simplification*: We propose simple tools to address the complexities of platforms in a progressive and systematic way. Yet, we do not sweep complexity away because we fully agree with Elif Shafak's advice: "Do not be afraid of complexity. Be afraid of people who promise an easy shortcut to simplicity." The shortcuts that we present in this book are not meant to be easy (some effort is required on your part) but efficient (your investment should be worth it).

We have benefited greatly from the input of students (at Louvain School of Management, Imperial College Business School, Aix-Marseille University, College of Europe, and Sacred Heart University Luxembourg), colleagues (special thanks to Chiara Farronato, Kayvan Lavassani, Daniel Trabucchi, and Jordana Viotto da Cruz), and practitioners (our gratitude goes in particular to Dimitri De Boose, Cédric Goffeau, Benoit Hanzen, Julien Paquet, and Olivier Simons). Finally, we are grateful for the unwavering support of our partners, Catherine and Magali.

Scan this code to access the tools and frameworks presented in the book

INTRODUCTION

Up to recently, few people were accepting rides from – or proposing rides to – absolute strangers. From an economic and social point of view, this situation was unsatisfactory, as assets were not put to their best use: People were traveling in half-empty cars, while other people would have gladly traveled with them. The reasons behind this matching failure were two-fold. On the one hand, a *lack of coordination* explained why demand and supply could not meet: It took hitchhikers a great deal of perseverance and luck to find a driver (or often, several drivers) to bring them to their destination. On the other hand, there was a *lack of trust* between people not knowing one another beforehand: Even if a hitchhiker was heading to a popular destination, along a busy road, they may just be ignored by most drivers or prefer to turn down the offer of the driver who would finally stop.

To try and solve these problems, a French entrepreneur, Frédéric Mazzella, created an online market for hitchhiking in 2006, called CoVoiturage (the French word for carpooling).[1] The website's main role was to coordinate supply and demand: An algorithm was matching people looking for rides

DOI: 10.4324/9780429490873-1

with people offering rides, while all these people were comfortably sitting at home. Although the site attracted many users, it eventually flopped because the trust issue had not been addressed properly. Both sides of the market were largely unreliable, with passengers not showing up and drivers overbooking or canceling offers at the last minute.

Drawing the lesson from this first venture, Mazzella revamped CoVoiturage by introducing a reciprocal rating system (whereby passengers can evaluate drivers and drivers can evaluate passengers) and making advanced online payment compulsory (to reduce no-shows and cancellations). With these two additional features (and a new name, BlaBlaCar), the platform quickly became a huge success: In 2021, the BlaBlaCar community had 100 million members worldwide, including 20 million in France (and more members joined in 2022 because of the explosion in fuel prices).

Platforms: what are they?

A definition

To start off on the right foot, we must define clearly what we mean by 'platform'. BlaBlaCar is the prototypical example of the platforms that we are going to study in this book. It exploits the following business opportunity: Individuals or organizations would benefit by interacting more with one another, but they fail to do so because they cannot afford the costs of organizing this interaction by themselves (costs of finding one another, coordinating their needs, achieving trust, etc.). By reducing these costs and acting as an intermediary, the platform is in a position to create value for all the participants (and for itself, if it is the objective). Moreover, the platform's value tends to increase with the number of participating users. In the BlaBlaCar example, passengers find the platform more attractive if more drivers join it and vice versa, as more win-win matches can be achieved. This is a manifestation of so-called *positive network effects*: The value of the interaction increases with the number of participants. It is by leveraging positive network effects that platforms create value for their users.

Given this description, we choose to define a platform as follows: *A platform is an entity that brings together economic agents with complementary needs and facilitates interaction among them.*[2] To do so, a platform deploys strategies to reduce the transaction costs that users must bear to interact (that is, costs related to search, matching, coordinating, contracting, building trust, etc.) and to add value to the interaction by leveraging network effects (for instance, through rating and review systems, payment services, data analytics, etc.). The platform operates a physical or virtual infrastructure, via which the interaction among users takes place.

Depending on whether users have the same or different interaction objectives, they are said to belong to the same or different groups (or 'sides'). Accordingly, a distinction is made between *one-sided* platforms (like social networks) and *two-sided* (or *multi-sided*) platforms (like those connecting hitchhikers and drivers, buyers and sellers, employers and employees, etc.). As we will discuss later, choosing the number of sides – that is, which users to connect and how – is a major decision for platform operators.

> **A platform is an entity that brings together economic agents with complementary needs and facilitates interaction among them.**

A platform economy

Over the past decade, platforms have spread through many industries and generated an increasing share of the global economy. The five names that spring to mind are Apple, Alphabet (Google), Microsoft, Amazon, and Meta (Facebook, Instagram, WhatsApp). These companies, which occupy the top of the list of the world's most valuable companies, have adopted a platform-based business model, either from the very start or at some later stage. Very large platforms also exist in the China-dominated part of the world; think of Alibaba, Tencent, Baidu, or Xiaomi.

These platforms pervade our everyday lives. Just take this book as an illustration. You may have bought it on Amazon, after having heard of it on some Meta's social network, or searched for it through Google search engine; if it is an e-book version that you bought, you may be reading it on an Apple or Microsoft tablet; also, the original manuscript was produced using a famous Microsoft software on an Apple MacBook by one author and a Microsoft-powered PC by the other author.

Despite the dominance of a few giant platforms, many smaller platforms manage to thrive. In the European Union, for instance, it is reported that over 10,000 digital platforms are in operation. Most of them are small and medium-sized enterprises.[3] If you ambition to swell their ranks, continue to read this book!

Most – but not all – platforms are digital

The rapid development of digital technologies and the increased adoption of smartphones have vastly expanded the scope of value creation and capture for platforms. Digital technologies allow platforms to reduce transaction costs substantially, manage network effects more actively, and add value to the interactions.

Even if the vast majority of platforms are, nowadays, digital platforms, the reality of platforms is centuries-old. One can say that the concept of a platform was born as soon as someone had the idea to organize a market in a town square, attract merchants and farmers on one side and city dwellers on the other, and invite them to engage in some form of exchange. Indeed, this description meets all the characteristics of our definition. First of all, a location identified and recognized by all as a central place is delimited: The marketplace in front of the church. The date and time are set to ensure a sufficient number of participants and, thus, increase the chances of doing business: Every first Saturday of the month. Finally, the whole organization is supervised: The public authority delimits and rents slots, manages access at the city gates, ensures the safety of participants, levies taxes on goods, etc.

Not all digital business solutions are platforms

As 'platform' has become a catch-all term, it is important to clarify what our definition *does not* encompass. In particular, not all digital business solutions relying on a digital infrastructure should be called a platform, at least in the way that we hear the word. For example, a company launches a webshop to engage in e-commerce; another company develops an intranet portal to ease access to corporate information for its employees; a hospital develops a mobile application allowing patients to book medical appointments, etc. Although these organizations would probably advertise their new solution as a 'platform', we prefer not to call them so. As solutions of that sort do not put users in contact with one another, the value that they create for their users is largely independent of how many users adopt them. That is, network effects are missing.

In contrast, the platforms that we consider in this book are, in essence, *managers of network effects*. They primarily act as intermediaries, not as merchants, resellers, or service providers, as we now explain.

> **Platforms are intermediaries whose primary role is to manage network effects.**

Platforms versus pipelines

It is clear from our definition that platforms *enable* transactions. That is, they create value by facilitating the interaction between different groups of external and independent participants. In contrast, traditional organizations create value by transforming 'inputs' into 'outputs', relying on resources and assets that they own. Such organizations are commonly known as 'pipelines' because they *control* transactions in a linear way.[4] In other words, platforms set up an infrastructure through which service providers and consumers can interact to exchange goods and services, whereas pipelines produce or resell the goods and services, and deliver them to the consumers.

> **Platforms enable transactions while pipelines control them.**

Relative merits

We observe that platforms and pipelines coexist in various sectors of the economy. Typical examples are Uber and Lyft versus taxi companies for short-distance mobility in many cities, Airbnb versus hotel chains in the short-term accommodation sector, or BlaBlaCar versus SNCF or Air France for long-distance travel in France. Such a competition between platforms and pipelines suggests that there are competitive advantages and disadvantages to enabling or controlling transactions.[5] In general, platforms fare better than pipelines in terms of *motivation* and *adaptation*. That is, by giving independent suppliers greater control, platforms can rely on the suppliers' motivation to meet the consumers' needs. Because suppliers are in direct contact with the consumers, they are also in a better position to spot changes in the demand and adapt their products or services accordingly.

In contrast, pipelines fare better than platforms in terms of *coordination*. By maintaining direct control over important aspects, such as product variety, advertising, prices, or responsibility for order fulfillment, pipelines coordinate better decisions that generate spillovers across products or services (for instance, if selling more of one product contributes to increasing the demand for another product).

To sum up, platforms do not provide products or services directly by themselves, but they do so indirectly by facilitating the interaction between those who make and those who consume (or those who co-create when the value comes from matching users). By leveraging network effects, platforms make the quality of the interaction grow organically. Yet, a potential downside, compared to pipelines, is the loss of control over part of the operations, which increases the risk of seeing users served below their expectations. The chief strategy officer of Alibaba Group, Ming Zeng, calls this the 'control paradox' of building a platform: On the one hand, "command-and-control has become a dominant way of thinking for most businesses"; yet, on the other hand, "[b]eing a platform means you must rely on others to get things done, and it is usually the case that you do not have any control over the 'others' in question."[6]

Not an either-or situation

While platforms and pipelines are quite different models, they are by no means incompatible. Some companies successfully combine the two models. Other companies travel the platform-pipeline spectrum in one or the other direction. The idea is to leverage the strong points of the two models according to the specificities of different activities or changing circumstances. Here are some examples.

Amazon is the most well-known company with a hybrid 'pipeline/platform' model. Amazon started as an online reseller of books and CDs (a pipeline model) and, only later, opened its infrastructure to third-party sellers by creating the Amazon Marketplace (a platform model). Recently, Amazon reinforced its pipeline position through the successive acquisition of Whole Foods Market (2017) and Metro Goldwyn Mayer (2021). These acquisitions turn Amazon into, respectively, a brick-and-mortar reseller of groceries and a movie producer. Arguably, Amazon can perform these activities more efficiently as a pipeline than as a platform.

Many companies that start as pure platforms choose to include some pipeline aspects into their operations at some stage of their development, as illustrated by Deliveroo, a food-delivery platform. The company started as a pure platform by connecting independent restaurants to diners via its ordering and delivery services. Yet, it quickly realized that its model was malfunctioning in urban areas in which restaurants are in short supply. In reaction, Deliveroo decided to build its own network of so-called 'Editions kitchens' to prepare food for delivery-only customers in these areas. In a similar move, Airbnb tries to grow its supply by partnering with real estate investors to turn housing buildings into Airbnb-friendly apartments that can host a combination of long-term tenants, long-term stays, and short-term trips.[7]

The move from a pipeline to a platform is also possible. Traditional companies can consider opening up to the platform model without necessarily questioning their core business or their founding principles. For instance, they can launch a new business unit that enables transactions instead of controlling them, without affecting the rest of their activities. This is what Marriott International did in 2019 when it decided to launch the 'Homes & Villas' program, offering 2,000 luxury properties worldwide. This new activity, which includes rentals managed by third-party companies, was a clear move to compete with Airbnb and similar platforms in the booming short-term rental sector.

It appears thus that there is no reason to oppose the platform and the pipeline models. Instead of facing an either-or situation, firms can consider a whole spectrum of possibilities, ranging from a pure pipeline business to a pure platform business. Between the two extremes, there is a richness of hybrid business models, which differ in the degree of control that the firm maintains over transactions. The possibility to navigate along this spectrum calls into question a principle dear to the advocates of the value-based theory of the firm. According to this theory, it is the possession of rare, hard-to-imitate, and non-substitutable strategic capabilities that allows a company to develop a sustainable competitive advantage. In contrast, platforms demonstrate that success can be achieved without owning any critical resource or differentiated asset but by connecting those who own such resources or assets.

Between the 'pure pipeline' and the 'pure platform' extremes, there is a richness of hybrid business models that differ in the degree of control that the firm maintains over transactions.

'Platformization'

By moving along the pipeline/platform spectrum, firms choose the level of 'platformization' that best suits their business. Platformization can be seen as the addition of platform-like elements to a pipeline. By 'platform-like', we mean that the new elements add value to the existing business by enabling interactions among external stakeholders (mainly suppliers, customers, and contractors). The objective is to add value by leveraging the network effects that result from the interactions.

Platformization can be achieved in two main ways.[8] The first method consists in encouraging interactions among existing customers, thereby inducing them to co-create value. One common way is to propose a review and rating (R&R) system whereby customers share information about the products or services that the pipeline offers. Positive network effects arise because the quality of the shared information increases with the number of participating customers. Coming back to the example of Amazon, the introduction of an R&R system was the company's first move away from its initial pipeline (reseller) model.

The second platformization method consists of opening the doors to independent third parties. This is what Marriott International did with its Homes & Villas program, which lets third parties manage rentals. The manufacturers of video game consoles also followed this strategy. Initially, they sold their console along with a set of games produced in-house; their business was thus fully integrated. It is only later that they opened the doors to third-party game developers. Network effects then resulted from the interactions between gamers and game developers. As participation grew in one group, the console became more attractive to the other group.

> Pipelines can be 'platformized' by encouraging interactions among existing customers and by opening the doors to third parties.

What is this book about?

What we do

Reid Hoffman, a co-founder of LinkedIn, once proposed the following metaphor: "Building a startup is like jumping off a cliff and assembling an airplane on the way down. Building a company is like assembling a

Cessna. Building a marketplace is like assembling a Boeing 747" (quoted in Lu, 2019).

Our objective with this book is twofold. First, we want to make sense of Reid Hoffman's analogy by explaining the number of ways in which platforms are complex and, as a result, harder to conceive, launch, and operate than other businesses. Second, we aim at providing you with a strategic guide to help you deal with this complexity. Hopefully, the rigorous analysis and practical tools that we present in this book should allow you to assemble a well-functioning airplane before you hit the ground.

> **"Building a startup is like jumping off a cliff and assembling an airplane on the way down. Building a company is like assembling a Cessna. Building a marketplace is like assembling a Boeing 747" (Reid Hoffman).**

You may ask why a specific guide is needed. After all, we are surrounded by a multitude of platforms, whose modes of operation are so largely commented that they become common sense. Moreover, strategic management academics and practitioners have developed a set of compelling models and frameworks to guide decision-makers in a large variety of environments.

Even if there is some amount of truth in these arguments, we beg to disagree on two counts. First, as someone once wrote, common sense is what tells us the earth is flat.[9] We mean here that the platform-based business model turns out to be much more challenging than it may appear at first glance. Second (and this is a direct consequence of the first point), the well-known tools of strategic management look rusted and inadequate when it comes to assisting decision-making in the platform economy. We believe thus that a new strategic toolbox is necessary to apprehend correctly the ins and outs of the platform-based business model. Of course, we do not mean to throw the baby out with the bathwater. The well-established tools (like the value proposition canvas or Porter's Five Forces) will stay, although they will have to be dusted, fixed, or reshaped. On top of that, we will forge brand new tools like the 'Linkage Map' for instance, which you will soon discover.

We also believe that this new toolbox is the distinguishing feature of this book. There is no shortage of good books about platforms out there.[10] These books will certainly entertain you with a rich variety of interesting examples and case studies (mostly success stories). Yet, it is not clear whether these books will teach you anything useful for your practice. Examples and cases are valuable if they lead to clear and meaningful lessons, which one can then transpose to different contexts. It is our contention, however, that such a transposition can hardly be made without using a proper set of tools and methods.

What we do not do

In the interest of transparency, we find it important to also indicate what this book is not about. First, this book is not intended to replace more comprehensive strategy or marketing manuals. Platform operators are faced with a whole series of questions, unknowns, and challenges. Most of those are common to any type of organization but some are specific to platforms. It is this set of platform-specific issues that this book focuses on. The book should, therefore, be seen as a complement to more general strategy books. That is, we propose new approaches wherever we believe that the complexity of platforms requires it. For the rest, the existing theories and tools remain entirely valid.

Second, the book is not meant as a practical guide that addresses technical issues (for instance, how to develop a digital platform infrastructure using this or that programming language). To find answers to these important questions, we refer you to the MIS (Management of Information Systems) section of your favorite bookshop. Our guide is positioned further upstream in the implementation of a platform. It deals with strategic rather than operational choices. In other words, our objective is to help you formulate an articulated business model for your platform (well ahead of developing a mock-up of its technical implementation).

Who is the book for?

This book is primarily intended for entrepreneurs (experienced or aspiring) who contemplate developing a platform-like venture by facilitating interactions and managing network effects among individuals or organizations. We believe that this book will allow entrepreneurs to ask the right questions at the right time and provide them with an adequate toolbox to address these questions systematically and productively. Of course, this book will not provide them with a ready-made recipe and a guarantee of success thanks to it (only charlatans would claim such things). Our goal is rather to make entrepreneurs understand where and why they could fail. As Warren Buffet once said: "Risk comes from not knowing what you are doing." With the rigorous analyses and the tools that we propose in this book, we believe that entrepreneurs should have a better knowledge of what they are doing and, thereby, limit the risk of failure.

The book is also of interest to two other types of managers. First, managers of existing platforms may want to take a critical look at past decisions and inform their new choices to optimize the growth of their business. Second, managers of existing pipelines may find the inspiration for the platformization of some aspects of their business. The tools that we propose should also allow these entrepreneurs and intrapreneurs to structure their thoughts.

Finally, the book is aimed at students in management and economics. In MBA and pre-experience master's programs, it can serve as the main text for a dedicated course on the management of platforms or as a complementary text for more general courses in Strategy, Entrepreneurship, or Innovation Management. It can also serve to acquaint bachelor students in various disciplines with the specificities of the platform economy, whose economic significance and ubiquity are growing by the day.

How is the book organized?

Approach

The book is self-contained and does not require any specific prior knowledge (although some background in management or economics may facilitate the understanding of some concepts). Throughout the book, we blend academic rigor with a no-nonsense approach. On the one hand, we incorporate the path-breaking insights from the academic research on platforms, which has burgeoned in economics and management science over the last 20 years; a list of selected references to these two strands of literature appears at the end of each chapter; we also propose further readings. On the other hand, the book is conceived as a pragmatic and efficient guide, which is written in a readable and jargon-free style. To facilitate the understanding of the concepts and tools, we illustrate them with a large number of real-world applications, which we formulate as short 'cases'. We also highlight the important take-aways from our analysis (as we already did in this introduction). Each chapter is articulated around a list of key questions, which are stated at the start of the chapter and answered in a few sentences at its end.

Our philosophy can be summarized by three keywords, all starting with the letters 'HUM'. First, there is humility. We do not propose recipes for success, just well-thought-out tools that should help you avoid the many traps that platforms have in store for managers. Second, there is humanity. Unlike many strategy books that envision business as a zero-sum game and use military metaphors to expose their arguments, we insist on the positive-sum game aspect (win-win) of platform businesses. Also, our strategic guide is as suitable for commercial for-profit platforms as it is for pro-social non-profit platforms. Third, there is humor. Although we provide you with serious analyses, frameworks, and models, we do not want to take ourselves too seriously (a very Belgian trademark). We have done our best to make the exposition as brisk and lively as possible. Writing this book was great fun for us and we hope that it will also be fun for you to read it! Having fun does indeed generate network effects. As Anthony Burgess once declared: "Laugh and the world laughs with you, snore and you sleep alone."

Outline

This book is composed of three parts and each part is divided into two chapters. The three parts follow a very logical sequence: value proposition, value creation, and value capture.

Part I of the book is concerned with the *value proposition*: What sort of value does the platform propose to its users? Because interactions are key for platform users, platforms cannot propose value on their own but must combine forces with their users. It is then crucial for platform operators to identify and understand the various types of network effects that may be at work among their users. To this end, Chapter 1 clarifies the concepts and proposes a new tool – the *Linkage Map* – to describe the network effects that a platform can manage. Knowing how users will affect one another allows then the platform to design its value proposition, that is, to state clearly and simply the benefits that it will provide its users with. Chapter 2 explains why this exercise is both trickier and riskier for platform businesses and presents a dedicated tool – the *Multisided Value Proposition Canvas* – to help managers deals with these difficulties.

Part II is concerned with the *value creation* process, which consists in translating the value proposition into a concrete offering for the platform's potential users. As a preliminary step, the platform must gauge the external factors that may either improve or damage its chances of creating value successfully. To perform a competitive analysis that fits the specificities of platforms, Chapter 3 extends existing tools to develop a more suitable one – the *Platform Value Net*. Then, as platforms co-create value with their users, the prerequisite for value creation is to convince users to join the platform. Yet, this is easier said than done as users accept to join the platform only if they expect other users to do so as well: A conundrum known as the 'chicken-and-egg' problem. Chapter 4 describes three generic strategies to address this problem and a specific tool – the *Lever Selector* – to determine which strategy is the most efficient to launch the platform given the circumstances.

Finally, Part III tackles the *value capture*. Value has been proposed and created; now it is time to capture it. That is, once the platform is launched, ways must be found to monetize the services offered to the users. Chapter 5 analyzes two main monetization strategies. The first strategy is to let users pay for the value they get on the platform; yet, pricing is tricky because the value for each user is conditional on the participation of other users. To deal with this complexity, the concept of *leverage-based pricing* is developed and an organizing tool – the *Platform Pricing Matrix* – is proposed. The second strategy consists of onboarding advertisers on the platform and making them pay for the attention (and, potentially, the personal data) of the primary users of the platform. Finally, Chapter 6 sheds light on the challenges facing platforms that are up and running – establishing trust among platform users, designing retention strategies to counter the risk of platform leakage, choosing an appropriate growth path, and monitoring the platform's activities in an informative way. To help you perform the latter task, we introduce one final tool, the *Multisided Balanced Scorecard*.

Online resources

A companion website – www.platformstrategies.org – provides supplementary resources. It allows you to download (for free!) blank versions of the various canvases proposed in the book. It also gives you access to a bank of case studies (which will be restocked regularly) and teaching resources (slides, readings, and videos). As actions speak louder than words, we hope to turn this website into a platform that promotes the sharing of knowledge about platform strategies. Your contribution is, of course, more than welcome!

Notes

1. For a more complete account of the story, see Botsman (2017).
2. Our definition follows what Gawer (2014, p. 1241) refers to as the *economics perspective* on platforms, which "posits that platforms fundamentally create value by acting as *conduits* between two (or more) categories of consumers who would not have been able to connect or transact without the platform." Gawer (2014, p. 1243) contrasts this view with what she calls the *engineering design perspective* on platforms, which "interprets platforms as purposefully designed technological architectures (including interfaces) that facilitate innovation."
3. EU Observatory on the Online Platform Economy website, September 2021 (https://platformobservatory.eu/).
4. See, for example, Van Alstyne *et al.* (2016).
5. We follow here Hagiu and Wright (2019).
6. See Zeng (2015).
7. See RentalScale-Up (2022).
8. For more, see Hagiu and Altman (2017) and Hagiu and Wright (2021a, 2021b, 2021c). The authors discuss a third platformization method, which consists in going down the value chain by creating interactions between the firm's customers and these customers' customers. Arguably, this method can be applied by a smaller set of businesses than the other two.
9. This quote is often attributed to Albert Einstein, although other sources contend that it should be attributed instead to the economist Stuart Chase.
10. As you may have already read some of these books, the fact that you are currently reading these lines means that you are still hungry to learn more – or differently.

Bibliography

Botsman, R. (2017). *Who can you trust? How technology is rewriting the rules of human relationships*. New York: Public Affairs.

Gawer, A. (2014). Bridging differing perspectives on technological platforms: Toward an integrative framework. *Research Policy* 43(7), 1239–1249. https://doi.org/10.1016/j.respol.2014.03.006.

Hagiu, A. and Altman, E.J. (2017). Finding the platform in your product: Four strategies that can reveal hidden value. *Harvard Business Review* 95:4, 94–100. https://www.hbs.edu/faculty/Pages/item.aspx?num=52837.

Hagiu, A. and Wright, J. (2019). Controlling vs. enabling, *Management Science*, 65:2, 577–595. https://doi.org/10.1287/mnsc.2017.2956.

Hagiu, A. and Wright, J. (2021a). Product-to-platforms (Part I). *Platform Chronicles* (February 9). https://platformchronicles.substack.com/p/product-to-platforms-part-i?s=r.

Hagiu, A. and Wright, J. (2021b). Product-to-platforms (Part II). *Platform Chronicles* (February 23). https://platformchronicles.substack.com/p/product-to-platforms-part-ii?s=r.

Hagiu, A. and Wright, J. (2021c). Product-to-platforms (Part III). *Platform Chronicles* (March 9). https://platformchronicles.substack.com/p/product-to-platform-part-iii?s=r.

Lu, D. (2019). Not all marketplaces are created equal: Tales of a marketplace founder. Hackernoon (January 13). https://hackernoon.com/not-all-marketplaces-are-created-equal-tales-of-a-marketplace-founder-9fc0fb802706.

RentalScale-Up (2022). How Airbnb wants to unlock the next generation of Hosts (March 29). https://www.rentalscaleup.com/airbnb-unlock-the-next-generation-of-hosts/.

Van Alstyne, M.W., Parker, G.G., and Choudary, S.P. (2016). Pipelines, platforms, and the new rules of strategy. *Harvard Business Review* 94(4), 54–62. https://hbr.org/2016/04/pipelines-platforms-and-the-new-rules-of-strategy.

Zeng, M. (2015). Three paradoxes of building platforms. *Communications of the ACM* 58(2), 27–29. https://cacm.acm.org/magazines/2015/2/182646-three-paradoxes-of-building-platforms/fulltext.

Part I

VALUE PROPOSITION

1

UNDERSTANDING AND ACTIVATING NETWORK EFFECTS

KEY QUESTIONS

- What are network effects and why do they lie at the heart of platforms?
- Why is it important to map the network effects that are at play on the platform?
- How can network effects be activated?
- What is a 'positive feedback loop' and why should a platform aim at triggering it?
- Why are users' expectations so critical for platforms?

As explained in the introduction, platforms can create value by linking economic agents (individuals or organizations) when, on the one hand, these agents can benefit from interacting but, on the other hand, they fail to organize the interaction by their own means. A common driver lies behind these two conditions: *network effects*. Roughly put, network effects arise when

DOI: 10.4324/9780429490873-3

economic agents enjoy benefits that depend on the decisions of other agents. Network effects are positive if the value of the interaction for every participant increases when more agents participate in the interaction. For example, if more users connect to a social network, there is more content to be shared, which makes the social network more valuable for each participant.

Yet, network effects also make the interaction harder to organize because, when making their decisions, economic agents generally fail to consider the effects that their decisions have on other agents (they create what economists call 'external effects'). It is then likely that although all agents would find the interaction valuable if it were to take place, none of them is sufficiently motivated to set the interaction in motion on their own. This is precisely where platforms can make a difference. First of all, by bringing participants on board, platforms make them realize the value that they generate for one another. Second, by deploying the right strategies at the right time (we will indicate how in the next chapters), platforms reduce a variety of transaction costs and, thereby, help participants coordinate their needs and facilitate their interaction. In a nutshell, platforms create value by managing network effects.

Obviously, it is not possible to manage network effects properly without having a correct grasp of the concept. Therefore, we start this chapter by giving a general description of network effects and their different types. We then propose a simple tool, called the 'Linkage Map', to identify systematically the various network effects that are (or could be) at work on a platform. Finally, we pave the way for the next chapters (which deal with value proposition, creation, and capture) by explaining how to activate network effects and make them generate autonomous and long-lasting consequences for the platform and its users alike.

> **Network effects arise when economic agents enjoy benefits that depend on the decisions of other agents. Platforms create value by managing network effects.**

What are network effects?

In many situations, economic agents do not value a product or a service for its own sake but for its ability to let them interact with one another. The prototypical example is the 20th-century version of the telephone, which was valuable insofar as it allowed its users to call and be called. Obviously, a telephone is perfectly useless for anyone unless there is potentially somebody else at the other end of the line. Some would say that it takes two to tango but, in fact, the more dancers there are, the merrier: The value of a telephone service grows with the number of its subscribers, as the communication possibilities increase for everyone. This is even truer for the modern version of the telephone. Even if they allow us to do far more than just calling or being called, smartphones – or, for that matter, their operating system (OS) – also become more valuable the more they are adopted.

You may be reading these lines on your smartphone right now and you may then think that your device is valuable irrespective of you being linked to anyone else. But if you think further, you will understand that the application that you are using to read this text is available (probably for free) precisely because your smartphone is popular. In this case, your smartphone is valuable because it serves as an intermediary (a platform) between end users and application developers. Here, network effects take a slightly different form: As a smartphone attracts more users, developers are keener to write apps that are compatible with the OS of that smartphone, which makes the smartphone more attractive for users, and so forth.

The smartphone example is illustrative of the two basic types of network effects, called *same-side network effects* and *cross-side network effects*. The term 'side' refers to the idea that in many environments, it is possible to sort out economic agents into distinct 'sides' (or groups) according to their role in, or their benefit from, an interaction. Think for instance of buyers and sellers in a trade situation, or employers and job seekers on a job board. The distinction between the two types of network effects has thus to do with the scope of the effects: Do they arise among users belonging to the same side or different sides? To draw the line between the two types of network effects in the context of a platform, we need to answer the following question: Does one user's decision as to whether and how much to interact on the platform affect the platform's value for other users on this users' own side or another side? In the former case, one talks of *same-side network effects*. In the telephone example, one additional subscriber generates a positive same-side network effect for the other telephone subscribers (as they can now communicate with one more person). In the latter case, one talks of *cross-side network effects*. In the smartphone example, one additional participant on each side – end users and app developers – generates a positive cross-side network effect for the participants in the other group (users benefit from a wider array of apps; app developers enjoy a larger potential market for their product).

As soon as a platform links distinct groups of users, it is called a *two-sided platform* (if there are just two sides) or a *multi-sided platform* (if there are more than two sides). Choosing how many sides to link is a major strategic decision for platforms, as we will discuss at length in the next chapters. As we made clear in the introduction, it is misguided to consider that platforms are necessarily two-sided or multi-sided. An organization that targets a single group of users and actively manages the same-side network effects that exist among these users is also a platform. Think, for instance, of Facebook in its early years when the social network focused on allowing students to interact, without any connection to advertisers or producers of content. This being said, it would be equally wrong to consider that two- or multi-sided platforms only manage cross-side network effects: As we show below, many of them do also manage same-side network effects. Finally, even if the examples we took so far suggest positive network effects, it must be kept in mind that negative network effects can arise as well, as we show in Case 1.1.

Case 1.1 Traffic-routing apps and network effects: a bumpy ride

Road congestion is the prototypical example of negative same-side network effects: Because traffic becomes slower when the road gets busier, each additional car makes driving conditions worse for other cars. In contrast, traffic-routing applications like Waze, Google Maps, or INRIX are supposed to generate positive same-side network effects: The larger the community of users, the better the service, because information about traffic conditions becomes more accurate and algorithms can be improved. But is it really so? Recent research suggests that the benefits of these apps may crucially depend on the number of their users.[1] When this number is small (as was the case in the early days), users can quickly reroute and beat the traffic, while non-users benefit too, as roads are globally flowing better. Yet, as the user base grows larger, it is feared that these applications may deliver smaller and smaller benefits to both users and non-users or, worse, become counterproductive.

While the impacts of the growing use of routing apps for traffic systems as a whole have not been properly evaluated yet, evidence already exists of increased stress put on local side roads. That is, if too many users try to avoid the same traffic jam by using the same alternative route, congestion is just displaced from one point to another, resulting in negative network effects.

One of Yogi Berra's famous quips perfectly sums up what is going on here: "No one goes there nowadays, it's too crowded." The question that naturally arises then is: Where do they go instead?

A crucial consequence of network effects, irrespective of their form, is that platform users care about the participation and the usage decisions of other users when they make their own decisions. In other words, the decisions of platform users are interdependent.[2] This means that any strategy that a platform designs to influence the decision of some users will also affect, through the network effects, the decisions of other users. It is thus critical for a platform operator to start by identifying the sources, the direction, and the intensity of the network effects that are – or can be – at play on the platform. We now propose some guidelines to conduct this assessment.

> **Network effects make the decisions of platform users interdependent.**

Drawing the Linkage Map

Given the importance of network effects for the users whom you aim to bring together, an essential preliminary step is to understand how your future users are likely to affect one another when being active on your platform. In particular, you need to answer the following basic question: *When an extra user joins the platform (or increases their activity level on the platform), do they make the platform more or less valuable for other users?* To refine the analysis, it is useful to separate the other users according to whether they belong to the same group as the extra user under consideration or another group. The idea is to distinguish the same-side network effects (how the extra user affects their fellow users) from the cross-side network effects (how the extra user affects users in other groups).

We propose a simple tool, the 'Linkage Map', to help you identify and understand the various network effects that exist on your platform (and, when relevant, beyond it). As you can see in Figure 1.1, the Linkage Map for a two-sided platform invites you to fill three different kinds of boxes[3]:

- The four boxes on the top-left are concerned with the various types of network effects that are at play on the platform;
- The box on the right deals with 'hidden' network effects, that is, network effects that are exerted by groups of agents that are not (or not yet) active on the platform;
- The box on the bottom has to do with the platform's external effects, that is, the way the platform affects other stakeholders than its own users.

We now explain what is to be recorded in these boxes, as well as the underlying thought process. To help you understand better, we take the case of Airbnb as an illustration. (If you want to draw the Linkage Map for your platform project, go to www.platformstrategies.org to download a blank version.)

Identifying network effects at play on the platform

The top-left corner of the Linkage Map contains four boxes. Each box corresponds to a different type of network effect: Two boxes cover cross-side network effects (from the group on the left of the platform to the group on the right, and vice versa), and two boxes cover same-side network effects (within the group on the left, and the group on the right). For each box, we invite you to follow a two-step procedure:

1. The first task is to indicate (in the top-right corner) the 'sign' of the network effects: Are they positive (+), negative (−), or negligible (∅). As explained previously, network effects are positive if an extra user adds value for other users, negative if an extra user reduces value, and negligible if an extra user leaves the value (almost) unchanged.

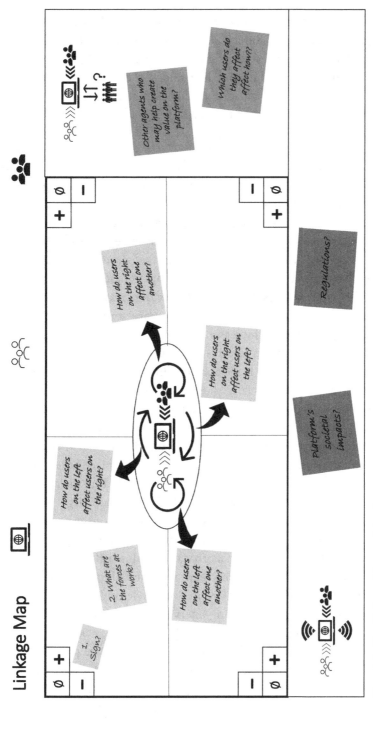

Figure 1.1 The Linkage Map explained.

2. The second task is to identify the mechanisms whereby an extra user adds (or reduces) value for other users. The question here is *how and why* does this extra user increase (or reduce) value for other users on the platform? Or, rephrasing, how and why do other users benefit (or suffer) from the participation of this extra user? If the effect is negligible, it is also important to explain why.

To describe how to fill in the four boxes, we take Airbnb as an illustrative case (see Figure 1.2). As it stands at the time of this writing, Airbnb connects two groups of users: hosts (whom we put on the left) and guests. We start with the *cross-side network effects from hosts to guests* (left to right). Recall that the question here is: *How does the participation of an extra host affect the way guests value the platform?* You will agree with us that it positively affects guests. Thus, to complete Step 1 (*Sign?*), we record a '+' in the corner. As for Step 2 (*How and Why?*), we simply observe that, on average, guests value the platform more highly when it gives them access to a wider array of accommodations to choose from. We wrote 'on average' because some guests may attach more value than others to increased variety; that is, they may *receive* differently the cross-side network effects that hosts exert upon them. What some guests appreciate in Airbnb is the ability to find all sorts of accommodation in all sorts of places (especially those places that lack traditional hotels); those guests put, therefore, a lot of value on any additional host joining the platform. Other guests, in contrast, may be happy with a limited supply of hosts because they travel repeatedly to the same destination or because they quickly tire of comparing options. These guests then place little or no value on extra hosts. The value may even be negative if they find the platform less convenient to use when the menu of options grows too large. Noting differences of this sort is not essential at this early stage of the analysis. But it may be wise to consider them later when designing strategies. For instance, one may want to deal with the fact that users value differently the participation of other users by providing them with more flexibility in how they use the platform. This is what Airbnb does by letting guests define their search options as they see fit, using filters or 'wish lists'.[4]

Moving clockwise, we look at *same-side network effects among guests* (within the right side). We mark a '+' at Step 1: These effects are positive, that is, guests welcome the presence of an extra user in their group. To answer Step 2, the main reason is the following. As reliable information about the

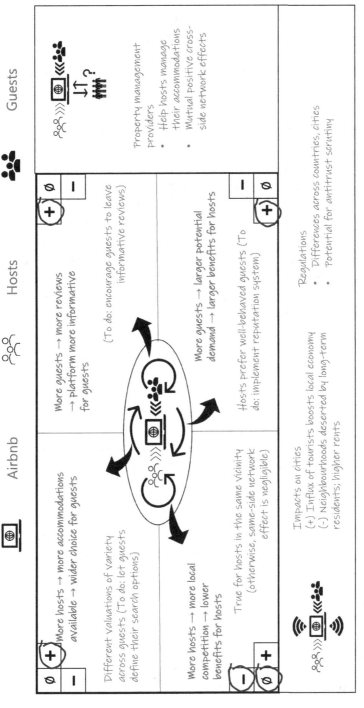

Figure 1.2 Airbnb's Linkage Map.

quality of accommodations and hosts is scarce, guests rely on the reviews written by other guests to make their choices; as more guests join the platform, better-informed choices can be made. Again, anticipating the design of strategies, we observe that platforms like Airbnb activate this sort of effect by encouraging users to leave informative ratings and reviews (we study the design of rating and review systems in Chapter 6).

We consider next the *cross-side network effects from guests to hosts* (right to left). Clearly, guests exert a positive cross-side network effect on hosts – that is, hosts welcome the presence of an extra guest on the platform (so, we record a '+' at Step 1), because an extra guest expands the potential demand for any host (the how and why at Step 2). Here again, this is an average trend. When discussing strategies later, you may refine your analysis by examining how these cross-side network effects may differ across users. In the present case, the profile of the extra guest is likely to matter. Hosts will indeed benefit more from a well-behaved guest than from someone who would, for instance, damage their property. Rating and review systems are also useful to address this issue. Thanks to these systems, hosts get to know the 'reputation' of each guest (which somehow summarizes their past behavior on the platform), while returning guests are encouraged to behave correctly.

Finally, let us move to the *same-side network effects among hosts* (within the left side). A nuanced answer is in order here. Starting with the why and how, we argue that competition among hosts can be a source of negative same-side network effects, but only among hosts in the same vicinity. To take an example, a host in city A (say Anchorage, Alaska) is much more concerned if Airbnb proposes one additional accommodation in this city than in some other city B (say Brussels, Belgium). That is, from the point of view of a host in A, another host in A generates a negative same-side network effect, whereas another host in B generates no same-side network effect whatsoever. The answers to Steps 1 and 2 would then be as follows: Same-side network effects on the hosts' side tend to be negative (hosts suffer from the presence of some other hosts) because *local* competition gets fiercer (with a clear emphasis on the word 'local').

The latter analysis may surprise you. At first glance, you may have thought (as some of our students do) that same-side network effects among hosts are positive. Isn't it true that as a host, I should welcome an extra host in my city because they contribute to making my city more attractive for guests, which is ultimately good for me? This is indeed true. Yet, what is described here is not a positive same-side network effect, but a chain of two positive cross-side network effects (an extra host attracts more guests and, in turn, more guests make hosts better off). Is this hair-splitting? No, because it is crucial to disentangle the various effects at work to design appropriate strategies.[5] For instance, a platform may want to control more directly the composition of a group of users to regulate the competition that exists among them. To the best of our knowledge, Airbnb has chosen not to go this route: Any host is welcome to register with Airbnb, whatever the level of competition in their vicinity.[6]

In sum, to draw the Linkage Map properly, you need to focus on the effects of having one extra user joining the platform, *while assuming that all other variables are held constant* ('ceteris paribus', as the Latin phrase goes). This method is borrowed from economics; the purpose is to put the finger on the effect of a single variable at a time. Naturally, the other variables are not constant in the reality (otherwise, they would not be called 'variables', would they?). Typically, if one user joins the platform, they are likely to lead other users to follow suit, who may attract yet other users in turn. This generates a so-called *feedback loop*. As we argue later, feedback loops are our main object of interest. What we want to stress here is that you cannot understand feedback loops – let alone act upon them – if you do not disentangle first the various effects that fuel them.

Uncovering 'hidden' network effects

The right box of the Linkage Map motivates you to uncover network effects that are not apparent at first glance. These 'hidden' network effects involve agents who are not directly connected to the platform, but whose actions are, nevertheless, of importance for some users on the platform. In the case of Airbnb, think of those providers of 'property management services' (such as cleaning, laundry, key exchange, booking management, etc.) who help hosts to manage their accommodation. In any given city, hosts and property management providers exert positive cross-side network effects on one another as they both benefit from each other's presence.

So, even if property management providers do not register with Airbnb, their presence and their actions affect the hosts' decision to join the platform and, thereby, affect Airbnb's business. This other group should therefore appear somehow on Airbnb's Linkage Map. Otherwise, the Linkage Map would not play its role, namely to help the platform figure out how to create and capture value by leveraging network effects. With this group positioned on the Linkage Map, the platform can examine the ins and outs of partnering with some actors in this group on some ad hoc basis (we refer here to the notion of 'complementors' that we develop in Chapter 3) or, more radically, of onboarding this group on the platform (as we will discuss in more details in Chapter 6).

In the short-term accommodation sector, platforms have made different choices in this regard. As for now, Airbnb is receptive to the group of property management providers but does not manage it directly; all it does (since 2015) is to list service providers in the 'Host Assist' section on its website. In contrast, HomeAway (another vacation marketplace) is more active: It suggests to its users some 'preferred' property managers, with whom it has a formal relationship.

As a further illustration, Case 1.2 describes how Lego, the Danish toy production company, uncovered hidden network effects and how it chose to manage them.

Case 1.2 How Lego weathered the Mindstorms storm

The Lego Group is probably not the company that springs to mind when talking about network effects and platforms. However, the following story shows that Lego was brought, somehow against its will, into a platform business model for one of its toys.

The toy in question is *Mindstorms Robotic Invention System*, a robotic set allowing users to program behavior into the bricks.[7] To Lego's great satisfaction, Mindstorms quickly gained popularity after its release in 1998. But to its great surprise, the enthusiastic adopters were not the 12-year-olds for which the toy had been designed but instead, grown-up geeks. This was not a problem as such until some of these geeks deciphered the code of the Mindstorms software and shared it on the Internet. A community of hackers started then to publish new advanced software for the Lego robots. From there on, network effects kicked in: As the software improved, Mindstorms attracted more users, and among them hackers, who contributed to improving the software even further. The value of the toy started thus to grow with the size of its user base.

Clearly, Lego did not anticipate these network effects. Yet, it had to decide what to do about them. The first option was to stop the network effects altogether by enforcing its intellectual property over the software (that is, by suing the hackers). This option was quickly rejected as it amounted to killing the golden goose: The more flexible and powerful the software, the more bricks Lego was able to sell; and who was in a better position to develop the software than the users themselves? Instead, Lego preferred to adopt a 'hacker-friendly' attitude. They embraced the group of hackers while controlling it at the same time. To do so, Lego made its software open source and encouraged users to submit their own adjustments, which the company later approved or even integrated into the official version of the robotic kit.

Even today, Lego's Mindstorms kits remain among the best programming education tools for young people who are passionate about robotics.

Gauging external effects

When you operate a platform, your focus is naturally on the users of the platform and the network effects that exist among them. This is indeed by exploiting these network effects that you can create and capture value. The previous boxes are designed to get you started in this direction. Now, even if other effects that the platform may induce for non-users are of second order, it may be worth paying some attention to them. This is the objective of the bottom box of the Linkage Map.

Take the Airbnb example once more. Studies show that the increased popularity of Airbnb (and other short-term rental platforms) generates important external effects in many cities: Some effects are positive (the influx of tourists benefits the local economy) while other effects are negative (neighborhoods are deserted by their long-term residents and rents tend to rise). Even if these external effects do not impact the platform business directly, they may do so indirectly via the reaction of regulatory authorities, whose mission is to preserve the common good. In the short-term rental sector, the list of restrictions that cities impose around the world is as long as your arm.[8] Similarly, when traffic-routing apps divert too many cars to local streets (see Case 1.1), municipalities sometimes take counteractive measures to protect the residents who live there.

In the previous examples, the regulatory interventions aim at limiting negative effects. The same logic may drive authorities to encourage the development of platforms that generate positive effects for the community. Take the example of 'smart cities', which use digital technologies to enhance the quality and performance of urban services. Smart cities often follow an open data strategy: They let third parties freely access and use their data sets to help them create new services for their citizens. Platforms may then seize this opportunity to start their business.

If your platform grows larger, it may also fall under the scrutiny of competition (antitrust) authorities. As we will discuss later, the feedback loops that positive network effects generate may lead to 'winner-takes-all' situations: On a particular market segment, a single platform ends up attracting most of the potential users, leaving no (or little) business to competing platforms. Competition authorities will then monitor closely the conduct of such dominant platforms to make sure that the competitive process is not endangered. Take, as evidence, the various investigations and cases that competition authorities around the globe opened against the largest digital platforms (Google, Amazon, Facebook, Apple, or Alibaba). You may never reach the size of these giants, but you should nevertheless be aware that strategies that are deemed legitimate for 'small' platforms may no longer be permitted for 'large' platforms.

In a nutshell, regulatory interventions end up framing the operations and performance of platforms. It would thus be short-sighted to ignore this kind of repercussions when designing the platform strategy. The first step in this direction consists in gauging the external effects that the platform may generate for other stakeholders than its own users. This is the type of information you will use to complete the bottom part of the Linkage Map.

> The Linkage Map helps you identify network effects at play on the platform, uncover hidden network effects, and gauge external effects.

Activating network effects and exploiting feedback loops

Now that the Linkage Map is drawn, you have a good idea of who can affect whom, and how, on your platform (and beyond). We wrote 'can affect' because the network effects that you identified are still virtual: They tell you what *would* happen if an extra user joins the platform. So, a prerequisite for network effects to materialize is that users do indeed join the platform and interact on it. This depends on the strategies that you will deploy, as a platform operator, to activate the network effects. In this section, we give a glimpse of these strategies (we will be more specific in the next chapters). We also explain how chains of network effects generate feedback loops and with which consequences.

How to activate network effects?

We defined platforms as managers of network effects. Obviously, if network effects remain virtual, there will be nothing to manage. So, your first job as a platform operator is to activate the network effects. That is, you must find ways to attract users to the platform and allow them to interact as smoothly as possible.

Attracting users to the platform will be the focus of Chapter 4. As interacting with other users is the main reason to join a platform, we will see that the main way to attract some users is … to attract other users! We will then endeavor to answer the following two crucial questions: Which users should be attracted first and through which strategies? Coming back to the example of Airbnb, it appears that the founders focused initially (that is, around 2009) on the host side: "The founders supported their hosts by uploading photos that showcase the properties. They also guided the hosts on how to create the best homestay experience."[9] So, the founders thought that it was more effective to use hosts as 'baits' to attract guests than the other way round. They also figured out that hosts needed some help to be attracted to the platform (and also for guests to find them attractive).

Making users interact repeatedly is another challenge that platforms must take up. In the next chapter, we will prompt you to identify the jobs that users will try to get done when joining your platform, the benefits they expect from these jobs, as well as the difficulties they may experience before, during, or after getting these jobs done. To address your users' needs, desires, and fears and manage network effects in a fluid and efficient way, you will have to take on one of several of the following functions:

- *Discovery and matchmaking.* You need to provide users with effective tools to find their 'match', that is the other user(s) they want to interact with. This can be done by equipping your website or app with a powerful search engine and adequate filters.
- *Trust building and risk mitigation.* Once users are matched, they still need to trust each other sufficiently to interact or conduct a transaction. Recall the story of *CoVoiturage* that we told in the introductory chapter. Although this ride-sharing platform facilitated the matching between passengers and drivers, it failed to take off because too many users could not be trusted. *BlaBlaCar*, created on the ashes of *CoVoiturage*, remedied this problem by introducing a two-sided rating and review system. By encouraging users to assess one another, such systems improve users' information about whom they may interact with and, thereby, mitigate uncertainty and risk. We return to these issues in Chapter 6.
- *Transaction facilitation.* Once users are matched with other users they can trust, you may want to facilitate their interaction, in particular when it involves a transaction (that is, the exchange of a product or a service against some compensation). You can then think of providing users with services such as payment, security, logistics, dispute resolution, record-keeping, booking management, etc.

> **Platforms activate network effects by accomplishing three essential functions: discovery and matchmaking; trust-building and risk mitigation; transaction facilitation.**

As indicated previously, platform-like intermediaries have been performing these essential functions for a long time. For instance, the count of Champagne (in France) began hosting trade fairs around ad 1180. Merchants and financiers from all over Europe joined because the count had managed to create a safe and reliable environment for trade, mainly by selecting participants, enforcing contracts, and resolving disputes.[10]

At that time, such a 'market design' process required considerable power and authority, which was very costly to acquire and exert. Nowadays, the rapid development of digital technologies has vastly broadened the scope of value creation for platforms. Digital technologies allow platform operators to cut into the costs of performing the three essential functions: for instance, AI-powered algorithms, search engines, and recommender systems facilitate matching, rating and review systems generate trust among anonymous users, while online payment and transaction monitoring systems make transactions smoother.

From active network effects to feedback loops

Go back to the Linkage Map of Airbnb that we detailed previously. Recall that the cross-side network effects among hosts and guests are positive in both directions: Hosts are better off when additional guests join the platform and vice versa. The participation of an extra user generates thus a *positive feedback loop*, that is, a self-enforcing process that magnifies the initial change: More users in group A attract more users in group B, who attract in turn more users in group A, and so on so forth.[11]

> **When combined, positive cross-side network effects between two groups of users create a positive feedback loop.**

This is the sort of self-reinforcing mechanism that a platform wants to initiate and fuel. Once value is created, positive feedback loops make it grow with little or no additional effort; in a sense, value is multiplied for free. Two metaphors are often used to describe this process. The first metaphor that comes to mind is a *snowball*. You need some energy to press snow into a small ball and push it from the top of the slope; then, as the ball rolls downhill, it takes on more snow, grows larger, accelerates, takes on even more snow, and so forth. That is, without any additional energy, the ball "grow[s] quickly in size and importance" (which is how the Cambridge Dictionary defines the verb 'to snowball'). The second metaphor is the *flywheel*, which the Cambridge Dictionary defines as "a heavy wheel in a machine that helps the machine to work at a regular speed." Peppler (2019) usefully complements the definition by stressing the following (emphasis added):

> *[i]t takes a lot of effort to get [a flywheel] started*, but once it starts to turn there are counterweights around the outside of the wheel that start to take effect and *it starts to build momentum almost by itself. From that point, the same effort can be placed on the flywheel and it will start to turn faster and faster.*

One way to evaluate how fast a positive feedback loop spins is to measure the time it takes for a particular platform to reach a given number of users. Here is how fast several technologies and applications that exhibit network effects hit 50 million users: telephone (75 years), radio (38 years), television (13 years), World Wide Web (four years), iPod (three years), Facebook (two years), Instagram (19 months), YouTube (ten months), Twitter (nine months), Angry Birds (35 days), Pokemon Go (19 days).[12]

As we already noted, there is a period before and a period after the Internet (and digital technologies in general). Before the Internet, network effects were rather slow to materialize because they were relying on the development of costly physical infrastructure and support systems (cables, switchboards, antennas, etc.). Nowadays, the global development of the Internet provides other digital technologies and applications with the necessary infrastructure for harnessing network effects at unprecedented speeds. 'Domino effects' are also at work: social networks would not exist without the Internet, nor smartphones without the telephone, and Angry Birds or Pokémon GO would not have become viral so quickly without the combination of social networks and smartphones.

Understanding feedback loops and their consequences

Now, let us not paint too rosy a picture and take these metaphors literally. First, both the snowball and the flywheel may make you believe that once the process is set in motion, it becomes irreversible. This is unfortunately incorrect: Feedback loops may also be negative. Second, it is wrong to think that as a platform operator, you can set the snowball or the flywheel in motion on your own; in fact, you rely on the combined efforts of the first users, who will not show up unless they believe that other users will share the workload with them; hence, the expectations that users form about other users' behavior are crucial.

Negative feedback loops

If things can spin fast in one direction, they can spin equally fast in the opposite direction. The combination of positive cross-side network effects between two groups of users also implies that if users on side A *leave* the platform, then users on side B will also be incited to leave, which will induce more side-A users to leave, and so on so forth. That is, negative feedback loops are the mirror image of positive feedback loops.[13] If positive loops allow you to gain users with little or no effort, negative loops make these users hard to retain. This demonstrates that *timing* is of the essence for platform management. Not just because success depends on making the right decisions at the right time (this holds for any business). But because the self-reinforcing nature of network effects dramatically amplifies the consequences of any decision (right *and* wrong) and, also, narrows down the windows for making the right decisions.

The power of expectations

Feedback loops heavily depend on users' expectations. For a positive feedback loop to get underway, new users have to join the platform on some side (say side A). But new side-A users will join only if they believe that they will be able to interact with side-B users. The problem is that potential side-B users may make the exact same reasoning: They will join only if side-A users join.[14] This situation may lead to two opposite outcomes, depending on which expectations users form about participation on the other side of the platform. On the one hand, users may have *optimistic expectations*: They believe that users on the other side will join and, as a result, they decide to join as well. On the other hand, they may have *pessimistic expectations*: They believe that no user on the other side will join and, consequently, they do not join either. This unfortunate outcome has been given several figurative nicknames, namely chicken-and-egg problem, cold start, or ghost town.

The remarkable thing is that, in both cases, what is expected turns out to be right. When participation is expected, participation does indeed take place; the reverse happens when it is not expected. The existence of these so-called 'self-fulfilling prophecies' stresses how critical it may be for platforms to find the right way to manage users' expectations. We will obviously come back to this issue in the next chapters. For now, we note in Case 1.3 that self-fulfilling prophecies are a real-life phenomenon and not just the product of a twisted theoretician's mind.

Case 1.3 The importance of expectations for a platform's take-off

Through a field experiment, Boudreau (2021) empirically estimates the role that expectations about the future size of a platform may play in the initial growth of that platform. Messages were sent to more than 16,000 potential users, inviting them to join a newly launched platform. The invitations included an indication of the current size of the platform, as well as randomized statements about its expected future size. The analysis of the decisions to join the platform following these invitations indicates that expectations do play a crucial role. Boudreau makes indeed two major observations. First, adoptions were significantly more affected by statements regarding the expected rather than the current number of users. Second, statements of a larger expected installed base caused more adoptions than did statements of a smaller expected installed base. This empirical evidence suggests that expectations can be self-fulfilling indeed.

> **Users' expectations as to the participation of other users give rise to self-fulfilling prophecies.**

Implications for value proposition, creation, and capture

We close this chapter by commenting briefly on the implications that network effects and feedback loops have for the management of platforms. In terms of *value proposition*, the main insight that we can draw from this chapter is that the value that users derive from a platform is heavily interdependent; in the presence of positive network effects, the value for each user grows with the number of users (or, more generally, with the intensity of interaction on the platform). This interdependence may make it difficult for entrepreneurs to formalize their business idea into a strong value proposition. In Chapter 2, we propose tools to deal with this difficulty.

Regarding *value creation*, one of the major findings of this chapter is that a great deal of the value is co-created by the users themselves, with the platform acting as a facilitator. The good news is that positive feedback loops generate 'free value'; the bad news is that pessimistic expectations may impede the creation of value altogether. By formulating a strong value proposition, you will generate positive expectations about the future development of your platform, a prerequisite to creating value. Another condition to create value is to differentiate from the competitors and take advantage of complementary forces that exist in the market. To help you in these tasks, we will assess, in Chapter 3, the competitive environment of platforms. We will revisit the traditional vertical view of the firm (squeezed between its suppliers and customers, and struggling with its competitors), arguing that when it comes to platforms, 'suppliers' and 'customers' are often misnomers, and complementors also need to be included in the picture. We will also examine the conditions under which network effects can be used to gain a long-lasting competitive advantage. In Chapter 4, we will focus on the strategies for launching a platform to overcome the curse of pessimistic expectations and ignite positive feedback loops.

Finally, as far as *value capture* is concerned, we will see how network effects shape the entire range of platform strategies. As values for different users are interdependent, so are the price and non-price strategies that are targeted to these users (Chapter 5). As negative feedback loops are just around the corner, establishing trust among platform users is a prerequisite for value creation and consolidation; similarly, retaining users is a major issue; finally, sustained growth supposes the continuous exploitation of network effects, either by adding more sides to the platform or by expanding the scale and scope of the platform, strategies that raise yet other challenges (Chapter 6).

> **Through their implications for value proposition, creation, and capture, network effects set platforms apart from other businesses.**

SHORT ANSWERS TO THE KEY QUESTIONS

- *What are network effects and why do they lie at the heart of platforms?* Network effects arise when the users of a solution (product, service, platform, ...) care about the participation and usage decisions of other users when taking their own decision. Network effects are positive if the value of the solution for each user increases the more users there are. Because network effects make users' decisions inter-dependent, they raise coordination issues among users. Platforms can then create value by bringing users together and managing net-work effects among them.

- *Why is it important to map the network effects that are at play on the platform?* As value on a platform is co-created by users, it is crucial to understand how they affect one another when interacting on the platform. The sign and sources of both cross-side and same-side network effects must be identified. It is also useful to look beyond the platform to uncover hidden network effects and gauge external effects on other stakeholders than the platform users.
- *How can network effects be activated?* Platforms activate network effects by bringing users together and accomplishing three essential functions: discovery and matchmaking; trust-building and risk mitigation; transaction facilitation.
- *What is a 'positive feedback loop' and why should a platform aim at triggering it?* A positive feedback loop describes a self-reinforcing mechanism, fueled by positive network effects, whereby users attract more users, who attract even more users, and so on. By triggering a positive feedback loop, a platform can let value grow organically, with little additional effort.
- *Why are users' expectations so critical for platforms?* Network effects imply that the value users attach to a platform depends on the par-ticipation of other users. As a result, users will decide not to join a platform if they expect no other user to join. For a platform to start, it is thus necessary that users form optimistic expectations about the participation of other users.

FURTHER READINGS

Despite its age, Chapter 7 (Networks and Positive Feedback) of Shapiro and Varian (1999) still provides readers with a remarkable introduction to network effects in the digital economy. More mathematically oriented readers will find in Belleflamme and Peitz (2018), a systematic and for-mal analysis of network effects in markets with platforms.

Notes

1. See Madrigal (2018).
2. It is in this sense that users are said to form a 'network', whence the term 'network effect'. Whether this network is based on physical connections (like phone lines), or virtual ones (like friendship links over a social network) is secondary.
3. If you add sides to the platform, you also add boxes to fill in. If your platform only has one side, then the picture becomes much simpler (as you only have same-side network effects to consider); yet precise identification of the sources of network effects remains important.
4. For instance, a guest looking for personal contacts will not put much value, if any, on additional 'commercially-oriented' hosts joining the platform. As they can filter accommodations when they search the platform, such guests face a higher chance to find like-minded hosts by selecting a 'private room' ("*Have your own room and share some common spaces*") or 'Shared room' ("*Stay in a shared space, like a common room*") instead of an 'Entire place' ("*Have a place to yourself*") or a 'Hotel room' ("*Have a private or shared room in a boutique hotel, hostel, and more*"), as described on Airbnb.co.uk (last accessed February 12, 2021).
5. Hosts on Airbnb face a typical situation of what Brandenburger and Nalebuff (1996) call 'co-opetition', which reflects the coexistence of cooperation and competition. Hosts cooperate to 'make the pie grow' (more hosts attract more guests, which is good for all of them) but compete to 'divide the pie' (each host's slice of the pie gets smaller as more hosts are present). Many platforms connecting sellers and buyers exhibit the same phenomenon.
6. In contrast, in the online education sector, platforms like EdX or Coursera initially accepted any proposition of MOOCs (Massive Online Open Courses) by universities or individual professors. But, as their offering became imbalanced, they started to refuse new MOOCs in more populated fields, while they encouraged MOOC creation in less populated fields.
7. We follow here Keegan (2001).
8. Airbnb is well aware of all this and has adjusted its strategy accordingly. As Ovide (2020) writes:

> the company has devoted a lot of its attention to cities and regulators that are concerned it is making neighborhoods and communities worse. In the

financial document for its stock offering, Airbnb included several pages of explanation of multiple cities' restrictions on Airbnb listings and the company's efforts to "promote responsible home sharing" and "healthy" tourism.

9. See Rabang (2019).
10. See Fisman and Sullivan (2016).
11. Same-side network effects also play their role. For instance, in the case of Airbnb, the positive feedback loop tends to be *accelerated* by the positive effects within the group of guests (as more guests, and the reviews they write, make the platform more attractive for other guests) but potentially *decelerated* by the negative effects within the group of hosts (because of local competition).
12. See Dadson (2017) and Noakes (2018).
13. We slightly abuse the term here, as a negative feedback loop is usually defined as a process whereby the effect of an initial change is dampened.
14. The same reasoning applies to platforms that cater to the needs of a single group of users (and thus manage positive same-side network effects); here, users must form expectations about the participation of other users in their group.

Bibliography

Belleflamme, P. and Peitz, M. (2018). Platforms and network effects. In Corchon, L. and M. Marini (Eds). *Handbook of game theory and industrial organization*. Cheltenham, Northampton MA: Edward Elgar.

Boudreau, K. (2021). Promoting platform takeoff and self-fulfilling expectations: Field experimental evidence. *Management Science* 67(9), 5953–5967. https://doi.org/10.1287/mnsc.2021.3999.

Brandenburger, A. and Nalebuff, B. (1996). *Co-opetition*. New York: Broadway Business.

Dadson, S.A. (2017). Reaching 50 million users: The journey of Internet and non-Internet products. TechToday-Medium. https://medium.com/techtoday/reaching-50-million-users-the-journey-of-internet-and-non-internet-products-7a531d36f4ea.

Fisman, R. and Sullivan, T. (2016). Everything we know about platforms we learned from medieval France. *Harvard Business Review*, March 24. https://

hbr.org/2016/03/everything-we-know-about-platforms-we-learned-from-medieval-france.

Keegan, P. (2001). Lego: Intellectual property is not a toy. Business 2.0 (September).

Madrigal, A.C. (2018). The perfect selfishness of mapping apps. The Atlantic (March 15). https://www.theatlantic.com/technology/archive/2018/03/mapping-apps-and-the-price-of-anarchy/555551/.

Noakes, S. (2018). 50 million users: How long does it take tech to reach this milestone? Posted on LinkedIn on February 8 (2018). https://www.linkedin.com/pulse/50-million-users-how-long-does-take-tech-reach-milestone-simon-noakes.

Ovide, S. (2020). Airbnb's biggest problem. *New York Times* (November 17). https://www.nytimes.com/2020/11/17/technology/airbnb-troubles.html.

Peppler, L. (2019). The amazing flywheel effect. Medium. https://medium.com/swlh/the-amazing-flywheel-effect-80a0a21a5ea7.

Rabang, I. (2019). The Airbnb startup story: An odd tale of airbeds, cereal and ramen. Bold Business. https://www.boldbusiness.com/society/airbnb-startup-story/.

Shapiro, C. and Varian, H.R. (1999). *Information rules. A strategic guide to the network economy.* Boston MA: Harvard Business School Press.

2

CO-CREATING VALUE WITH PLATFORM USERS

KEY QUESTIONS

- What sort of value does a platform propose?
- Why is it so important for a platform to formulate a compelling value proposition?
- For whom should the value proposition of a platform be formulated?
- Are existing value proposition canvasses adapted to platforms?
- How many value propositions should be formulated: One or several?

Now that we have a better understanding of network effects, it is time to dive into the first step of this entrepreneurial journey, namely the design of a strong value proposition. The concept of value proposition is credited to Lanning and Michaels (1988), who defined it as "a clear, simple statement of the benefits, both tangible and intangible, that the company will provide". More than a simple slogan, a value proposition is a well-thought expression of the reasons and motivations that bring

DOI: 10.4324/9780429490873-4

customers to prefer a given product or service over existing alternatives in the market.

Designing an effective value proposition turns out to be both riskier and trickier for platform businesses than for other businesses: *Riskier* because if the value proposition is not clearly laid out, the business may simply not take off; *trickier* because the aspirations of various groups of users need to be carefully blended. This chapter aims to help you rise to the challenge. We return first to the basic questions that you need to answer, namely 'Why?', 'What?', and 'To Whom?'. After stressing that answering the why (that is, stating the platform's mission) necessarily comes first, we discuss the specificities of platform businesses regarding the other two questions. We then propose a specific tool – the '*Multisided Value Proposition Canvas* (MVPC)', to assist you in identifying, in a systematic way, how your platform can meet the needs of its users. Finally, we show how to use the canvas to phrase a compelling value proposition statement for your platform.

Why? What? To Whom?

The Why comes first

When telling about their idea, many entrepreneurs start describing what the platform is about: How easy it will be to register, how user-friendly the interface will be, how much valuable information you will access, how fast you will get a successful match, and so on. All this is fine of course, but these entrepreneurs miss the most important thing: the purpose. As is the case for any type of business, it is usually easier to answer the *What* and the *To Whom* questions than the *Why* question. Yet, if people do not understand *why* your new solution is needed and makes a lot of sense (the purpose), they will generally not care about *what* you are proposing and *to whom* (the value proposition).

Before conveying your value proposition, you should first let people know about the purpose. People need to understand the journey your mind took, from the initial observation – "something doesn't work well here!" – until the conclusion and your decision to do something about it – "a platform could easily fix this!". They need to follow your reasoning because if they do not agree on the purpose, they will not be convinced by the solution either.[1]

The absence of a strong purpose is much more worrying for a platform than for a pipeline business. For the latter, a weaker purpose will translate into lower sales and revenues, but eager users will allow the product to persist; it is not because sales are lower that the intrinsic value of the product is reduced. In contrast, the value that users attach to a platform crucially depends on the participation of other users; that is, if fewer users are attracted to the platform in the first place, then the value of joining the platform becomes even lower for future users, starting the type of negative feedback loop that we described in the previous chapter. Consequently, it is the very existence of a platform that may be in danger if its purpose is not strong enough! In other words, while consuming a traditional product is generally an individual decision, interacting on a platform is by nature a collective process. So, the presence or absence of a significant purpose means 'More or Less' for a pipeline, but 'All or Nothing' for a platform.

> **The presence or absence of a significant purpose means 'More or Less' for a pipeline, but 'All or Nothing' for a platform.**

Although what we just wrote may sound a little scary, we want to persuade you that this knife-edge situation may also turn into an incredible opportunity (and so, that it is worth your while to continue reading this book!). Indeed, by giving a clear purpose and by convincing potential users of the raison d'être of the platform, you may generate positive expectations that will greatly facilitate the launch of the platform. As explained previously, these positive expectations may generate 'self-fulfilling prophecies': If people believe that your project will succeed, then chances are high that it will actually do.

In sum, it is crucial to think carefully about the purpose of your proposed solution and to make sure that users perceive correctly your vision. If you fail, your project is stillborn, as illustrated in Case 2.1. But if you succeed, your platform may snowball (a positive feedback loop) thanks to the network effects generated by the first participants that you managed to convince.

Case 2.1 Why Zillionears failed

In the business press and management books, you are much more likely to find accounts of successes than failures. Although this is perfectly understandable, this is also regrettable, as there is often a lot to be learned from managers who are brave enough to explain why their business did not fare as well as they hoped.

Among those managers is Jordan Nemrow, who exposed honestly the reasons behind the failure of Zillionears, the startup he founded. We reproduce here a few excerpts of a post that he published (Nemrow, 2013). As illustrated in the parts that we emphasize, the purpose of his startup was not really thought through (it was more like wishful thinking). As a result, the purpose was poorly conveyed to the potential users. Worse, users eventually formed a totally wrong perception of what the platform was about. You can thus take what the founders of Zillionears did as an example of what you should *not* do.

> The product was a flash sale platform for musicians to release their music using dynamic pricing (zillionears.com). To us, this software was a no-brainer for musicians to use. The artists get to engage their fans while enticing their community to share with friends. So we talked to *a few* artists who said they thought it was a cool idea. BOOM! Our idea had been validated! After that moment *we basically stopped talking to artists for a year* and built (and rebuilt) the software until we thought it was acceptable.
>
> [...] there was our main problem. Our market demographic was musicians, and although a few of us had worked around the industry, we concluded recently *we were not music SALES domain experts.*
>
> [...] *people didn't really LIKE anything about our product.* No one that used the service thought it was that cool. In fact, some people that participated in the sale didn't even like our "dynamic pricing" system.
>
> [...] Finally, the day came for our second beta (which was totally gonna kick ass for sure). The artist we had on board set up his sale page and was ready to go. Only problem is *he totally misunderstood what our software was all about.*

Value co-creation

Once the purpose (*Why*) is clear, it is crucial to building a value proposition (*What* and *To Whom*). The question is: *What kind of value does your platform bring to users and the market?* The answer to this question has to be formalized into the value proposition (VP), that is, a convincing expression of the appeal of a product or service to customers, usually integrated into the sales force and the advertising message. This statement should be strong enough to convince people that they will enjoy greater value by participating in the platform than not.

Platforms fundamentally differ from pipelines in the way they create value. From a traditional value chain perspective, value is created by the firm that owns the manufacturing or assembling process of a product or a service. Through the successive operations (sourcing, design, build, distribution, etc.), the value grows incrementally along the chain, which is controlled by the firm. The fact that the outcome matches the initial value proposition is the entire responsibility of the firm. In other words, even if the firm relies on subcontractors and partners, it has full ownership over the offering that is delivered to the clients and over its ability to capture value by setting a price that makes the business profitable.

Things are different for platform-based businesses. There are two sources of value to consider. On the one hand, the platform generates value by creating an optimal matching environment. This value is mostly independent of what is being transacted. Actually, a platform exists mainly because it enables transactions among users at a lower cost than in a decentralized setting. As explained previously, platforms reduce search and transaction costs through various features and mechanisms. In the end, users value using the platform because of the convenience it provides them with (large choice, user-friendly interface, automated processes, trusted actors, etc.).

On the other hand, there is the value assigned to the underlying object of the transaction. Here, the platform has much less control as it does not provide the services or the goods by itself; it relies instead on a group of independent third parties. Take the example of Kickstarter. This crowdfunding platform allows entrepreneurs to raise funds from a large number of small investors (also called 'backers'). The value that backers attach to a given project featured on the platform depends on the project (innovativeness, fit with the backer's needs, etc.) and on the entrepreneur proposing it (communication skills, robustness of the business plan, etc.); even if the platform plays an important role by selecting which projects to feature, it can hardly influence the venture's success rate over time.

> **Because platforms do not control transactions but simply enable them, they co-create value with their users.**

To be successful, a platform must combine both sources of value: A great matching environment (the platform operator is in charge) and a transacted object that meets users' respective needs (the platform users are in charge). Against this backdrop, it seems logical to consider platform users as co-creators of value rather than pure value consumers. Even in the absence of a so-called transacted object, participation in a platform is a source of value creation. Because of users' voluntary activity on social media for instance – writing posts, sharing pictures, commenting on news, etc. – value is generated in the form of audience and data, which are respectively valued by advertisers (the higher the traffic on your platform, the higher the willingness of advertisers to target your visitors) and brands (more data enable consumer profiling and improve the brands' marketing strategies).

In comparison with the manager of an integrated business (a pipeline), you, as a platform operator, will necessarily lose some degree of control over value creation. However, by selecting wisely the users and leveraging the power of cross-side network effects, you can count on extra value, which you could not have generated on your own as a pipeline manager. This reinforcing process is the positive feedback loop that we described in the previous chapter: The value created by the first users makes the platform more attractive for other users who, in turn, generate more value and so on, so forth. If you manage to initiate this process, then the value will flow organically.

Connected user groups

Now that you have a better understanding of how value is created on a platform, you may feel equipped to formulate your value proposition. However, before doing so, you need first to identify who you want to target with this proposition, that is, who your customers will be. This may look like a plain and easy question; yet, as we now argue, platforms add a layer of complexity that deserves some further thinking.

For a traditional business, the two most important outside stakeholders to interact with are the client (who buys and consumes your product or service) and the supplier (who provides you with the resources that are required to build or assemble that product or service). They both represent two distinct points on a linear value chain within a given industry. Your ability to create value between these two points drives the success of your business.

In contrast, for platform businesses, it seems more appropriate to talk of 'connected users' rather than 'clients and suppliers'. Analyzing the value creation process on a platform through the lens of a vertically integrated model does not make much sense. Indeed, it would mean that 'suppliers' would be represented by those who help you in building and running the platform (back-end developers, data service providers, front-end designers, etc.) and that 'clients' would encompass all the users who register to the platform. The main problem with the latter interpretation is that putting all platform users on the same 'side' is misleading since it would suggest that they all have the same needs.

Actually, platforms most often cater to different types of 'clients', who can be seen as belonging to different 'sides'. A 'two-sided platform' means that the platform is connecting two different user groups. Usually, one group is represented by the 'producer' side (those actors having something to offer) and the other group is made of actors belonging to the 'consumer' side (those looking to consume what producers have to offer). What brings users together can be of any nature: exchanging a product (e.g., items on Amazon.com) or a service (freelance labor on TaskRabbit), transferring money (funds pledged by the crowd on Kickstarter), building relationships (dating on Tinder), or monetizing attention in the case of advertisement, which often represents an additional side on a given platform to make the whole system financially viable (as we will discuss in Chapter 5).

> **Change your vocabulary: replace 'suppliers' and 'clients' with 'connected user groups'.**

In some particular cases, the roles of consumers and producers are interchangeable insofar as consumers can also produce content, goods, or services. This is largely noticeable in the so-called sharing economy. That is the reason why, to define and circumscribe a given user group, it is important to focus on what users *do* on the platform, rather than on who they *are*. This is an important point because it expresses the fact that depending on the role that the user plays on the platform, the same person will be receptive to very different arguments or incentives to join and remain on the platform. In other words, behind the same person, there are potentially two (or more) user profiles that, when active on the platform, have very different expectations. As a result, it will be necessary to adapt the formulation of the value proposition.

The Multisided Value Proposition Canvas (MVPC)

In recent years, several frameworks have been developed to help entrepreneurs reflect on which elements should be included (or not) in their value proposition. The most famous tool is probably the *Value Proposition Canvas* (VPC) proposed by Osterwalder *et al.* in 2014. After presenting this tool, we argue here that it can hardly be applied to platform businesses because it does not address adequately the specificities that we just highlighted. Therefore, we propose an alternative tool that is more appropriate for nascent multisided platforms. In essence, the MVPC aims to identify the complementarities and potential conflicts between the wants and needs of the different groups of users to formulate a set of interlocked value propositions.

Existing tools and their limitations

Some efforts have been made to offer actionable tools to practitioners, using frameworks and visual representations to depict the value proposition compellingly. Among others, based on their famous *Business Model Canvas*, Alex Osterwalder and his co-authors have built a more specific framework, called the VPC,[2] by which they show how the value proposition should fit the customer profile, namely a description of the market segment that the products and services target. The Business Model and Value Proposition canvasses are powerful tools: They are easy to understand and make it possible to visualize in one glance concepts that may otherwise remain quite abstract. This explains why they have become very popular, especially inside the business community where they are often used in the context of innovation, entrepreneurship, and design thinking workshops.

The VPC is made of two different parts. On the right is the customer segment circle and, on the left, is the value proposition square. Those two parts come directly from the Business Model canvas, even if they were not detailed there. The VPC, therefore, makes it possible to refine the analysis. Concerning the customer segment, the authors ask three questions: What jobs does a customer try to get done? (*Customer Jobs*); What kind of difficulties does a customer experience before, during, or after getting the job done? (*Pains*); Which benefits does a customer expect or desire while consuming your product or service? (*Gains*).

Once you have completed this part of the tool, you are invited to reflect on your value proposition in three complementary directions, which mirror the right-hand side of the tool. 'Products and Services' represent the solution that you put in place to address what the customer needs to get the job done. For instance, Airbnb is offering its users a simple and efficient online reservation tool. Yet, enabling transactions by setting up the necessary infrastructure can be done in various ways. How will the platform work? What is the approach chosen by the platform to solve an efficiency gap in the market? What are the guiding principles that will support the design of the platform's key processes?

To answer this kind of question, it is necessary to associate specific features and functionalities of the products and services with the various customer's needs. In particular, you need to design 'pain relievers' and 'gain creators'. *Pain relievers* are those features and functionalities that help the customer overcome the pains you identified previously. The goal is to soothe the perceived risks and fears that may prevent the customer from joining the platform. Pain relievers, therefore, allow you to phrase your value proposition reassuringly by emphasizing, for instance, how the platform makes the life of its users more comfortable and how effortless it is to join the platform.

Gain creators, on the other hand, are those features and functionalities that create additional value to the solutions that customers can currently find, referring to the gains you identified on the right-hand side of the canvas. It is important to understand that gain creators are not just the mirror image of pain relievers. On top of erasing imperfections (which pain relievers are meant to do), you also need to find strongly differentiating elements that provide real added value in the way users' needs are met. So, gain creators make your value proposition sound alluring (and not just reassuring) by showing how the platform provides its users with unique and extensive benefits.

Now, the question we ask here is whether the VPC is suitable for building the value proposition of a platform. To put the tool to the test, we asked our students to apply it, scrupulously, to a well-known platform, namely

Airbnb. Several iterations of this exercise converged to the results presented in Figure 2.1.

At first glance, one might be tempted to say that the result meets the expectations and that it is fairly easy to find elements to place in each box. However, on closer inspection, some major shortcomings come into sight. Purely on semantics first, we should avoid using the terms 'products and services', as they do not seem to fit well here. As highlighted in the above section on co-creation, the platform is not selling a product, nor is it delivering a service designed on its own to a particular segment of clients. In fact, the platform is enabling transactions without being directly involved in the production of the underlying good or service (that is, in the case of Airbnb, a room or accommodating guests).

The same remark applies to the other half of the canvas. Consistent with what we noted earlier, we prefer to employ the term 'user' instead of 'customer' in the context of a platform. Moreover, some platforms can be joined for free, and some others exist outside the business world. Hence, being active on a platform does not necessarily mean behaving like a customer who is paying for a product or a service.

These details on wording put aside, there is actually a bigger issue that has nothing to do with terminology. The chart in Figure 2.1 is missing an important part of the platform's business model. More exactly, it completely ignores half of the picture. We keep on using the case of Airbnb to illustrate

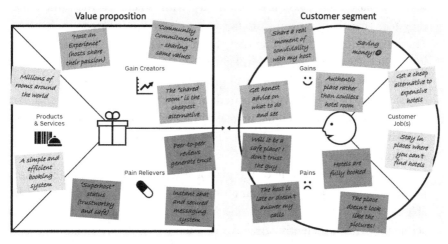

Figure 2.1 The Value Proposition Canvas applied to the case of Airbnb.

a point that many practitioners still miss. The platform intends to bring together two different groups of actors, namely travelers and hosts. Now, take a look at the canvas in Figure 2.1. You will easily notice that those who filled it out focused exclusively on the travelers' point of view. Indeed, all jobs, pains, and gains mentioned on the sticky notes refer to needs, expectations, and situations that are experienced by a traveler, like for instance finding an alternative to expensive hotel rooms, getting genuine contacts with locals, being afraid that the place does not look like the pictures, etc. This is quite understandable insofar as most of our students had probably more experience as guests than as hosts. It is obvious that if we had asked owners of properties listed on Airbnb to do a similar exercise, the answers obtained would have been very different.

> **The Value Proposition Canvas invites you to consider a single group of users, which is unsatisfactory for a multisided platform.**

Yet, as far as Airbnb is concerned, there is no reason to neglect the hosts' point of view when defining its value proposition. To be successful, Airbnb must attract both travelers and hosts to its platform. These two groups are distinct: Most users belong to a single group, and even if some users may wear the two hats, they do so alternatively and, each time, with different expectations. Hosts typically look for additional revenues; they also often want to share their passion for their city with others. At the same time, they fear that their future – unknown – guests, may degrade their place. These aspirations differ substantially from those that were reported for the guests in the canvas presented in Figure 2.1. Worse, there may be conflicts between the wishes of the different groups of users: What is wished for on one side may be exactly what is feared on the other side, and vice versa. For example, travelers will prefer increased flexibility on payment terms (no deposit nor pre-payment), while hosts would typically go for the opposite (up-front payment).

In the end, it is the role of the platform to find the best possible compromise between these conflicting objectives. That is, a platform must be able to confront the two viewpoints and find a balance that is perceived as acceptable and sufficiently attractive by each party. As we document later in Case 2.2, the Covid-19 crisis impacted this balance on Airbnb, which reacted by increasing flexibility for travelers to cope with the uncertain evolution of the sanitary situation. To find the right balance between the connected user groups, you must rely on a more suitable tool than the one we used so far. Hopefully, the improved canvas that we propose in the following section should do the trick.

A new tool adapted to platforms: the MVPC

To overcome the limitations that we just pinned down, we propose an alternative that remains actionable and intuitive. One part of the analysis consists in performing the first half of the above exercise for *each user group* targeted by the platform. That is, you need to make out the Jobs, Pains, and Gains of every group that your platform is connecting. You may be tempted to complete the rest of the exercise as you go along. It seems indeed natural, once you have identified jobs, pains, and gains, to design appropriate solutions, pain relievers, and gain creators, and to formulate, on that basis, a set of distinct value propositions for the different groups. Yet, this is where you would go wrong. The reason is simple: As the service that the platform offers is precisely the interaction between the groups, the various value propositions are necessarily intertwined. So, the other – and critical – part of the exercise is to reconcile the expectations of the different groups.

The MVPC that we propose in Figure 2.2 keeps the same building blocks as the original version but organizes them differently. The first change is that there is now room for two groups of users.[3] We place the platform at the center of the model, in line with its natural position as a market intermediary between different connected user groups. The second difference is the integrated nature of the model. The elements that were separate in the original model, although echoing each other, are now joined, and aligned (that is, jobs with solutions, gains with gain creators, and pains with pain relievers). This should make it easier to understand the responses that are provided by each of the stakeholders to any given issue. Finally, this new version incorporates the reality of value co-creation by bringing to the fore the platform's pivotal role in helping users to meet each other's needs.

The MVPC is a 3×3 table that should help you answer two critical questions: *Who needs what?* and *Who does what to meet these needs?* The three columns address the 'Who?' question: The outside columns are for the two user groups, while the middle column is for the platform that connects them.

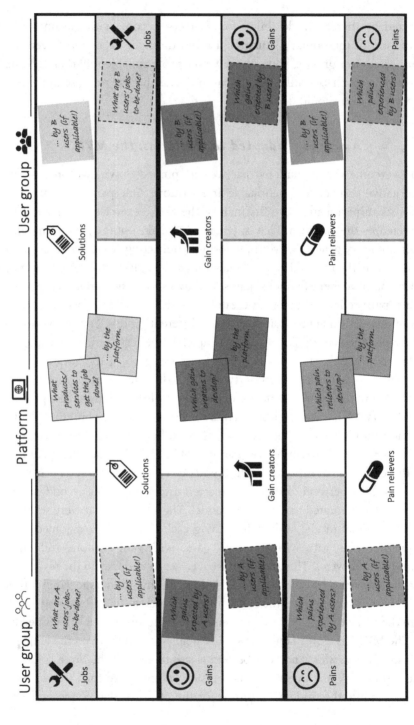

Figure 2.2 The Multisided Value Proposition Canvas explained.

As for the horizontal blocks, they address the 'What?' questions. They correspond to the three main categories of the initial VPC: The first block is for the jobs to be done and their solutions, the second for the gains and the corresponding gain creators, and the third for the pains and the corresponding pain relievers. Each block is further divided into two lines, with each line focusing on one user group: The top line concerns the user group in the left column and must be completed from left to right, whereas the bottom line concerns the user group in the right column and must be completed from right to left. As we explain below, this ambidextrous exercise will facilitate the horizontal and vertical reading of the table, thereby allowing you to extract meaningful information from the listed elements.

Let us now describe what you should list in the various cells of the table (you can find a blank version of the canvas on www.platformstrategies. org). For the sake of illustration, we continue to use the case of Airbnb (middle column), putting guests in the left column and hosts in the right column. Figure 2.3 summarizes our analysis.

Starting from the top, we first consider the jobs to be done and their solutions (first horizontal block). The first line takes the guests' point of view and is divided into three boxes. Moving from left to right, the first box records the guests' needs (that is, the jobs they try to get done), while the next two boxes record the solutions to these needs (that is, a set of products and/or services) that are jointly proposed by the platform (second box) and users in the other group (third box). In our example, whenever a guest wishes to find an alternative to a hotel room to spend one night in some place (first box: the 'job to be done'), Airbnb offers, via its website, a wide array of accommodations to choose from, coupled with a set of search, booking and payment tools (second box: solutions provided by the platform), while the selected host offers the underlying service, that is one night in the booked and paid accommodation (third box: solutions provided by users in the other group and facilitated by the platform).

You can then move to the second line and take the viewpoint of users in the other group (here, the hosts). You complete the boxes following the same principle, with the only difference being that you need to start from the right. That is, you report the hosts' needs in the right-hand box, the solutions brought by guests in the left-hand box, and, as before, the solutions proposed by the platform in the middle box. In our example, a job that hosts try to get done is earning additional income by renting out

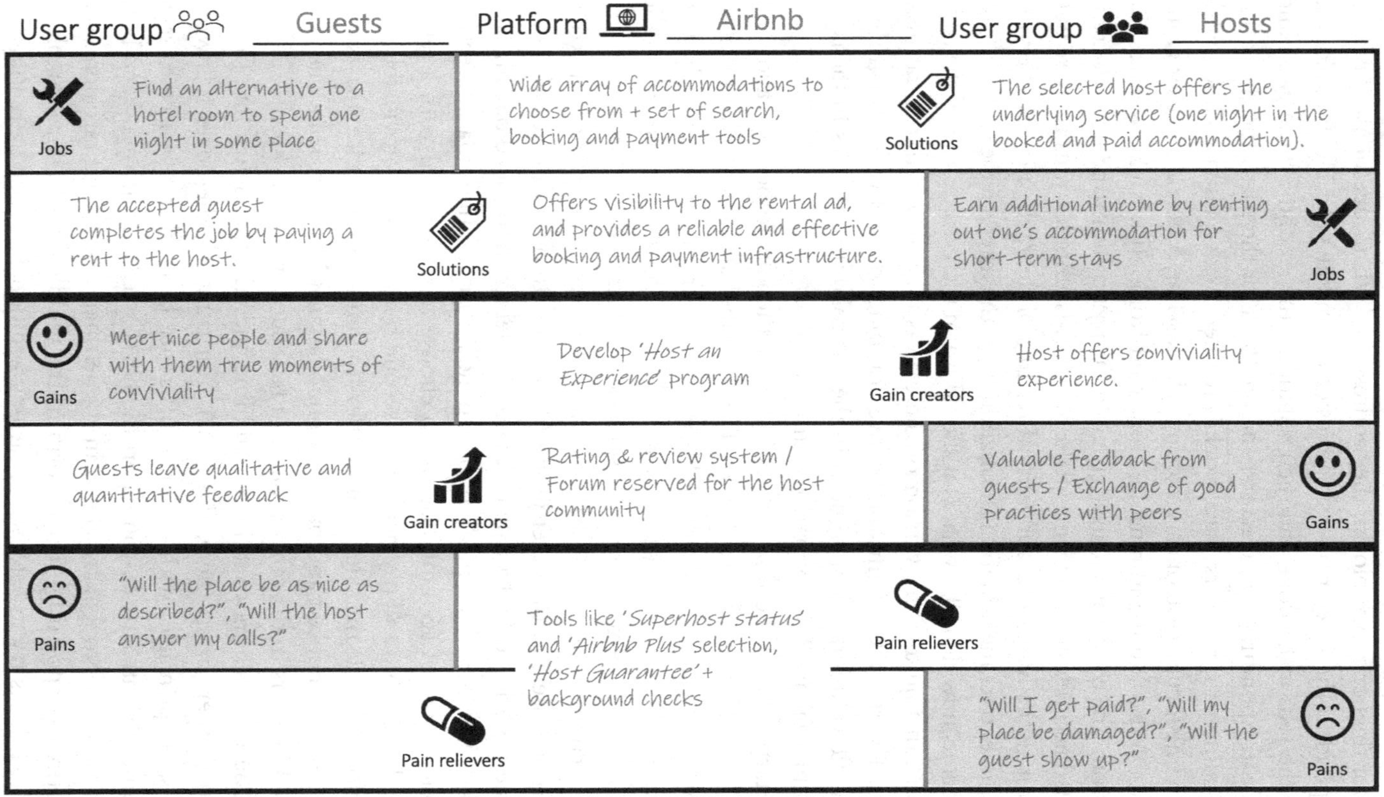

User group (Guests)

Jobs — Find an alternative to a hotel room to spend one night in some place

Solutions — The accepted guest completes the job by paying a rent to the host.

Gains — Meet nice people and share with them true moments of conviviality

Gain creators — Guests leave qualitative and quantitative feedback

Pains — "will the place be as nice as described?", "will the host answer my calls?"

Pain relievers —

Platform — Airbnb

Solutions — Wide array of accommodations to choose from + set of search, booking and payment tools

Offers visibility to the rental ad, and provides a reliable and effective booking and payment infrastructure.

Gain creators — Develop 'Host an Experience' program

Rating & review system / Forum reserved for the host community

Pain relievers — Tools like 'Superhost' status and 'Airbnb Plus' selection, 'Host Guarantee' + background checks

---

User group (Hosts)

Jobs — The selected host offers the underlying service (one night in the booked and paid accommodation).

Earn additional income by renting out one's accommodation for short-term stays

Gains — Host offers conviviality experience.

Gain creators — Valuable feedback from guests / Exchange of good practices with peers

Pains — "will I get paid?", "will my place be damaged?", "will the guest show up?"

Pain relievers —

Figure 2.3 The Multisided Value Proposition Canvas for Airbnb.

their accommodation for short-term stays; the platform is instrumental in meeting this need by offering visibility to the rental ad and by providing a reliable and effective booking and payment infrastructure, while hosts complete the job by paying rent to the host.

The second horizontal block is dedicated to gains and gain creators. It works on the same principle as the previous block: The first line considers the group on the left-hand side and lists the gains for this group (left box), followed by the gain creators provided by the platform (middle box) and/ or the other group (right box); and similarly, but in a mirror way, for the second line, which considers the group on the right-hand side. For example, we saw in the original model applied to Airbnb that one of the sources of satisfaction from the guest's point of view is to meet nice people and share with them true moments of conviviality. This is something to write down in the upper-left box of this block (answering the question: *Which gains do guests expect?*). The space on the right is then naturally reserved for the elements that will contribute to fulfilling this desire of the guest. In the upper-middle box (the platform), you can list the *Host an Experience* program developed by Airbnb. Through this program, Airbnb invites hosts to offer a very personalized service consisting in organizing a dedicated activity to share their passion with their guests. In the upper-right box (the host), you can indicate the conviviality experience that the host can offer. As for hosts, they value feedback from guests, but also the exchange of good practices from peers to improve the quality of their offer. This is what you can list in the lower-right box of this block (answering the question: *Which gains do hosts expect?*). In the lower-middle box, you will then list what Airbnb is implementing, such as the rating system or a forum reserved for the host community. Finally, in the lower-left box, you can mention both qualitative and quantitative feedback that guests will provide.

The last iteration of this process concerns pains and pain relievers. On Airbnb, pains that are often observed on both user sides are more related to a behavioral risk coming from the opposite user group than from the service offered by the platform. On the host side, legitimate questions are: "Will I get paid?", "Will my place be damaged?", "Will the guest show up?", etc. And on the guest side, "Will the place be as nice as described?", "Will the host answer my calls?", etc. Trust is thus an essential factor for platforms and is crucial in the wider perspective of the overall match-making role that they play. Therefore, tools like the *Superhost* status and the

Airbnb Plus selection which increase confidence on the guest side, or the *Host Guarantee* and the background checks that make the service safer for hosts, are good examples of pain relievers offered by the platform. Also, the user-friendly booking system that Airbnb provides and the various tasks that this system automates (sending confirmation notifications, issuing invoices, updating prices, etc.) relieve the pain that the administrative workload exerts on hosts.

It is not because we described the MVPC line by line that you must fill it out in that way. For instance, some of our students found it more natural to list all the jobs, pains, and gains (in the gray boxes) before thinking about the solutions, gain creators, and pain relievers (in the white boxes).

Making the most of the canvas

A good thing with the MVPC is that it saves you from the temptation of writing a separate value proposition for each user group. The elements that you listed in the MVPC are indeed too tightly interwoven to allow for such a misguided formulation of the value proposition. Instead, you need to embrace the complexity of the canvas to figure out the value that your platform proposes to all its users. To do so, we invite you to scan the elements you have listed both horizontally and vertically.

The horizontal scan is meant to analyze, for each job, gain, or pain identified for a given user group, how to distribute work between the other group of users and the platform to get the job done, create the gain, or relieve the pain. That is, you should first gauge what you can achieve by simply facilitating the interaction between the groups, thereby letting them meet each other's needs. Next, you should think of what extra roles the platform should play to help users help one another more efficiently and, if applicable, to meet unanswered needs.[4]

The second scan you need to perform is vertical and concerns the middle column. In each block, the two boxes in the middle column tell you what the platform can do to meet the needs (jobs, gains, or pains) expressed by the two groups of users. Viewing them together, you must now check to what extent addressing the needs of one group facilitates or, in contrast, impedes addressing the needs of the other group. The more the former case prevails, the better: It is indeed simpler and cost-effective to design solutions that get the jobs done (create gains or relieve pains) for both groups at the same time. For instance, any solution that improves the matching of the two sides does just that. However, addressing the needs of one group might sometimes only be done at the expense of the other group; similarly, what creates gains (or relieve pains) on one side might generate pains (or limit gains) on the other side. That is, situations are win-lose instead of win-win. This is often so on marketplaces, when the cake (that is, the value of transactions) to be divided between the demand and the supply sides has a fixed size. Then, any decision of the platform that enlarges the share for one group necessarily reduces the share for the other group (think, for instance, of a fee that is charged, either to sellers or to buyers, for every transaction conducted on the platform). It is thus crucial first to pinpoint such potential conflicts and next, to find the best compromise. As Case 2.2 illustrates, the latter task is inevitably tricky, and circumstances may force platforms to adjust their initial choices.

Scan the MVPC horizontally to distribute the value co-creation between your users and you and vertically to identify potential complementarities or conflicts between the needs of different user groups.

Case 2.2 When Airbnb cancels its hosts' cancellation policies

In the short-term accommodation sector, cancellation policies are inevitably a source of tension between the two sides of the market: Travelers (or guests) prefer increased flexibility on cancellation (no penalty in case of late cancellation), while landlords (or hosts) typically favor the opposite (no compensation for last-minute cancellation). It is the role of the platform to find the best possible compromise between these conflicting objectives.

Regarding cancellations by guests, Airbnb decided not to decide. As situations and preferences differ widely, Airbnb preferred letting hosts choose the policy that fit them best within a preset menu (at the time of this writing, the menu goes from 'Flexible' – free cancellation until 24 hours before check-in – to 'Super Strict 60 days' – 50% refund for cancellation at least 60 days

before check-in). For a long time, hosts and guests alike appreciated this flexible approach. And then came the Covid-19 pandemic
and its attendant traveling restrictions and stay-at-home policies.
Facing massive cancellations all around the world, Airbnb decided,
in mid-March 2020, to let guests cancel their reservations for a
full refund and no cancellation fees. Naturally, this decision was
heavily criticized by those hosts whose stricter cancellation policies had been unilaterally overridden. To calm the uproar, Airbnb
announced a fortnight later that the company would pay hosts a
quarter of what they would normally receive through their cancellation policy. Later, in September 2020, Airbnb decided to revamp its
'Extenuating Circumstances Policy' by eliminating circumstances
that used to be covered (notably, unexpected disease or illness),
while adding other circumstances not included before (notably,
government-declared emergencies or government-imposed travel
restrictions).

Phrasing a compelling value proposition

Filling in the MVPC allowed you to get a clear view of the users' needs,
and to understand how best to meet these needs. Now that you have all the
ingredients near at hand, it is time to grind and mix them to cook a strong
value proposition that users on both sides will find appealing and convincing. We show you how to do so in this section.

Characteristics of a strong value proposition

First, a good value proposition does not require any further explanation. It
should be clear after reading it once. More than being easy to understand,
a strong value proposition is intuitive, in the sense that people should react
by finding it obvious. This reaction is often achieved when someone says:
"Why didn't I think of that before?".

Second, the value proposition should be concise. If it is too long, people
will tend to forget it. The goal is to make sure people quickly associate
the value proposition with your business. Of course, there is a trade-off

between including all your great arguments that make your platform a top service and the fact of keeping it short. Remember that having a concise and straightforward value proposition does not mean you cannot explain how you are going to keep your promise. There are for sure places (like a section on a webpage) where you can display more details about the value proposition without making the phrasing too dense.

Third, a strong value proposition should be *unique*, as it is meant to differentiate yourself from rival platforms, or any form of competition. Avoid mainstream buzzwords and ready-made formulas when writing a statement about your service. If you cannot find and emphasize those aspects that make your platform truly special compared to existing solutions in the market, it may mean that your service is perfectible, or worse, irrelevant. You may then want to return to the MVPC and refine your analysis of the users' needs.

Fourth, you should be careful not to overstate how much value your platform can deliver. Remaining *honest* is key if you want to build a sustainable business. People are not stupid: If they feel like the platform does not fulfill the initial promise, they will leave and sometimes publicly denigrate the solution, which can be synonymous with death in the context of a young venture (especially a platform one, as we discussed previously). Conversely, being able to surprise platform users with a service that is above their expectations can lead to more traction and positive spillovers in the long run.

Finally, a strong value proposition is relatively *stable*; it must be visible and easily recognized by people. It is important to repeat it and show it at all touchpoints with existing and potential future participants on the platform. Unless you change your strategy or decide to remove or add a key feature in the service you deliver, the value proposition ought to remain unchanged; otherwise, people may be confused or perceive a lack of conviction and steadiness.

A strong value proposition is intuitive, concise, unique, honest, and stable.

Defining a strong value proposition can thus be a challenging task. This explains, as described in Case 2.3, why many platforms are looking for quick wins, especially by taking advantage of the notoriety of a third-party player that has succeeded in establishing itself in the market.

Case 2.3 'Lookalike' value propositions

One common way to formulate an intuitive and concise value proposition for a new platform is to compare oneself (or being compared by others) to an existing and successful platform. For instance, Splacer's value proposition is worded as follows: "Find Your Space—Discover & Book Unique Spaces for Your Upcoming Activity". Although this statement is already quite clear, the press made it even clearer by dubbing Splacer "the Airbnb for event space". Similarly, Attestation Légale (ALG) proposes the following on its web page: "Join the ALG network: a simpler, more secure way of doing business." This is a vague statement, which only becomes more explicit when reading the description of the services that the platform offers. Yet, the press found (or was suggested) a more direct way of presenting the platform: "Attestation Légale: the administrative LinkedIn for businesses." In these two examples, the analogy to well-known platforms makes it easier for potential users to identify quickly what the new platform is about.

By the same token, it may also be efficient to position the new platform not as identical but as antithetical to an existing platform. For instance, the messaging application Jack Media introduces itself as follows: "Jack is a communication tool that combines instant notification and delayed delivery. The waiting period between the moment a Jack is delivered and the moment it can be read creates anticipation." This becomes clearer when Jack is presented as the 'anti-Snapchat'.

Are such lookalike value propositions effective? The message they convey is certainly intuitive and concise; no question about that. What is more problematic though is uniqueness, as the platform will always be in the shadow of its well-known precursor. Stability may be at stake as well: Any trouble that the famous predecessor faces may contaminate its lookalikes (when Uber sneezes, many 'Uber for X' startups catch a cold).

From the MVPC to the value proposition

The authors of the VP canvas propose a fairly simple way to start from the framework and then arrive at a value proposition formulation. They suggest the following: "Our [*Products and Services*] help(s) [*Customer segments*] who want to [*Jobs to be done*] by reducing/avoiding [*Pains*] and increasing/enabling [*Gain*]" (Osterwalder *et al.*, 2014). Though helpful, this method for formulating the value proposition must be adapted to the specificities of platforms. In particular, if you follow this method too closely, you may shroud the primary function of the platform, namely its capacity to bring together actors who are looking for each other. As we explained many times already, it is of paramount importance to convince users that the platform will allow them to find other users to interact with. Otherwise, the platform may never get off the ground.

So, before extolling all the nice features that the platform may have in terms of design, ergonomics, etc., we advise you to bring to the fore what you listed in the top block of the MVPC (see Figure 2.2) to demonstrate how the platform meets the needs of its users by organizing and managing the interaction among them. As an illustration, here is how Etsy explains how it works: "Our global marketplace is a vibrant community of real people connecting over special goods. The platform empowers sellers to do what they love and helps buyers find what they love."[5] Noticeably, the first sentence aims at reassuring potential users about other users' participation: The platform is a *vibrant community connecting* people. Then, the second sentence clearly describes whom the platform aims to connect (buyers and sellers) and how it differs from other marketplaces (buyers and sellers are *real people* trading *special goods* that *they love*).

Note that you can underpin statements of this sort with quantitative elements (for example, "We are the market leader with X thousands of users and no other platform can do better" or "98% of our users are satisfied with our services and say that they can easily find what they are looking for") or qualitative consideration via, for example, testimonials of users who are delighted by the platform (for example, "Since I joined the Y platform, my turnover has increased by 60%").

> To be compelling, the value proposition of a platform should emphasize the interaction that the platform facilitates and manages, before describing, potentially in separate statements, how the platform creates gains and relieves pains for its users.

Once the 'platform aspect' of your business is clearly displayed, it is important, in a second step, to address the users' gains and pains in more detail. As gains and pains differ across groups, it is often sensible to differentiate the communication aimed at the two groups. Many platforms choose to walk this route. In practice, they often use tabs on their website or app to direct each group of users to a different subset of pages. Coming back to Etsy, we observe that the previous general statement is followed by two specific statements, one for sellers ("With low fees, powerful tools, and support and education, we help creative entrepreneurs start, manage, and scale their businesses") and one for buyers ("From the specific to the unexpected (or custom-made), our search tools help buyers explore all the special one-of-a-kind items offered by Etsy sellers"). As we see, these statements explain in more detail how gains are created, and pains are relieved for each group.

As illustrated in Case 2.4, the online food ordering platform Just Eat Takeaway. com followed this two-step procedure to formulate its value proposition.[6]

Case 2.4 The value proposition of Just Eat Takeaway.com

In its general communication, *Just Eat Takeaway.com* introduces itself as follows: "Just Eat Takeaway.com is a leading global online food delivery marketplace, connecting consumers and restaurants through its platform in 23 countries. We offer an online marketplace where supply and demand for food delivery and ordering meet." Words like *global*, *marketplace*, *connecting* or *platform*, and a phrase like 'supply and demand (...) meet' are all meant to create positive expectations about the extent of participation on both sides.

As for *Just Eat Takeaway.com* website, we observe that it is more aimed at consumers than at restaurant owners. This is logical given that the former largely outnumber the latter and use the website on a more regular basis. After explaining how the service works, the platform enunciates the value that it proposes to consumers: The three sections – 'Your Bonus', 'Your Guarantee' and 'Your Benefits' – correspond, respectively, to the gain creators, the completed jobs, and the pain relievers. As for restaurant owners who want to collaborate with the platform, they must go to the bottom of the home page, click on the 'Signup a restaurant' tab, and access pages that adopt a more businesslike tone.

The value proposition is broken down into three parts. First, three arguments answer the *Why* question by using quantified and therefore very concrete elements (that is, "Get more customers – Restaurants on Just Eat take 4,000 orders a year on average"; "We'll do the marketing – More than 12 million hungry people come to Just Eat every month"; "Save with exclusive perks – You can save up to £13,000 a year with exclusive partner discounts from wholesalers, utilities providers and insurers"). Then, there is a storytelling element with flattering video testimony from a satisfied restaurant owner ("The Partner Perks system is really good. It's a great way that Just Eat have sat down and thought, how can we add value to our product? It's a win-win deal"). Finally, the platform lists seven "What you get" benefits (that is, your restaurant on the Just Eat apps and website, an order pad tablet and printer, personalized data and business best practice, cashback up to 7% at suppliers, up to £1,000 off electric delivery bikes and scooters, an average saving of £1,150 a year on energy bills, and free Just Eat merchandising).[7]

Same-side heterogeneity

As the last example showed, platforms may prefer to differentiate their value proposition across user groups instead of trying to phrase an all-encompassing, one-size-fits-all, message. In some cases, it may even be useful to go one step further, as user profiles may differ widely within a particular user group. Although users in the same group share the same objective in joining a platform, they may be quite dissimilar in terms of expectations or ambitions. The way users generate – or are affected by – network effects may also vary within a group, as we illustrated when describing hosts and guests on Airbnb in Chapter 1.

When this 'same-side heterogeneity' (as we call it) is marked, a platform may find it useful to segment a user group into several sub-groups. A striking example of such a strategy is the segmentation that eBay operated on the sellers' side in the 2000s, as described in Case 2.5.

Case 2.5 Segmentation of sellers on eBay

Sellers on eBay do not form a homogeneous group and the platform has several terms to categorize them.[8] The first main difference is made between professional and private sellers. Professional sellers, called 'business sellers', are sellers who chose a professional status while registering on the platform; they are either self-employed or set up as a small and medium enterprise (SME). Private sellers are more linked to a 'garage sale' logic (C2C), involving the sale of second-hand items, whereas business sellers are clearly associated with a 'commercial sale' logic (B2C), which mostly involves selling new items.

In addition to this distinction based on status (private or professional), eBay also tends to use volume and frequency of sales as segmentation criteria. Sellers with a high level of sales are called 'top sellers'. Of course, most of these are professionals. However, some private sellers stand out in this respect. They are then called 'job sellers'. Similarly, it is possible to encounter business sellers who do not sell much on eBay, either because selling on eBay is not their main professional activity (as is the case, for instance, for a part-time self-employed worker), or because they sell more through other channels (for instance, a shopkeeper).

Once same-side heterogeneity is observed and translated into some segmentation of the users, a platform must integrate this segmentation in the choices it will make. As far as the value proposition is concerned, the question is whether the platform wants to address all subgroups or rather focus on only some of them. If the platform chooses to pursue a niche strategy by limiting access to a specific category of users (for example, premium service, urban location, services by professionals, etc.), this should clearly appear in the value proposition, as it is both a way to distinguish the platform from the competition and to send a clear message to interested parties.

As we will discuss later, such a niche strategy may also be sensible to address the challenges of launching the platform (Chapter 4), before thinking of expanding its scale and scope (Chapter 6). Catering to the specific needs and expectations of various subgroups will indeed force the platform to adapt its services. For example, when eBay (see Case 2.5) opened up to business sellers, it quickly put in place tools to facilitate and automate the mass import of listings, a functionality that was of no use to the casual private sellers.

For readers with a background or experience in marketing, what we just discussed may resonate with the type of market segmentation that consists in identifying subsets of buyers sharing similar needs and behaviors in order to reach them with a distinct marketing mix (that is, price, channel, product attributes, etc.). The *Persona* method, in particular, makes it possible to draw up a typical profile of a customer belonging to a specific market segment. This approach makes it then much easier to build a VP by ensuring that it fits perfectly, both in content and in form, with the customer's preferences and consumption habits.

Although this method remains perfectly valid to design the value proposition of a platform, it must be adjusted to incorporate network effects. Our previous analysis indeed taught us two important lessons: First, the main motivation for users to join a platform is to interact with other users; second, any platform decision geared toward users in one group inevitably affects users in other groups. This means that you cannot usefully create segments or personas within a group of users if you ignore the cross-side network effects on and from the other group of users.

Coming back to the example of eBay, distinguishing business sellers from private sellers is sensible not only because the two segments have different needs (such as advanced tools for businesses) but also because they affect buyer participation differently (that is, they exert cross-side network effects with different intensities). As evidence, here is the answer that Curchod and Neysen (2009) got from the eBay management team in Belgium to the question "Are business sellers strategic clients for eBay?":

> Absolutely! And obviously for several reasons. As a marketplace, the crucial thing for us is, one, to make sure that the sellers make enough deals

with quality buyers and, two, for the buyers to make sure that there is an abundant and quality supply. And in that second part, business sellers play a central role. Even if business sellers represent maybe not more than 2 or 3 percent of all our users in Belgium, they totalize between 20 and 25 percent of the transactions.

> **To sharpen the value proposition, it may be useful to create segments or personas within a group of users. But, to do so properly, cross-side network effects must be kept in mind.**

To conclude this chapter and link it to what is coming, let us stress that when it comes to formulating your value proposition, the thought process (identifying your users' needs and finding how to meet them) is as important as the final result (a public statement of the benefits that you provide). This means that you should not put the MVPC away once the value proposition is written down. The next two chapters of this book will indeed invite you to revisit your canvas and, potentially, your value proposition. Chapter 3 will teach you how to study the competitive environment of your platform. The analysis of your potential competitors may reveal that your idea is not as unique as you thought initially or, in contrast, that allying with other organizations may allow you to push your project one step further. You may then want to reconsider the elements you listed in the MVPC in light of these new findings. Later, in Chapter 4, you will think of which group of users it is best to attract first to launch your platform. Once this group will be identified, you may decide to give more prominence in your value proposition to the benefits that your platform brings to this group.

As you see, nothing goes linearly with platforms: It is a world of feedback loops and dynamic thinking. Hopefully, with our guidance, you will not go around in circles.

> **SHORT ANSWERS TO KEY QUESTIONS**
>
> - *What sort of value does a platform propose?* On a platform, most of the value is co-created by the users through their interaction. But, for this to happen, the platform must first organize these interactions

and then manage them. Thus, a platform proposes value by orchestrating the co-creation of value by its users.

- *Why is it so important for a platform to formulate a compelling value proposition?* Because a platform, unlike a pipeline, generates value by connecting users. So, in the absence of a compelling value proposition, the platform will fail to convince users to join, and no value will be created.
- *For whom should the value proposition of a platform be formulated?* For platform businesses, it seems more appropriate to talk of 'users' rather than 'clients/suppliers', and of 'platform sides' rather than 'market segments'.
- *Are existing VPCs adapted to platforms?* Unfortunately, no. The existing tools generally focus on a single group of users and neglect the interaction with other groups. Our MVPC provides a solution in this regard.
- *How many value propositions should be formulated: One or several?* This is probably not the right way to ask questions. Even if a value proposition must be concise, it can combine several articulated statements. We recommend proceeding in two steps: First, it is crucial to emphasize the interaction that the platform facilitates and manages; second, one must describe, potentially in separate statements, how the platform addresses the needs of its users.

FURTHER READINGS

The book by Osterwalder *et al.* (2014) is certainly a must-read to think properly and systematically about the design of a value proposition. For a review of the literature on platforms' value propositions, see Belleflamme and Neysen (2021).

Notes

1. In *Start With Why*, Sinek (2011) discusses the benefits of focusing on the purpose first, arguing that customers do not buy *what* you offer, but instead *why* you offer it. As he writes:

   When companies talk about WHAT they do and how advanced their products are, they may have appeal, but they do not necessarily represent something to which we want to belong. But when a company clearly communicates their WHY, what they believe, and we believe what they believe, then we will sometimes go to extraordinary lengths to include those products or brands in our lives.

2. Strategyzer AG and Strategyzer.com. See also Osterwalder and Pigneur (2010) and Osterwalder *et al.* (2014).
3. The canvas we propose here is designed for two-sided platforms (which are the most common ones). Adapting it to platforms with more than two sides is perfectly feasible, although readability may become an issue.
4. You can think of adjusting this 'division of labor' at later stages; for instance, you can add functionalities to your website or app, so that the platform will provide more solutions on its own. This is what Airbnb did. So, you should not be misled by our previous example, as we clearly described Airbnb's situation at the time of this writing and not when the platform was launched.
5. See www.etsy.com/about (last accessed May 2021).
6. According to Wikipedia, "Just Eat Takeaway.com N.V. (formerly Takeaway.com; founded as Thuisbezorgd.nl) is a Dutch multinational online food ordering and delivery company, formed from the merger of London-based Just Eat and Amsterdam-based Takeaway.com in 2020."
7. See https://restaurants.just-eat.co.uk/ (last accessed March 2021).
8. We follow here Curchod and Neysen (2009).

Bibliography

Belleflamme, P. and Neysen, N. (2021). A Multisided Value Proposition Canvas for online platforms. *Journal of Business Ecosystems* 2(1), 1–14. https://doi.org/10.4018/jbe.2021010101.

Curchod, C. and Neysen, N. (2009). Disentangling positive and negative externalities on two-sided markets: The eBay Case. Working Paper 09/03. Louvain School of Management. https://cdn.uclouvain.be/public/Exports%20reddot/iag/documents/WP_3_Curchod_Neysen.pdf.

Lanning, M.J. and Michaels, E.G. (1988). A business is a value delivery system, McKinsey Staff Paper, No. 41.

Nemrow, J. (2013). The lessons I learned from my failed music startup... *Digital Music News* (April 12). https://www.digitalmusicnews.com/2013/04/12/startup/.

Osterwalder, A. and Y. Pigneur (2010). *Business model generation: A handbook for visionaries, game changers, and challengers.* Hoboken NJ: Wiley.

Osterwalder, A., Pigneur, Y., Bernarda, G., Smith, A. and Papadakos, T. (2014). *Value proposition design: How to create products and services customers want,* Hoboken NJ: John Wiley & Sons.

Sinek, S. (2011). *Start with why: How great leaders inspire everyone to take action.* New York: Penguin Publishing Group.

Part II

VALUE CREATION

3

ASSESSING A PLATFORM'S COMPETITIVE POSITION

KEY QUESTIONS

- Why is the traditional competitive analysis ill-suited for platforms?
- How can we define a platform's competitors and complementors?
- What is the difference between the rivals and the substitutes for a platform?
- How does the Linkage Map fit into the competitive analysis of a platform?
- How can network effects be turned into a competitive advantage?

The first part of the book was concerned with value proposition, which is more complex to conceive for platforms than it is for other businesses. Because interactions are key for platform users, platforms cannot propose value on their own: They propose value jointly with their users. Therefore,

DOI: 10.4324/9780429490873-6

we suggested drawing first the *Linkage Map* of your platform (to understand how your users will affect one another) and next, filling in the *Multisided Value Proposition Canvas* (to help formulate your value proposition).

It is now time to start translating your proposition into a concrete offering for your potential users – that is, to move from value proposition to value *creation*. We just recalled that platforms cannot propose value on their own. Even more so, they cannot *create* value on their own: Platforms *co-create* value with their users. The consequence is plain and simple: As there is no value without users, the prerequisite for value creation is to convince users to join the platform. Yet, this is easier said than done as users will accept to join your platform only if they expect other users to do so as well: A conundrum known as the 'chicken-and-egg' problem, which we address in Chapter 4.

Before launching your platform, there is yet one important step to take. As for any business, you cannot start operating if you do not have the first clue about a strategy. And to decide which strategy is the most appropriate, you need first to understand the context you are moving in. This is why analyzing your environment and assessing your competitive position remains key. It is indeed crucial to acknowledge the external factors that may either improve or damage your chances of success. And once you have a clear view of your competitive position, you can think of how to assert it. This is what this chapter is about.

As explained in the introduction, it is not the purpose of this book to (re)introduce all the concepts and frameworks belonging to what is usually called *strategic diagnosis* or *strategic analysis*. Of course, we invite entrepreneurs to take the time to conduct analyses that may help them uncover interesting insights about the environment, using well-known tools (such as PESTEL). However, we believe that the peculiarities of markets with platforms give us grounds to discuss and review some aspects of competitive analysis.

In this chapter, we first briefly review the traditional tools of competitive analysis and point at their limitations when it comes to assessing the competitive environment of platforms. Then, to remedy these shortcomings, we propose a more appropriate tool, called the *Platform Value Net*. Finally, we examine how a platform can assert its competitive position, first by choosing to compete for or in the market and then, by turning network effects into a competitive advantage.

The traditional competitive analysis

We argue here that the traditional competitive analysis (which we first briefly review) faces several shortcomings when it comes to assessing the competitive position of platforms.

From Porter's Five Forces to the Value Net model

Identifying the 'outside' players is important insofar as they condition the moves that the platform can or should make. In the strategic management literature, one framework has become extremely popular: the *Five Forces model*, developed by Michael Porter (1979), which aims at identifying all the competitive forces that surround a given organization. The focus is thus set on potential sources of negative impact for the firm, lowering its ability to make profits within the industry it belongs to.

The five competitive forces are as follows. First, **rivals** or direct competitors (1) represent the most obvious threat since they target the same market segments with a similar value proposition (they offer the same kind of products and services). The more you are surrounded by large and powerful direct competitors, the more difficult it will be for you to be profitable (lots of alternatives exist for your customers and, thereby, there is negative pressure on prices). The question here can be formulated as follows: *To what extent do my existing rivals prevent me from being successful?*

Suppliers (2) and **customers** (3) may also exert negative pressure on you because of their bargaining power. Different reasons, like the number of players or the standardized nature of the product, might explain why the relative bargaining power is not equally distributed among buyers and suppliers. For instance, if you are in a situation where you have strong suppliers with highly differentiated raw material or production goods on the one hand, and that you can only count on a few buyers in a B2B niche segment, on the other hand, you are not in a position to take the law into your own hands. The question here is: *To what extent do my clients and suppliers impose their conditions?*

Another force is represented by the **new entrants** (4), which can be seen as potential competitors in the future. This category comprises players that are currently outside the game (active in another geography for instance), but that could decide to enter the market with a similar offer soon, thereby becoming rivals. The more attractive a particular industry is at the moment, the higher the risk of observing new players entering your playground. New entrants also include players that do not exist yet (that is, entrepreneurs with emerging business ideas) and firms that belong to other industries. These players might appear suddenly and completely disrupt the industry. The question is: *To what extent could players that are currently outside of my market become my next biggest competitors?*

Finally, **substitutes** (5) constitute another potential source of issues if the related threat is not anticipated and well understood. Those players compete differently than rivals in the sense that they answer the same needs, yet through a different value proposition. With substitutes, the focus is not set on products or services but rather on customer needs. In other words, if someone addresses the same customer need through a different offering than yours, then chances are high that you are confronted with a substitute. For instance, imagine that you operate a leisure park. While performing a competitive analysis, you should not limit yourself to considering only other parks that offer similar activities. You should rather extend the scope to the closest movie theatre, for example, and consider it as a substitute. Indeed, both of you address people's need for entertainment, although you do not belong to the same industry and do not mobilize the same resources to fulfill that need. You are competing with one another for getting access to the same golden resource: People's leisure time. Let us take another example. An electric scooter manufacturer and a car manufacturer do not belong to the same industry and neither do they offer the same range of products. Though, under certain circumstances, they compete with one another as they both provide means to fulfill mobility needs. In urban areas, clients might consider electric scooters as a decent alternative to small electric cars. Concerning substitutes, the question you need to answer is: *To what extent is it easy for my clients to find a valid alternative to the solution I currently offer?*

The Five Forces model, which we just depicted shortly, centers around potential sources of negative impacts for the firm – that is, forces that hamper the firms' capacity to create value. Brandenburger and Nalebuff (1996) proposed an extension of Porter's model, called the *Value Net model*, that introduces the possibility for third-party organizations to help the firm in the value creation process. In other words, the Value Net model also considers the potential *positive* impacts of the environment by uncovering collaboration opportunities with players that are usually perceived as opponents.

To describe this coexistence of competition and cooperation, Brandenburger and Nalebuff coined the portmanteau term *coopetition*. This hybrid concept lies at the heart of their model, as they introduce a new group of players to look at, namely the **complementors**. This category includes organizations providing products or services that *increase* the value that customers attach to your product or service if they can consume them together. For instance, when buying a flight ticket online, you often have the opportunity to subscribe, at the same time, a travel insurance covering risks linked to delay, cancellation, discontinuation, or lost luggage. The insurance company behind this service can then be seen as a 'complementor' to the airline company.

The other categories of players remain similar across both models as the Value Net model also encompasses suppliers, customers, and competitors. There is a little twist, though: While Porter's model makes a distinction between rivals, substitutes, and new potential entrants, the model proposed by Brandenburger and Nalebuff merges those three groups of players into a single category, simply called 'competitors'. Figure 3.1 illustrates the similarities and differences between the two models.

Having introduced these two popular strategic tools, our intention now is to explain why, in our view, they perform poorly when it comes to conducting a competitive analysis for platforms.

Traditional models are ill-suited for platforms

In Chapter 2, we described the difficulties we faced in applying the value proposition canvas in the context of platforms. Similarly, here, we believe

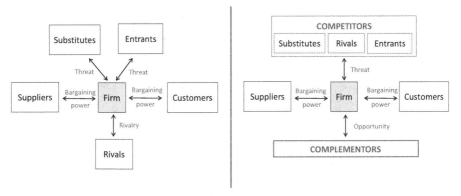

Figure 3.1 From the Five Forces to the Value Net.

that none of the two models that we just presented fits our purpose. The main reason is that two categories of actors – suppliers on the one hand and customers (or buyers) on the other hand – refer to the traditional value chain representation of a pipeline firm, which buys raw material and intermediate goods from suppliers and transforms or assembles them into some product or service of higher value for its customers or clients. In contrast, a platform hardly transforms or assembles anything, as it primarily facilitates transactions among independent users. In this context, assessing the bargaining threat of 'suppliers' and 'buyers' (as indicated in the Five Forces and Value Net models) does not make much sense. Worse, it may lead to misleading conclusions. To illustrate this possibility, we applied the Five Forces model to the case of Airbnb. Figure 3.2 summarizes our analysis.

Let us start with the categories of players that do not raise any particular issue. We think of *rivals*, *new entrants*, and *substitutes* (collectively named 'competitors' in the Value Net model). Who they are and how strong they are (or could be) must be similarly assessed for platforms as for any other business. If you had performed the exercise, you would probably have singled out the same competitors as we did, and you would have concluded that the threat they exert on Airbnb is quite high.

Note that the category of *complementors* in the Value Net model is as relevant for platforms as for other businesses. There exist plenty of examples of platforms that open their infrastructure to third-party services to enrich the user experience and provide a higher service level. For instance, services

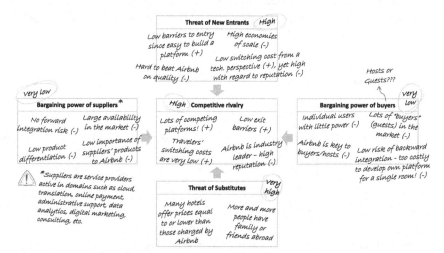

Figure 3.2 The Five Forces model applied to Airbnb.

like the ability to purchase insurance or to pay instantly via a secured and seamless payment mode are often provided by third-party players, which might be assimilated to complementors.

That leaves us with two categories that are more problematic to analyze in the case of platforms, namely 'suppliers' and 'buyers'. Let us explain why. In the traditional logic of pipelines, *suppliers* are the providers of the inputs that the organization under study uses for its production. In the case of a digital company like Airbnb, the suppliers we can directly think of are those firms that provide services and solutions for the implementation and maintenance of the platform infrastructure and processes (web design agencies, developers, cloud service providers, digital marketing consulting services, translators, etc.). It is fair to say that the bargaining power of these suppliers is weak, as they have no particular stake in the platform's purpose and activity. They are completely disconnected from the product or the service exchanged on the platform and belong to a different industry. This can be verified for almost any platform. An immediate consequence is that there is no risk of forward integration. For instance, a translation agency offering services that can accelerate the geographical expansion of the platform has no reason to be interested in entering the market in which the platform operates. In addition, those types of suppliers might offer services that are either easily accessible in the market, lowly differentiated, or that could be easily replicated in-house by acquiring the right competencies. For instance, by hiring qualified developers, a platform will not have to look for expensive IT consultants.

So, if we consider suppliers in this traditional – vertical – way, we should conclude that suppliers do not exert any substantial power on Airbnb and, by extension, on platforms in general. However, we may not have identified the 'true' suppliers of the platform; that is, those actors that genuinely equip the platforms with the means to create value. As we now argue, these actors are to be found in the ill-defined 'buyers' category.

The traditional competitive analysis considers the group of *buyers* as homogeneous. In the eyes of a retailer, for example, buyers represent all the end consumers, which often hold little bargaining power because of their isolated position as individuals. Buyers start getting more power when they unite to form consumer groups or consumer rights organizations. Yet, on platforms, it is unclear who should exactly be considered a buyer. In the case of Airbnb, should it be guests, hosts, or both of them? To some extent, both groups can be seen as 'buyers' of the platform's services.

This observation led us, in the previous chapter, to rename all of them as 'users'. Another argument for such a change of vocabulary is the following. On platforms that facilitate transactions (like Airbnb), users who are on the demand side (here, guests) probably see themselves as buyers of the users who are on the supply side (here, hosts), but not of the platform itself. There is thus a fundamental difficulty in assessing the relative bargaining power of 'buyers' if this category remains a hotchpotch of distinct user groups having their respective constraints, needs, and expectations.

Moreover, evaluating separately the bargaining power of each user group is also fraught with difficulty, owing to the tight interdependence between the various groups. As explained in Chapter 1, the presence of cross-side network effects makes the participation of one group conditional on the participation of the other group. Hence, from that perspective, users in each group have considerable bargaining power, as they can induce a negative feedback loop by leaving the platform, thereby jeopardizing its profitability. Also, insofar as the various user groups *co-create* value with the platform, they can be seen as both *co-consumers* (buyers) and *co-producers* (suppliers) of the service that the platform provides. In the case of Airbnb, that makes us conclude that hosts and guests must be considered as both buyers and suppliers.

In sum, we contend that because they are designed for vertically structured industries (in which suppliers and buyers act at distinct steps of a value chain), the Five Forces and Value Net models are ill-suited to analyze platforms (on which users co-create value and act thus as suppliers and buyers at the same time). An alternative route must then be found to analyze properly the competitive environment of platforms. We propose such a route in the next section.

The Five Forces and the Value Net are strategic models that are designed for pipelines, but not for platforms.

The Platform Value Net

The tool we propose to perform a meaningful competitive analysis of a platform business is called the *Platform Value Net* model. It is presented in Figure 3.3 for the classical case of a two-sided platform (you can download a blank version from www.platformstrategies.org).

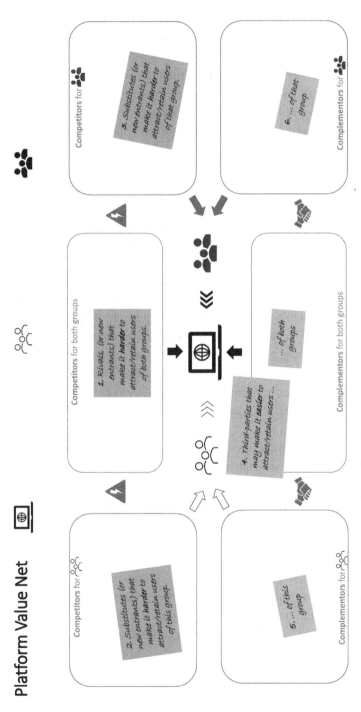

Figure 3.3 The Platform Value Net model explained.

Our tool borrows part of its name from the tool designed by Brandenburger and Nalebuff (1996) because it considers the same categories as this model but with two important twists. First, as we explained above, we abandon the traditional distinction between buyers and suppliers; we replace them with the various user groups that the platform aims at connecting. Second, because a platform's main challenge is to attract users, we regard competitors and complementors in a specific way. Starting with competitors, we see them as all entities or solutions that *make it harder for the platform to attract or retain users.* That is, referring to the Multisided Value Proposition Canvas that you completed previously, competitors provide alternatives that do the jobs, create gains, or relieve pains for your users. They may do so for users in all groups simultaneously or just for users in a particular group. This is why the top half of Figure 3.3 has three boxes: In the middle box, we invite you to identify the competitors that might prevent you from attracting any user – irrespective of the group they belong to; in the side boxes, you should report competitors that may draw away users of one particular group, while exerting no direct impact on users in the other group. Such a clear separation among competitors is meant to guide the platform's strategy when it comes to reducing the competitors' threat. It is important to stress that competitors in the side boxes are as threatening as those in the middle box: If you cannot attract users in one group, you will reduce the attractiveness of the platform for users in the other group.

We see complementors in a symmetric way. That is, complementors are all entities or solutions that *make it easier* for the platform to attract and retain users. If combined with your offering, the products and services that complementors propose will *help* you do the jobs, create gains, or relieve pains for your users. The complementarity between your offering and theirs will create additional value for your users, thereby driving users to stick by you. As for competitors, complementors might relate to all user groups or one user group in particular. The bottom half of Figure 3.3 is thus the mirror image of the top half: The middle box concerns the complementors that may help you attract and retain any type of user, while the side boxes are for complementors that can be instrumental to attract users in one group while being irrelevant or not supportive in the eyes of users in the other group.

> **View your competitors as entities and solutions that make it harder for you to attract and retain users and your complementors as entities and solutions that make it easier for you to attract and retain users.**

The Platform Value Net model is meant to give you a bird's eye view of your competitive environment and, thereby, enable you to test the robustness of your value proposition and design the right set of strategies for launching and growing your platform. Yet, to realize the true potential of this tool, you must identify and partition your competitors and complementors in the right way. To guide you in this process, we now detail the various parts of the model and illustrate them with a set of real-life examples.

Competitors in a platform environment

Competitors can be characterized along two dimensions. First, as we just explained, it is important to separate competitors according to whether they provide alternatives to both groups of users or just to one group. Second, in the spirit of Porter's Five Forces model, it is useful to distinguish between rivals, substitutes, and new entrants. Theoretically, that would make six (that is, 2 × 3) groups of competitors to consider. Yet, in what follows, we choose to distinguish among three categories of platform competitors:

- We define as **rivals** those competitors that connect the same groups of users as the platform and, thereby, make it harder for the platform to attract any user (irrespective of the side they belong to); rivals are called 'direct' if they use the same business model as the platform or 'indirect' otherwise;
- We define as **substitutes** all alternative solutions that meet the needs of users in one particular group without connecting them to users in the other group;
- **New entrants** are more transversal as they comprise potential rivals and substitutes that could appear in the future.

The three categories of platform competitors are illustrated in Figure 3.4. We now describe them in more detail.

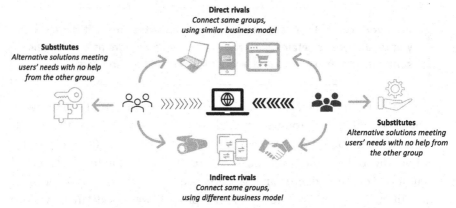

Figure 3.4 Categories of platform competitors.

Rivals (posing a threat on both sides)

Rivals intermediate between the same groups of users as the ones that you target. They have therefore the potential to divert any user from your platform. In what follows, we distinguish between direct and indirect rivals according to whether their value proposition is similar to or different from yours. Arguably, direct rivals pose a bigger threat, but indirect rivals should not be neglected. We also warn you that you could become your own rival if you are not careful. Finally, we discuss a major feature of the competitive environment that determines the intensity of rivalry.

Direct rivals. The competitors that will probably spring to mind are those platforms that mirror your offering: They address the needs of the same users and they do so in a relatively similar way. You will definitely put them in the central top box of the Platform Value Net, as they have the potential to divert users of all groups from your platform. For instance, in the European online food delivery sector, the Dutch platform Just Eat Takeaway.com needs to monitor its two biggest competitors, which are (at the time of this writing) Uber Eats and Deliveroo.

Indirect rivals. Looking at direct competitors exclusively would lead to a short-sighted view since other actors might also respond to the needs of your user groups while adopting a different business model. To avoid pretending that everything in the garden is rosy, you must identify such indirect rivals and assess their competitive threat. In particular, you should keep an eye on platforms whose user base overlaps with yours, even if their scope is different from yours. For instance, food-delivery platforms should not neglect the competition exerted by search engines (Google Search, Baidu, etc.) or social networks (Yelp, Facebook) that make it possible for customers to order food from restaurants in their neighborhood.[1] There also exist platforms – such as La Belle Asiette (France) or FoodyBuddy (India) – that allow diners to invite chefs to cook for them at home. Such platforms are indirect rivals for food-delivery platforms insofar as they offer similar services by connecting restaurants to diners (though the experience is enhanced for both sides and the connection is more direct).

Another danger would be to fall into, what we call, the 'purely online trap'. Because the digital platform phenomenon is booming nowadays, many entrepreneurs or platform operators tend to overlook the physical embodiment of platforms. We believe, however, that the offline world is still alive and kicking. As a consequence, your indirect rivals might be 'good old pipelines'. For instance, many restaurants develop their own delivery service and make local consumers aware of it by distributing folders in their mailboxes. This type of offline connection between restaurants and diners is a competing solution that meets the needs of the two user groups and, therefore, poses a threat to a food-delivery platform. Indeed, neither the restaurants using this solution nor their loyal customers are likely to join the platform, which limits the cross-side network effects that the platform can activate. Case 3.1 suggests ways to cope with such 'offline competitors'.

Case 3.1 Takeaway.com: a 'phygital' platform?

Instead of opposing the online and offline environments, you should probably try to shape your platform business model to get the best of both worlds. Trade fairs, job fairs, and other similar exhibitions remain very popular among the general public. Hence, it can be very dangerous to build your case arguing that your platform has the potential to displace a physical platform just because it is digital. Rather than assuming a complete substitution, you should strive to create distinctive offerings, identify complements, and find the mix of functionalities that users are looking for, whatever the environment. The business literature has coined terms like 'omnichannel' and 'phygital' to stress the need of integrating the two worlds.

In the food-delivery business, Takeaway.com (short for Just Eat Takeaway.com) is an example of a platform that follows this route: in contrast with competing platforms, Takeaway.com lets restaurants deliver the food themselves and focuses on facilitating the other aspects of the transaction between restaurants and customers (search, recommendations, ordering, and payment). Although the company hires its own couriers, the share of meals that they deliver remains limited. The purpose is more to parade couriers around in their shiny orange outfits and on their electric bikes to increase brand recognition.

Self-competition. Recall that we define competitors as entities and solutions that make it harder for you to attract and retain users. The part we stress here is: 'and retain users'. Attracting users on your platform is pointless if you do not manage to retain them, at least to the stage at which they start generating revenues for you. What you want to avoid is that users rely on your services to find one another but then decide to conduct the transaction outside the platform. This is particularly damaging if you charge users only for completed transactions (which is often a wise strategy for nascent platforms, as we discuss in Chapter 4). If you do not want to become your own worst enemy, you must design carefully the services you offer to prevent what is known as 'bypass' (we will show you how in Chapter 6). Bypass does not seem to be an issue for food-delivery platforms (as it requires the coordination of three parties – diner, restaurant, and courier). The threat is more serious, however, in the short-term accommodation sector: It is not uncommon for hosts and guests who have successfully matched thanks to a platform to repeat transactions and complete them outside the platform.

To make sure that you see what to put in this box (and the next), we perform the exercise for the recurring case of Airbnb (see Cases 3.2 and 3.3).

Case 3.2 Airbnb's direct and indirect rivals

Direct rivals are platforms that facilitate the transactions between hosts and guests similarly, like HomeAway, HomeExchange, Couchsurfing, Homestay, OneFineStay, Casamundo, Belvilla, or

Abritel. Indirect rivals are accommodation booking portals, like Booking.com, Expedia, Tripadvisor, Trivago, or Tripping.com. There are also other types of intermediaries – both online and offline – that allow hosts and guests to find each other; we can think of social media, newspapers with classified ads in the offline (and online) world, or rental agencies for short-term accommodation.

Intensity of rivalry. As we will discuss in the last section of this chapter, the threat that rivals pose – that is, their ability to drive users away from your platform – is inversely related to the capacity that users have to 'multihome'. When users can multihome (that is, when it is relatively inexpensive for them to be active on several platforms at the same time), rival platforms cannot completely steal them away from you. Such users continue to exert cross-side network effects on users in other groups, albeit to a smaller extent. For instance, a host that registers its accommodation on both Airbnb and HomeAway increases the attractiveness of Airbnb for guests. However, the availability for Airbnb guests might be reduced because this host also accepts guests from HomeAway. In contrast, when users must singlehome (because multihoming is either too costly or prevented by platforms), then any user that registers with a rival platform is entirely lost. Note that homing possibilities are likely to differ across sides. For instance, in the short-term accommodation industry, multihoming costs are arguably larger for hosts (from, for instance, syncing calendars to avoid double-bookings) than for guests.[2] This means that rivals can exert an asymmetric threat on the different user groups that your platform aims at connecting.

Rivals pose a threat on both sides of the platform by connecting your user groups in similar or alternative ways; they can be platforms with the same scope as yours or with a larger scope; they can also be pipelines or offline solutions.

Substitutes (posing a threat on a single side)

As mentioned earlier in this chapter, what matters with substitutes is to identify the alternative means that your different user groups can use to achieve a similar outcome as the one you are proposing. By 'alternative means', we have in mind that users in one group manage to have their needs answered *without interacting with users in the other group*. For instance, home cooking is a clear substitute for food delivery on the buyer side: Diners answer their needs (eating a — hopefully — tasty meal) without using the service of a restaurant (and therefore of an intermediary like a food-delivery platform). Going one step further, some platforms dispense with the seller side altogether and focus instead on facilitating the interaction within the group of buyers. One example in the food sector is Neighborplate, a US platform that proposes both to 'Order home-cooked meals' and 'Cook for your neighbors'.[3] This form of 'food-sharing' is another substitute for food delivery. Similarly, on the seller side, restaurants can make takeaway meals available to diners in neighboring supermarkets. Here, an anonymous pipeline approach is preferred over a one-to-one platform approach.

Case 3.3 Airbnb's substitutes

Substitutes on the *guest side* are rather easy to identify. Cheap hotels immediately come to mind, as they provide guests with an alternative to the accommodations they can find on Airbnb. The same goes for other alternatives like hostels, camping, or even staying with family or friends abroad. To uncover substitutes on the *host side*, we need to answer the following question: Who may offer hosts a service that would make them less interested in entering into a partnership with Airbnb, yet without proposing an appropriate solution to guests? This question brings us back to the understanding of users' needs and expectations. Hosts accept to rent their room or house via Airbnb because it represents a source of (additional) revenues. As this is the main motivation, we look for alternative ways to earn money through rental services. Stays booked through Airbnb last generally a couple of days, sometimes a couple of weeks, rarely more. As a result, house owners may find it more attractive to rent their property for a longer period (at least six months or one year). In this situation, real-estate agencies may help owners to find a tenant, which in a sense represents a missed opportunity for Airbnb and other platforms specialized in short vacation periods. Since people looking to rent a house or an apartment for a longer period belong to a different segment in the market – and therefore not interested in Airbnb's services, real-estate agencies and platforms like Immoweb for instance (see Case 3.4), can be seen as substitutes on the host side.

New entrants

New entrants are organizations that have the *potential* to meet the needs of your users (all or some of them). They cannot be considered rivals or substitutes because they do not operate in your market segment right now, but they may do so in the future. As new entrants are, by definition, hard to spot, you should assess more generally the threat that entrants pose – that is, you should evaluate the ease or difficulty with which entry can take place in your market segment.

Your own experience may serve as a first indication. If you had to go to great lengths to gain a foothold in your market, you may assume that other organizations would experience similar difficulties (if not greater considering that you entered first). Yet, latecomers may be better-equipped than you were (for instance, because existing activities provide them with useful assets). More importantly, they can learn from your earlier moves: Willy-nilly, innovators often smooth the path for their followers.

So, instead of projecting your experience onto potential entrants, you should try to assess objectively the so-called 'barriers to entry' that may shelter you from new competitors. In his seminal work, Bain (1956) identifies three main sources of barriers to entry: (1) Product differentiation; (2) Absolute cost advantages of established firms; and (3) Economies of scale.

Erecting the first two barriers – product differentiation and cost advantages – is largely in your hands. As discussed in Chapter 2, you must aim at designing an original, unique, and well-articulated value proposition to demarcate your business from existing and future competition. Also, you should make every effort to operate as efficiently as possible. As this holds for any type of business, we will not elaborate further here. In contrast, the third barrier – economies of scale – deserves a closer look as it plays out differently for platforms than for other businesses.

Economies of scale are achieved when producing more of a product or service allows you to lower the unit cost of production. Large upfront capital investments are a source of economies of scale because, as the scale of production increases, the initial fixed cost is spread on more units, which reduces the cost per unit. In general, online businesses require smaller initial capital investments than brick-and-mortar businesses. This is even truer for platforms that focus on intermediation, which necessitates little physical asset. One may therefore be tempted to conclude that economies of scale are less important in markets with platforms, which would make platforms more exposed to the threat of entry than pipelines.

However, even if growth does not reduce the unit cost of operating a platform, it increases the users' willingness to pay to join it because of the presence of network effects. In other words, network effects can be viewed as 'demand-side scale economies'. In the case of network effects, an expansion of a platform's user base increases the benefit that goes to each user while, in the case of scale economies, this expansion reduces the unit cost of production. A growing platform is thus in a position to capture a larger margin, either because the users' willingness to pay increases (network effects) or because the unit cost of delivering the service decreases (scale economies). So, even absent scale economies, network effects have the potential to raise barriers to entry and, thereby, confer a competitive advantage to bigger platforms. To which extent and at which conditions? We explore these issues in more detail in the last section of this chapter.

Complementors in a platform environment

According to Brandenburger and Nalebuff (1996), complementors are organizations whose products or services complement one another, in the sense that customers perceive a larger value when they consume these products and services together. We first identify the value (but also the costs) that complementors can add to a platform. Then, we explain that you can sometimes find complementors where you least expected to find them. Finally, as we did for competitors, we stress the importance of distinguishing among complementors according to which group(s) of users they contribute to attracting.

Platform complementors: what for?

As we explained previously, complementors are entities or solutions that make it *easier* for the platform to attract and retain users. Whichever their nature (platforms, pipelines, or other), complementors can help you grow your business because they reinforce network effects in two major ways. First, having complementors around enhances the value perceived by your users when interacting on the platform. Think for instance of a digital marketplace that partners with an online payment system. One famous example is eBay, which acquired PayPal in 2002 (but spun it off into a separate company in 2014). The presence of this complementor speeds up the payment process, which increases the value that users obtain from the transactions they conduct on the marketplace. As a result, each additional seller becomes more valuable for any buyer, and vice versa. Second, complementors also allow a platform to connect with a wider range of potential users. For instance, when a news mobile application like BBC News is directly connected to a social network application like Twitter, each platform gains access to the audience of the other, which creates mutual benefits (BBC News users can share with more, while Twitter users have more to share). Here, network effects are enhanced because there are more additional users than before (while the value of an additional user is unchanged).

> **Complementors contribute to enhancing network effects on a platform by bringing in new users and by making users more valuable to one another.**

By enhancing network effects, complementors also help you erect entry barriers and keep new entrants at bay. In particular, your ability to build strong ties with local complementors represents a shield against global players. As Case 3.4 illustrates, the partnerships concluded by Immoweb (the leading real estate platform in Belgium) can be seen as part of a defensive strategy against global players that have the technical and financial means to enter its turf by launching new dedicated platforms (think, typically, of tech giants like Google or Facebook).

Case 3.4 Immoweb and its complementors

As the leading real estate platform in Belgium, Immoweb benefits from a solid position and reputation within the market. The
intermediation between sellers and buyers of real estate goods
represents its core business for more than 20 years. Over the
past couple of years though, the company decided to diversify its
range of activities with additional linked services that should be
valued by its existing user base. Therefore, the platform negoti-
ated partnerships with various players including real estate agents,
construction firms, insurance companies, and utilities. All these
partnerships aim at building an ecosystem around its main platform. Whether it relates to financial services (mortgage loans),
legal advice (lease agreement), energy consumption (smart meter-
ing), or any other service related to the real estate sector, the goal
is clearly to intensify the number of transactions and diversify the
sources of revenues. This is all the more useful as the pure matchmaking activity over the Internet increasingly appears as a com-
modity that global platforms can easily 'envelop' (that is, they can
bundle their functionalities with those of smaller platforms to take
advantage of overlapping user bases; we return to such strategies
in Chapter 6).

Another positive consequence of tying your services with those
of complementors is that bypass becomes less profitable for your
users. As you propose a wider and more convenient set of services (one-stop shopping), users would forego more value if they
decided to complete transactions outside the platform.

For all the previous reasons, opening your platform to complementors
increases what your users are willing to pay for your services. Moreover, it
is often more cost-effective to let third parties provide value-added services
rather than doing so yourself. Indeed, these services can be of a very different nature, requiring specific knowledge and resources. Also, building
the entire architecture takes time and may distract you from your core

intermediation activity. Partnering with complementors appears thus as a very desirable strategy as it may allow you to widen your margins on both ends (by making your users pay more while reducing your costs).

However, you should not underestimate the costs of linking complementors to your platform. First, to ensure their participation, you will have to cut a win-win deal with your complementors. The stronger their bargaining power, the larger the share of the added value they will capture and the less profitable the partnership will be for you. Second, even if a complementor's offering is not overlapping with yours, its service should be aligned with the needs of your community. At the end of the day, your users will decide whether there is any interest for them in consuming the services together. For example, when eBay decided to buy Skype, the company assumed that a calling functionality would add value to the marketplace by improving the communication between sellers and buyers. However, it turned out that very few eBay users adopted Skype in the context of their retail activity. As a result, eBay decided to part from the calling business (despite a growing user base). One explanation behind this decision may be the following. If you overestimated complementarities, integrating third-party services may prove counterproductive, as it may confuse your users or damage their experience on the platform.

Finally, a platform faces significant risks when connecting low-quality complementors to its user base. Your users will indeed assume that you have endorsed the offerings of any third party they can interact with on your platform. As a result, they will hold you accountable for any mishap related to these offerings.[4]

Turning potential competitors into complementors

Identifying complementors may turn out to be trickier than expected. Sometimes, the positive implications are not obvious at first sight. This is especially true if you stick to a traditional pipeline reading grid. Your instinct might then be to fight those external players that seem to illegitimately thrive on your platform's success. However, as these players are outside your control anyway, it may be much wiser to try and turn the threat into an opportunity, as Case 3.5 illustrates.

Case 3.5 Comple-titors

In the spirit of 'co-opetition', we coin here a new portmanteau word, namely 'comple-titor'. We want to blend the meaning of complementor and competitor because a platform may well find useful complementors in the group of its competitors. As evidence, we reproduce here a few excerpts of examples found in the literature, which we believe illustrate particularly well the challenge of recognizing that some players that appear at first as a threat can, in the end, become helpful complementors.

IKEA and IKEAhackers.net

IKEA [...] faced a choice to smother or fuel a platform when IKEAhackers.net went mainstream. The fansite shared creative ways to recombine, or hack, IKEA's already modular products. Originally viewing the site as a legal and public relations risk, IKEA shifted script and embraced its biggest fans. Empowering fans as potential product developers instead of shutting down or taking over the unexpected platform, IKEA built trust and ultimately extended its brand reach (Brown, 2016).

The Forum Athletic Club and Cyc Fitness

The Forum Athletic Club has replaced its own cycling classes with the Cyc Fitness classes offered at its gym. Cyc's spinning classes have proved more popular with members and allow the Forum to focus its resources on other services while converting Cyc from a competitor to a complementor. The underlying logic is that if substitution from third parties is inevitable, bringing them onto your platform may expand its overall appeal to your customers (Hagiu and Altman, 2017).

Apple and its apps

The first iPhone was a closed-system product with a handful of apps produced by Apple. As it became more popular, hackers began to 'jailbreak' the phone so that they could install their own apps. [...] Apple first reacted to the hacking by going on the defensive: It made the phone's operating software more secure and threatened to avoid the warranty if a jailbreak had been applied. Eventually, though, Jobs saw the wisdom in creating a more open platform, and a year after launching the iPhone, Apple opened the App Store (Zhu and Furr, 2016).

Complementors for whom?

Like we did for the competitors, it is useful to separate complementors according to whether they may assist the platform in attracting users in any group (the middle box) or just one group (the left and right boxes). We use, once more, Airbnb as an illustration (see Case 3.6).

Case 3.6 Airbnb's complementors

For Airbnb, being able to connect with complementors is very important, especially if it wants to reduce the threat of hotels on the guest side, as noted in Case 3.2. Many guests may see hotel rooms as a superior option because they are bundled with services that accommodations on Airbnb do not offer (such as food, daily cleaning, front desk, breakfast included, etc.). The platform must therefore think of providing guests with similar services, for instance by concluding a partnership with a food-delivery platform active in the same market. For that matter, it makes sense to put food-delivery platforms in the 'Complementors for guests' box.

Similarly, Airbnb may think of potential partnerships or agreements that would be beneficial for hosts. For example, because it has been demonstrated that the quantity and the quality of the pictures are key decision criteria to explain the success of Airbnb, the access – facilitated by the platform – to local professional media service providers might be seen by some hosts as a decisive argument to join the platform. The same goes for other service providers like insurance companies and digital marketing agencies.

Finally, when complementors have a positive and direct impact on users irrespective of the sides they belong to, those services (like professional cleaning for example) are to be assigned to the middle box 'Complementors for both groups'.

The reason we advise you to separate complementors into these three categories is the same as for competitors: It will help you design your set of strategies. This exercise should indeed clarify the cost-benefit analysis of linking with this or this complementor. For instance, even if it seems a priori more productive to partner with complementors that contribute to attracting users in both groups, we will see in the next chapter that it may sometimes be more efficient to focus on users in one group and exploit the leverage that they exert on the other group. In that case, linking with complementors relative to that particular group should be seen as a priority. We will also discuss in Chapter 6 the form that such a relationship should take. Should the platform partner with a selected subset of complementors? Should it take a whole category of complementors on board as a new user group? Or should it produce itself the services that complementors provide? Again, the best mode of organization may depend on which group of users is considered.

Network effects and competitive advantage

Now that you have completed the Platform Value Net, you should have a pretty good view of the competitive landscape around your platform. You are then equipped for what is coming in the rest of this book: You will learn how to launch successfully your platform (Chapter 4) and gain a sustainable foothold in the market (Chapters 5 and 6). But before getting there, you should use the information you collected previously to evaluate to which extent you can turn *network effects into a competitive advantage*. As we explained in Chapter 1, network effects have the potential to consolidate a platform's competitive position thanks to the positive feedback loops they generate – recall the analogy we drew with a snowball or a flywheel to describe the self-reinforcing mechanism whereby more users attract more users. Yet, to unlock this potential, you must first connect the Platform Value Net to the Linkage Map and make sure that you do not confuse one model for the other. Next, you must assess whether network effects on your platform are *strong* and *defensible*; that is, whether they give rise to a significant and sustainable competitive advantage.[5]

Connecting with the Linkage Map

As seen in Figure 3.3, we put a simplified representation of the Linkage Map at the center of the Platform Value Net. This is to stress the strong complementarity between the two tools. To make the most of this complementarity, it is important to realize that the two tools invite you to take distinct standpoints. The Linkage Map looks *inward* as it aims at describing the *relationships between users on the platform* (as its main goal is to identify the network effects that exist either across the two groups of users or within each group). In contrast, the Platform Value Net looks *outward*, with the objective to highlight the *relationships between the platform and external players*.

We see two potential pitfalls if you mistake one tool for the other. First, it would be confusing to mention platform users as competitors or complementors in the Platform Value Net.[6] Users may compete with one another (like Airbnb hosts in the same city) or complement one another (like Airbnb guests leaving ratings and reviews). Yet, these relationships are best reported as same-side network effects in the Linkage Map, because they take place within – and not outside – the platform boundaries.

Second, you should not let cross-side network effects blur the lines between the competitors (or complementors) that concern both groups and those that concern just one group. For example, as cheap hotels may take guests away from Airbnb, they should be put in the 'Competitors for hosts' box. Yet, because of cross-side network effects, the platform becomes less attractive for guests as soon as it loses some hosts. One could then be tempted to place cheap hotels in the 'Competitors for guests' box as well, as they make it harder for Airbnb to attract guests. But if cheap hotels are placed in both boxes, then their true place should be in the 'Competitors for both groups' box. Pursuing this line of reasoning, all competitors would be reported in the central box, which would lead to a much less informative representation of the competition. To avoid such a trap, you need to recall that the Platform Value Net focuses on external players that have a direct impact on the platform, while the Linkage Map indicates how these impacts may be indirectly channeled to other users (that is, through network effects).

Strength of network effects

The Linkage Map that you drew gives you a fair idea of the nature and strength of the network effects that operate on your platform. A priori, stronger network effects (cross-side and/or same-side) will give rise to a more powerful feedback loop. But things are a bit more subtle than they look.

First, the strength of network effects is not just a function of the number of users that are active on the platform. Who these users are, what they do, and how they complement one another may be as important as how many they are. Specifically, on platforms that gather providers and consumers, the quality of the underlying products or services that are offered via the platform is of paramount importance because a single rotten apple may suffice to spoil the whole basket in no time. There are multiple examples of rotten apples one can think of: counterfeited goods on an e-commerce platform, substandard housing on a holiday booking platform, weak business cases on a crowdfunding platform, fake profiles on a dating platform, etc. Of course, achieving an ex-ante assessment of the quality of something you do not control can be a daunting task. One possibility, as we will discuss in Chapter 6, is to rely on the consumer side (reviews) or on a third-party (accreditation) to handle this issue. Whatever the instruments you use, the challenge is to find the right balance between quantity (larger numbers of users to fuel network effects) and quality (better pools of users to avoid reputational damages). Case 3.7 illustrates this trade-off in the case of reward-based crowdfunding.

Case 3.7 Quantity–quality trade-off for crowdfunding platforms

Catarse is a Brazilian reward-based crowdfunding platform. It allows entrepreneurs to pitch creative projects to a pool (a 'crowd') of backers; in exchange for their contribution, backers receive a 'reward', in the form of early access to the financed product or some special perks.

Up to 2016, the platform's staff was approving every project manually. This process guaranteed that all projects responded to minimum quality requirements. Yet, as this process was costly and difficult to scale, it was perceived as an impediment to the platform's growth and competitiveness. In 2016, Catarse relinquished the staff screening, leaving to the 'crowd' the decision to 'select' projects, that is, to participate or not to their funding.

Viotto da Cruz (2019) reports that this change led to an increase in the entries on the entrepreneurs' side, which was not necessarily accompanied by a comparable increase in participation on the backers' side. First, entrepreneurs were facing more competition for the attention of backers (that is, the negative same-side network effects got stronger). Second, the lack of screening allowed many low-quality projects to appear on the platform. The fact that these projects ended up not receiving any funding shows that the crowd selection worked fine. But the cost was high, as the presence of such low-quality projects undermined the backers' trust in the whole pool of projects presented on the platform (that is, the positive cross-side network effects exerted by entrepreneurs on backers somehow weakened).

The strength of network effects may also depend more on the composition than on the size of the groups of users joining the platform. For instance, buyers often value a marketplace for the variety of product categories they can find there. To keep the feedback loop powerful, the marketplace should then focus on attracting sellers in new or poorly populated product categories, with the view to increasing variety. In contrast, attracting one more seller in a category that is already well-populated would exert little cross-side network effects on buyers and so, add little fuel to the feedback loop. Similarly, users of e-scooter platforms are happy if one or two scooters are available for them to use in their vicinity; having a third or a fourth one does not add much value.

Second, the geographical scope of network effects matters. Here, the question is whether users care about other users in all locations or only in their vicinity. In other words, is proximity an important dimension for users? It is, for example, on food-delivery platforms. Imagine someone living in a remote place in the countryside, far from any city center. Even if the platform has thousands of registered restaurants, that person will not see any interest in joining the platform, as she will not be able to benefit from the service. In contrast, proximity is not so much of an issue on platforms that offer dematerialized services. On Wikipedia, for instance, anyone benefits from the addition of new articles or the improvement of existing ones irrespective of where they are.

Why does it matter? In the case of Wikipedia, network effects are said to be 'global', in the sense that an additional user in location X exerts network effects on users in any location Y or Z. A feedback loop can thus be ignited anywhere and be fueled from anywhere, which makes it very powerful. In contrast, in the case of food delivery, network effects are only 'local', meaning that feedback loops must be ignited in each location (X, Y, and Z) and cannot spread from one location to the next (what starts in location X stays in location X). The conclusion is thus that network effects can be turned more easily into a competitive advantage when they are global rather than local.[7]

By analogy, network effects are stronger (and thus more likely to generate a competitive advantage) if they can be 'ported' across different market segments that the platform caters to or across different services that it offers. To understand this point, take the example of Uber. In 2014, Uber launched its food-delivery service, Uber Eats, which connects three groups of users, namely restaurants, diners, and couriers. Later, in 2020, Uber launched Uber Direct, a parcel-delivery service, which also connects three groups of users, namely senders of parcels, recipients of parcels, and couriers. Because couriers are mostly common to the two services (they can deliver parcels alongside meals), the positive cross-group network effects that they exert on restaurants and diners through Uber Eats can be ported, at little cost, to parcel senders and recipients through Uber Direct. Uber is thus strengthening the network effects that it manages and, thereby, it gains an advantage over its competitors. It is indeed more profitable for Uber to organize the delivery of food and parcels jointly than it is for two separate platforms to do so.[8] As a result, a platform that specializes in parcel delivery would have a hard time entering the market.

Finally, it is important to evaluate *how long* a feedback loop remains powerful. This depends on how the value of network effects evolves with the number of users who are already on the platform; that is, how does the additional value of, say, the 10,000th user compare with the value of the 1,000th or 100th one? If additional users keep on providing roughly the same value to other users as the platform grows in size, then the feedback loop will remain powerful; but if the value of additional users decreases quickly as more users join the platform, then the feedback loop will fizzle out.

> Network effects tend to be stronger if the platform cares about attracting the right users (and not just more of them), if users can co-create value across locations or market segments, and if additional users keep on providing roughly the same value as the platform grows.

Defensibility of network effects

Even if you manage to gain a competitive advantage, you may still struggle to maintain this advantage in the long term. In particular, you must be aware of two typical situations in which your advantage may wear away relatively fast. First, the benefits of the feedback loop generated on your platform may spill over to rival platforms. Second, other platforms may reproduce the conditions that gave rise to your feedback loop. The first situation has to do with the *specificity* of the network effects and the second with their *replicability*. As we now explain, network effects are more defensible the more specific and the less replicable they are.

Specificity of network effects

Network effects are said to be specific to a platform if users must be registered with this platform to enjoy the benefits of these effects. That is, no interaction can take place between users registered with different platforms. In that case, a platform that grows larger necessarily does it at the expense of competing platforms. Then, with the reinforcing power of feedback loops, dominant positions quickly arise: The big platform gets bigger while the small platforms get smaller. Competition among platforms, therefore, leads to a winner-takes-all situation. As competing platforms are forced to leave the market, the competitive advantage that specific network effects generate is highly defensible. In such situations, platforms are said to compete *for* the market.

Yet, defensibility rhymes here with uncertainty. In this cut-throat environment, the emergence of a single winner is the only sure thing. The identity of the winner, on the other hand, is largely unpredictable, which means that having the most convincing value proposition is no guarantee of success.[9] It might then be wiser to make network effects on your platform somehow less specific. This means that you could let users from other platforms reap some of the network benefits generated on your platform. There are basically two routes to achieve this. First, you can agree with your rivals to make your platforms technically interoperable; this can be done by adhering to common standards or by opening APIs (Application Programming Interfaces). In that case, users can interact across different platforms. For instance, users of smartphones powered by any operating system (OS) can call one another if they use regular phone lines; they can also do so when using one of the many 'Voice over IP' applications that are available for all major OSs (such as Skype, WhatsApp, or Viber).[10] Another example is Facebook, which announced in December 2019 its intention to facilitate the portability of photos from the social network to rival online services.[11] Whenever this will become a reality, the positive network effects resulting from photo sharing on Facebook will somehow benefit users of other platforms as well.

The second route consists in lowering the costs for users to multihome, that is, to be active on several platforms at the same time. In this case, interaction is still limited to users belonging to the same platform but, as multihoming is relatively inexpensive, users can easily reap network benefits from several platforms. In the case of ride-hailing services, for example, travelers can easily request a ride simultaneously on more than one app. Whichever route is followed, the competition among platforms changes in the same way: As network effects are no longer specific to each platform, feedback loops do not necessarily lead to dominant positions, meaning that competing platforms may well coexist on the market.[12] Platforms no longer compete for the market but in the market.

To sum up, there is a trade-off between defensibility and uncertainty. By keeping network effects specific, you take a gamble: Either you win a sustainable competitive advantage or you lose everything. In contrast, if you opt for interoperability or if you facilitate multihoming, a better value proposition will earn you a competitive advantage, but this advantage will be harder to maintain. Your confidence in the superiority of your value proposition and your attitude toward risk will decide which path you follow.

Replicability of network effects

A related issue regarding the defensibility of network effects is the extent to which rival platforms can replicate the way you generate positive feedback loops on your platform. We see two factors that influence this replicability. First, the nature of the matching between the different groups of users can make a difference. In particular, if efficient matching requires the simultaneous presence of many users in both groups at any given time, then feedback loops are more defensible, as smaller platforms cannot offer a service of the same quality. This is so in the ride-hailing industry: Waiting times are shorter on big platforms (like Uber, Didi, or Lyft) because many passengers and drivers are constantly using them. In contrast, car-sharing platforms on which rides can be booked well in advance do not require the synchronous matching of the two groups, which makes them an easier target for new entrants.

Second, the defensibility of feedback loops also depends on the users' ability to coordinate their decisions. When users have a hard time coordinating their decisions, network effects create so-called 'collective switching costs': Users find it costly to switch to another platform because they fear losing the benefits of network effects if too few other users switch alongside them. If so, network effects lead to a defensible competitive advantage because, even if a rival platform with better features wants to enter the market, it is quite unlikely that users will coordinate on it. In contrast, if users can easily communicate (and there is no other source of switching costs), then massive migration to rival platforms becomes a real threat, as illustrated in Case 3.8.

Against this backdrop, you may want to implement tactics that reinforce collective switching costs. One way is to make existing users value the possibility to interact with users they do not know about (for instance, by improving the search features or the recommendation system); as coordinating with yet unknown users is obviously more complex, migration becomes less of a threat.

Case 3.8 How communication missteps cost WhatsApp's millions of users

In January 2021, WhatsApp announced, in a rather confusing way, an upcoming update of its privacy policy. Although the changes were meant to allow businesses using WhatsApp for customer service to store logs of their chats on the servers of Facebook (WhatsApp's parent company), many users understood that they would have to accept the sharing of sensible profile information with Facebook if they wanted to continue using the app. This misperception was quickly amplified by social media and led millions of users to migrate, in a matter of days, to competing apps like Signal or Telegram. The irony here is that the instant messaging service that WhatsApp offers generates strong network effects but also makes it very easy for its users to switch to rival apps. It is indeed within their WhatsApp group that most users (the authors included) coordinated their adoption of Signal or Telegram.

Network effects tend to be more defensible if they are specific to the platform and if they are hard to replicate by rival platforms.

One very last step. Before moving to the next chapter, we advise you to return to your value proposition and have a critical look at it. The Platform Value Net should have given you a broader perspective about the contours that your project should take. For instance, now that you have a better idea of who your competitors are (or could be), you may want to double-check if your value proposition is as unique as you initially thought. On a more positive note, now that you have spotted several potential complementors, you may think of services or functionalities that could be added to your offering thanks to the complementors' collaboration.

SHORT ANSWERS TO THE KEY QUESTIONS

* *Why is the traditional competitive analysis ill-suited for platforms?* Mainly because it refers to the value chain representation of a

pipeline firm, which buys raw material and intermediate goods from suppliers, transforms or assembles them into some product or service of higher value, which it then sells to its customers or clients. In contrast, a platform hardly transforms or assembles anything, as it primarily facilitates transactions among independent users. By the way, in the context of platforms, 'users' is a more adapted term, which englobes 'buyers' and 'suppliers'.

- *How can we define a platform's competitors and complementors?* A platform's competitors are those entities and solutions that make it harder for the platform to attract and retain users. A platform's complementors are those entities and solutions that make it easier for the platform to attract and retain users.

- *What is the difference between the rivals and the substitutes for a platform?* Rivals pose a threat on both sides of the platform by connecting your user groups in similar or alternative ways. Substitutes pose a threat only on one side of the platform; that is, they let users in one group manage to have their needs answered without interacting with users in the other group.

- *How does the Linkage Map fit into the competitive analysis of a platform?* The Linkage Map describes the relationships between users on the platform. Thereby, it complements the Platform Value Net, which highlights the relationships between the platform and external players. While the Platform Value Net focuses on external players that have a direct impact on the platform, the Linkage Map indicates how these impacts may be indirectly channeled to other users (that is, through network effects).

- *How can network effects be turned into a competitive advantage?* To generate a significant and sustainable competitive advantage, network effects must be strong and defensible. Network effects tend to be stronger if the platform cares about attracting the right users (and not just more of them), if users can co-create value across locations or market segments, and if additional users provide roughly the same value as the platform grows. Network effects tend to be more defensible if they are specific to the platform and if rival platforms have a hard time replicating them.

FURTHER READINGS

Porter (1989) and Brandenburger and Nalebuff (1996) remain essential readings to inform any competitive analysis. For an introduction to the economics of competition between platforms, see Belleflamme (2020).

Notes

1. An example from another sector is AutoScout24, the European leader in automotive classifieds: Although platforms like eBay are much less specialized, they represent a credible alternative because they propose used cars among all kinds of other second-hand items.
2. Giannoni *et al.* (2021) analyze a sample of more than 3,900 hosts from the region of Corsica in France. According to their estimate, roughly half of them only use Airbnb (the other half use at least one additional distribution channel).
3. See https://neighborplate.com/ (last accessed September 2021).
4. For more on this, see Hagiu and Altman (2017).
5. For this part, we follow Hagiu and Wright (2020a, 2020b).
6. Unfortunately, the management literature does nothing to lighten the confusion. Many scholars do indeed call 'complementors' the independent service providers on a transaction platform or marketplace. For instance, Chen *et al.* (2022) write:

   In a platform ecosystem (e.g., Android's ecosystem), we can distinguish between the platform (i.e., Android), platform owner (i.e., Google), platform providers (e.g., Samsung and Huawei), and complementors (e.g., app developers). Both platform providers and complementors are "producers" in the ecosystem, while "consumers" are end-users.

   In our vocabulary, both app developers and end-users are seen as users of the platform.
7. Another way to see this point is to compare the competitive positions of Uber and Airbnb. If Uber is the dominant ride-hailing service in some cities, this does not give the company much traction to extend its dominance to other cities. The reason is that the interaction between drivers and riders takes place in a given city, making each city a distinct market. In contrast, Airbnb guests have no interest in hosts located in their city; what matters for them is to be able to travel anywhere. The market is thus global, which

protects the dominant platform – Airbnb – from the entry of potential contestants.

8. This can be seen as a form of economies of scope on the demand side (as they stem from an increase in the users' willingness to pay). We return to this concept in Chapter 6 when examining platforms' growth strategies.

9. In his seminal paper, Arthur (1989) describes four common features of the competition between platforms when network effects are specific: *Path-dependence* (the outcome depends on how adoptions build up), *inflexibility* (the left-behind platform needs to bridge a widening gap), *non-predictability* (the process locks into the dominance of one platform, but which platform is not predictable in advance), and *potential inefficiency* (the platform that wins the market needs not to be the one that creates the largest value in the long run).

10. Yet, the performance of some apps may vary across OSs, which may cause problems (such as synchronization issues) when calls are made between users of different devices. Note that there also exist applications that are only available to users of devices running on a given OS (like FaceTime, which Apple deploys exclusively on the iPhone); in that case, there is no interoperability.

11. It is worth stressing that Facebook announced this move as an effort to comply with European privacy laws and to appease the regulators, who fear that its control over data may hinder competition. This illustrates what we mention in Chapter 1 about big platforms falling under the scrutiny of regulators and competition authorities.

12. This does not mean that competition in contexts of multihoming is always low. For instance, social networks do not really compete for users, as they know that multihoming is the norm. But they compete quite fiercely for the *time* that users spend on their platform. Indeed, time is not an extensible resource and is ultimately what is of interest to users on the other side of the platform, namely advertisers.

Bibliography

Arthur, W. B. (1989). Competing technologies, increasing returns, and lock-in by historical events. *Economic Journal* 99, 116–131. https://doi.org/10.2307/2234208.

Bain, J. S. (1956). *Barriers to new competition*. Cambridge MA: Harvard University Press.

Belleflamme, P. (2020). An introduction to the economics of platform competition (I, II, and III). IPdigIT (April). http://www.ipdigit.eu/2020/04/an-introduction-to-the-economics-of-platform-competition-part-1/.

Brandenburger, A. and Nalebuff, B. (1996). *Co-opetition*. New York: Broadway Business.

Brown, C. (2016). 3 Questions to ask before adopting a platform business model. *Harvard Business Review*. https://hbr.org/2016/04/3-questions-to-ask-before-adopting-a-platform-business-model.

Chen, L., Yi, J., Li, S., and Tong, T.W. (2022). Platform governance design in platform ecosystems: Implications for complementors' multihoming decisions. *Journal of Management* 48(3), 630–656. https://doi.org/10.1177/0149206320988337.

Giannoni, S., Brunstein, D., Guéniot, F. and Jouve, J. (2021). Multichannel distribution strategy of Airbnb hosts. *Annals of Tourism Research Empirical Insights* 2, 100017. https://doi.org/10.1016/j.annale.2021.100017.

Hagiu, A. and E. Altman (2017). Finding the platform in your product. *Harvard Business Review* 95, 94–100. https://www.hbs.edu/faculty/Pages/item.aspx?num=52837.

Hagiu, A. and Wright, J. (2020a). Seven questions to evaluate network effects moats. *Platform Chronicles* (December 2). https://platformchronicles.substack.com/p/network-effects-and-defensibility.

Hagiu, A. and Wright, J. (2020b). How defensible are Zoom's network effects? *Platform Chronicles* (December 15). https://platformchronicles.substack.com/p/how-defensible-are-zooms-network.

Porter, M.E. (1989). How competitive forces shape strategy. *Harvard Business Review* 57(2), 137–145. https://hbr.org/1979/03/how-competitive-forces-shape-strategy.

Viotto da Cruz, J. (2019). Platform governance and complementors' quality: Evidence from crowdfunding websites. Unpublished manuscript.

Zhu, F. and Furr, N. (2016). Products to platforms: Making the leap. *Harvard Business Review* 94, 72–78. https://hbr.org/2016/04/products-to-platforms-making-the-leap.

4

LAUNCHING A PLATFORM

The big challenge

KEY QUESTIONS

- What is a Minimum Viable Platform?
- Which users should be attracted first to launch a platform?
- How costly is it to attract a particular group of users?
- Which launching tactics should be deployed in practice?
- When is 'not being a platform' the best way to start a platform?

The first three chapters helped you lay the groundwork for your platform. Going through the Linkage Map, the Multisided Value Proposition canvas, and the Platform Value Net, you gained a solid understanding of who your users are, what they need, and how you can beat the competition to meet these needs. You should thus be ready to launch your platform. Yet, the previous chapters also taught you that platforms are complex creatures. They are complex to design and – perhaps even more so – to launch. This is

DOI: 10.4324/9780429490873-7

why the present chapter is meant to help you navigate this complex launch phase.

We start by discussing a recommendation that you may have come across already when reading about the management of platforms: 'Start small!'. Although we agree with the general principle, we explain that it is not easy to put it into practice. The main reason is that any nascent platform can only attract users by attracting other users. In the case of two-sided platforms, this means that to attract users in group A, the platform must attract users in group B, but to attract users in group B, it must attract users in group A. This conundrum is known as the 'mutual baiting problem' or, more figuratively, the 'chicken-and-egg problem': Because chickens hatch from eggs and eggs are laid by chickens, one wonders which came first. As far as platforms are concerned, the conundrum is more about which, of the chicken or the egg, *should* come first. That is, knowing that you have to start somewhere, which users should you target in priority to start your business? In the second part of this chapter, we provide you with a rigorous method for answering this tricky question; we call it the 'Lever Selector' because the objective is to select the group of users that proves the most efficient lever to attract the other group(s) of users. Finally, we describe three generic strategies that platforms can deploy at the launch stage, depending on the circumstances they are faced with. Moreover, we propose, for each strategy, a set of specific tactics.

Start 'small'

"The best way to get big is by first going small." Here is the lesson that Rachitsky (2019) draws from the interviews he conducted with founders and early employees of 17 successful platforms (such as Airbnb, DoorDash, Thumbtack, Etsy, and Uber). All these companies (with the notable exception of Thumbtack – we explain why later) initially 'constrained' their operations. That is, they started to operate within a well-defined category of products or services and/or within a bounded geographical location; some of them also carefully chose the time of their entrance into the market. This is reminiscent of the three unities that govern French classical theatre – unity of action, unity of place, and unity of time (the play should have one principal action, occurring in a single place, and within a day). Rachitsky (2019) provides some illustrations of these principles: only three categories of items could initially be sold on Etsy (category constraint/ unity of action), Airbnb first focused on New York (geographical constraint/unity of place), while Instacart thought that it would attract more demand if it launched in the Winter (period constraint/unity of time).

This mantra of starting small also echoes the concept of Minimum Viable Product (MVP), which Ries (2011) popularized as part of the Lean Startup methodology. The MVP is a version of a product that contains the minimum set of features to make it appealing to early adopters. The goal is to generate feedback from the first customers and use it to improve the product iteratively while minimizing the cost of the whole process. Applied to platforms, the concept becomes the 'Minimum Viable Platform', which Choudary (2014) associates with the idea that platforms should focus first on what constitutes the 'core interaction' between its users. In the case of Uber, for instance, the core transaction is the matching of drivers and riders in a given location. This is what Uber tried to achieve from the outset; other features (like fare splitting or gamification) were only introduced at a later stage.

It seems thus wise to start with a small – or minimal – platform that tries to meet nothing more than the main needs of its users and does so with a limited set of features and, if proximity between users matters, in a limited location. Yet, this minimum platform also needs to be 'viable', in the sense that it delivers enough value to its users. And this is where Minimum Viable Platforms crucially differ from minimum viable products: As platforms co-create value with their users, their viability requires the participation of sufficiently many users. That is, to be viable, the minimum platform must be … large enough. Sander Daniels, a co-founder of Thumbtack, vividly illustrates this issue:

> The conventional wisdom was to narrow focus to a category (like Amazon did with books) or geography (like Yelp did with San Francisco). We didn't get funding for many years in part because we did the opposite – we did all categories and all geographies from the beginning. People thought that wouldn't work, that we were boiling the ocean. In retrospect *it was the only way to build a marketplace in our space at scale – being broad in category increased the frequency of use of our product from once every couple years (how often do you need to hire a house painter?) to 8–12 times a year (the number of Thumbtack services an average American household hires annually). And being broad in geography allowed us to scale our marketplace as*

fast as possible, giving us the revenue, traffic, and thus experimental velocity we needed to bootstrap a great product. In our case we wouldn't have survived had we done it any other way.

(Quoted in Rachitsky, 2019; emphasis added)

In sum, it is certainly a wise move to limit the scope of your platform at first (that is, to limit the transactions you facilitate, the features you offer, and the categories or geographies you cover). You would indeed waste precious resources if you were trying to solve every need of your users at once. Yet, you should not limit your scope too much either, because it is precisely by bringing users together that you can meet their needs. Therefore, you need to grow a sufficient audience, which may imply that you cover enough categories or geographies to start with (as in the case of Thumbtack).

Start small ... but not too small. That is, limit the scope of your platform to avoid wasting resources while remaining sufficiently broad to grow a large enough audience.

One understands that it is more complex to design a Minimum Viable Platform than a minimum viable product. Another main difference between the two types of MVPs is the following. Product developers can improve their products gradually by responding to the feedback they obtain from successive working versions. In contrast, such an iterative process does not seem feasible for platforms. The service that a platform offers – that is, interaction possibilities – cannot be built step by step, as it only materializes when it is jointly consumed by its users. As we saw in Chapter 1, network effects give an all-or-nothing nature to platforms. This leaves you with little room for maneuvering, as you need to come up straight with the right Minimum Viable Platform (and with the right value proposition, as we stressed in Chapter 2). All this cannot be done without careful planning, especially regarding the way to attract your first users, as we now discuss.

The chicken or the egg: which should come first?

Any entrepreneur who wants to launch a platform understands intuitively what the chicken-and-egg problem means and how taxing it is. Chapter 1 provided us with some useful ingredients for solving this apparently intractable problem. In particular, we learned how to map and gauge the links that connect users on the platform, as well as the feedback loops that result from these links. The next logical step is to activate the links.

The objective is naturally to start – and take advantage of – positive feedback loops (while keeping negative loops, if any, on a tight leash). Consider the typical case of a platform that facilitates the interaction between two groups that exert positive cross-side network effects on one another. As group A members (say, providers) attract group B members (say, customers) and conversely, a positive feedback loop can in principle be started anywhere. Yet, it is in general more profitable to start the loop with one group rather than with the other. As the proverb goes, a good beginning makes a good ending. As the co-founder and CEO of Bsit (a Belgian-based platform that helps parents find trustworthy babysitters) once declared:

> . By connecting the two sides of a marketplace – parents on one side and babysitters on the other – we knew that the mistake we couldn't make at launch was to work on both simultaneously. The solution? Gather a community of 'sitters' first and only then focus on demand.
>
> (De Boose, 2018)

Why did Bsit choose to focus first on babysitters and not on parents? In more general terms, the million-dollar question here is: "Which user group should be attracted first to launch a platform?". This is what we want to uncover now.

To make our point, we can draw a simple but very effective analogy with levers. Figure 4.1 depicts a lever: It is a beam, resting on a fulcrum (or pivot), that is used to lift a load with one end by exerting an effort on the other end. In our case, by acquiring users from one group (the effort), you take advantage of the cross-side network effects (the beam on the fulcrum) to attract users from the other group (the load). The question "Which user group should be attracted first?" can then be rephrased as "Which user group generates the most efficient lever?". If you fix the load (that is, if your objective is to attract, say, one more user in the other group), you can play with two variables: The vertical force that is exerted at the other end of the beam and the length of the beam itself.

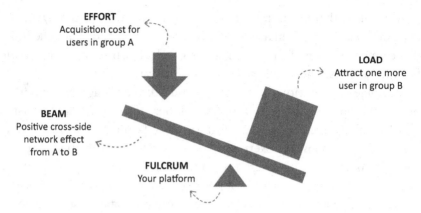

Figure 4.1 The lever analogy applied to platforms.

The force exerted on the beam can be understood here as the effort that is required to attract one more user. This notion is very close to a concept widely used in marketing, namely the 'customer acquisition cost' (CAC). In this case, the CAC represents the cost of attracting and convincing an additional customer to join the platform at launch. For the same reasons that we substituted *user* for *customer* and *supplier* (see Chapter 2), we prefer to speak here, more generally, of 'user acquisition cost' (UAC) rather than 'CAC'. Other things equal, the lower this cost, the more efficient the lever. Hence, focusing on this variable, it pays more to choose the group with a lower UAC. Indeed, for the same starting budget, the lower the UAC, the larger the number of users the platform can attract.

The length of the beam is the second variable to play with. Everyone knows the physics principle that the longer the lever, the easier it is to lift the load. In this case, we propose to see the length of the beam as the strength of the cross-side network effects. Again, other things equal, the stronger those cross-side network effects, the more efficient the lever. Focusing on this variable, it pays more to choose the group that exerts stronger cross-side network effects on the other group. The idea behind this reasoning is that one additional user in that particular group allows you to gain more users on the other side than one additional user in the other group does. In other words, you choose that group because it exerts a stronger 'attraction power' (AP).

In the rest of this section, we analyze these two variables and we design a simple tool to help you decide on which group you should concentrate your efforts on when launching the platform.

> To launch a platform, it pays to focus on the group with a lower user acquisition cost and/or a stronger attraction power.

Comparing user acquisition costs

As there is no single user on board at the very start of a platform, no network effect of any sort is at work. It seems thus reasonable to assume that the first users anticipate that they will not interact with anyone on the platform and have thus little reason to join. This means that it takes a lot of convincing to get the first users on board. To do so, you can resort to traditional means, such as advertising, public relations, cold-calling, or canvassing for users. Less traditionally, you may sometimes need to 'bribe' the first users by offering them direct subsidies, as illustrated in Case 4.1 (we will analyze later on when such a tactic is appropriate).[1]

Case 4.1 Epic pays developers to give away their games for free

Epic Games is a US video game company founded in 1991. In the last couple of years, it encountered a massive success via its game called *Fortnite*, one of the world's largest games that reached 350 million accounts in 2020. Based on this success, the company decided to break away from third-party platforms and launch its own video game download platform, *Epic Games Store*.

To grow its gamer community, Epic Games relies on a strategy that is quite common in the gaming industry, namely offering games for free and hoping that players will eventually spend money on paid items (for instance by unlocking special features) or on subscriptions to games that remain out of the free-to-play range. Since its launch, Epic Games has given away over 100 games. Yet, from the platform's viewpoint, the games in question are not free and the developers must logically be compensated.

This is how Epic Games disbursed $11.6 million to offer 38 titles in open access on its store between December 2018 and September 2019. In response, over the same period, the platform registered almost 5 million new accounts, which translates to Epic

Games paying $2.37 for each new gamer it signed up. According to the company, 90% of its total community of users were attracted first via free game giveaways (among which 7% end up making a purchase).

The question of interest here is toward which group of users you should direct the main bulk of your marketing campaign. The best way to answer this question is to compare the 'UAC' for the two (or more) groups of users that your platform aims to connect. As the name indicates, the UAC is the cost related to acquiring a new user. The classical 'CAC' is often measured through the ratio between the expenses allocated to marketing during a given period and the number of new customers acquired during this period. For instance, in Case 4.1, we see that the UAC for EPIC was equal to $2.37 (that is, $11.6 MIO spent on free titles to acquire five MIO new users).

Yet, this way of evaluating the CAC is not terribly useful for your purpose. At this early stage, you cannot observe (*ex post*) how much you have spent per acquired user. What is crucial for you is to forecast (*ex ante*) how much you *will have to spend* to acquire a new user. To do so, you must first identify your potential users and find out how to advertise your platform to them. Then, you must put yourself into their shoes and figure out how you can get the better of their potential reluctance to join your platform. In this spirit, we invite you to evaluate the following three types of costs:

- The *costs of prospecting users*: You have to identify the users who may be interested in joining your platform, as well as the right channel to reach them;
- The *costs of easing users' adoption*: Once you have identified the target users, you need to compensate them for the costs they have to bear when joining the platform;
- The *costs of establishing trust*: Once users are convinced to join, you still need to ensure that they will feel comfortable interacting on the platform.

> **On a platform, the UACs mainly come from prospecting users, easing users' adoption, and establishing trust.**

To help you figure out which group of users exhibits the lowest UAC, we now discuss the factors that affect these three types of costs, so as to understand why they may differ across groups.

Costs of prospecting users

As for any new venture, your first task is to identify your target audience. Of course, you have already performed a rough segmentation by identifying the groups of users that wish to interact. Yet, you still have to determine more precisely, within each group, whom you should target in priority, and which marketing channel you should use to approach them. It is quite likely that the answers to these questions will differ across groups. For instance, there may exist official, public, and freely searchable databases in which users in one group are registered; users in that group will then be easier to identify than users for whom no such registers exist. Charles Armitage, the founder of Florence – a platform connecting independent nurses and elderly care homes in the UK – illustrates this point by explaining how the platform managed to get its first customers:

> On the care home side, I found a list of all care homes in London; I sat down with a phone and just called them up. (...) On the side for the nurses, we went around Facebook, called in some favors, and found some nurses too.[2]

It appears in this example that care homes were relatively easier to identify than nurses. The takeaway is the following: *An increased difficulty to identify potential users in a given group increases the UAC of this group.*

Second, the appropriate channels to reach users may also differ in cost. Typically, prospecting costs tend to be lower for groups composed of users that are relatively similar and interchangeable. Such users can be approached through large-scale, and relatively cheap, advertising campaigns. In contrast, when users in a group have their specificities and when their potential interest in your platform may vary a lot, you may have no other choice than to contact them in person and canvass their custom, which will obviously be quite costly. For platforms linking buyers to sellers, buyers usually fall in the first category and sellers in the second. Online recruitment platforms (such as Recruit, LinkedIn, CareerBuilder, Monster, 51Job, and the like) provide another example: They connect companies to job seekers, with the former being way easier to identify (for instance through official listings) than the latter. In short, *the UAC tends to be larger the more difficult it is to get in touch with potential users in a massive and relatively automated way.*

A larger difficulty in both identifying and getting in touch with a potential user of the platform inflates the prospection cost and, thereby, the UAC.

Costs of easing users' adoption

One of the main adoption barriers for users comes from the pessimistic expectations they may have about the lack of participation of other users. Continuing with the example of an online recruitment platform, why would a job seeker use a given platform if they expect that no company will ever advertise any job opening on this platform? The same reasoning applies to companies: Why would they bother advertising their job openings if they expect no job seeker to visit the platform? This is the crux of the 'chicken-and-egg' problem.

One way to break this vicious circle is to provide users with so-called *stand-alone benefits.* There are typically two sources of value for users on a platform: The value from interacting with other users (the *network benefits*) and the value from consuming platform services that do not depend on the presence of other users (the *stand-alone benefits*). Clearly, the chicken-and-egg problem strikes harder the larger the value that users place on network benefits. Reversing the argument, it is easier to attract users if you can provide them with stand-alone services (as it breaks the constraint of having to attract other users simultaneously). In other words, the cheaper it is to offer stand-alone services to one group, the lower the costs of easing this group's adoption. For instance, by making it possible to watch Blu-ray and DVD movies on its PlayStation, Sony provided end-users with benefits that are independent of the number and variety of games that are compatible with the console. As it is hard to imagine how Sony could have come up with an equivalent stand-alone benefit for game developers, we can say that, from this viewpoint, it was less costly for Sony to ease the adoption for end-users than for game developers. Hence, *the more difficult it is to provide a group of users with stand-alone benefits the larger this group's UAC.*

Another adoption barrier may result from *specific assets* that users need to possess or acquire to start operating on the platform. By specific assets, we mean resources (including knowledge, capabilities, and time) that require investments that are specific to the participation in the platform and have thus little or no value in any alternative use. In the example of ride-hailing platforms, it is clear that because drivers need to use their own car, they are exposed to much larger costs than riders if they want to use the platform. From this perspective, it is costlier for the platform to acquire drivers because it will need to compensate them somehow to convince them to join. Similarly, entrepreneurs who try to raise funds on crowdfunding platforms have to go through much more trouble than funders to be active on the platforms. In other words, *the more the participation in the platform is conditional on users investing in specific assets, the larger the UAC for these users.*

Finally, as explained in Chapter 1, same-side network effects may also exist on some platforms; that is, users in a given group may attach more or less value to the platform depending on the level of participation of fellow users of their group. If same-side effects are positive, then the cost of attracting users in a group decreases with the number of users that the platform has already attracted in this group. The opposite prevails in the presence of negative same-side network effects. If you apply this reasoning to, for instance, video game platforms, it appears that easing users' adoption is less costly for gamers than for game developers. This is so because there exist positive same-side network effects among gamers (the more gamers, the broader the possibilities to play multiplayer games) and negative same-side network effects among game developers (as they compete to attract gamers). We note thus that *the presence of positive (negative) same-side network effects within a group reduces (raises) the UAC of users in this group.*

Having to make specific investments to benefit from the platform's services and not being able to benefit from stand-alone services are two factors that increase the UAC.

Costs of establishing trust

Identifying potential users and making their adoption easier are only the first steps: One still needs to make sure that users feel comfortable interacting on the platform. Even if digital platforms have been around for a while, it remains challenging for many people to use a platform instead of a more traditional alternative. For instance, it took a big leap of faith for the first passengers to climb into the back seat of an Uber or Lyft ride instead of a cab. The main issue here is trust: The employees of an established taxi company are, a priori, more trustworthy than the independent drivers registered on some unknown ride-hailing platform. As drivers also have reasons to distrust riders, the costs of establishing trust look pretty similar across the two groups of users in this very instance.[3]

Yet, there are other situations in which the trust issue is clearly asymmetric because the members of one group already enjoy some outside reputation whereas the members of the other group do not. Think again of online recruitment platforms: Because companies have a name and reputation to defend, while job seekers are largely anonymous, the adoption cost (that is, the risk of misplacing one's trust) is arguably larger for the companies than for job seekers.

Practically, we want to assess how trust – or, to be exact, the lack of it – may prevent the different groups of users from joining the platform. The higher the risk associated with a lack of trust between users, the larger the UAC from the viewpoint of the platform. It is indeed reasonable to assume that attracting users who are suspicious and fearful of malicious behavior from other users is costlier than attracting users who tend to trust other users.

> **The more reasons a user has to distrust others or fear the consequences of fraudulent behavior, the higher the UAC.**

The risk in question can be seen as the product of two factors: On the one hand, the probability that users in the other group would behave in a harmful way and, on the other hand, the extent of the harm that such behavior would cause. Quantifying these two factors is by no means an easy task. Yet, remember that our aim here is not to measure these factors accurately, but to compare this risk across the two groups, to identify which users are a priori more reluctant to join – and thus more expensive to convince. This must be done on a case-by-case basis since, as noted above, trust is asymmetric. As we just saw for Uber, comparing the extent of potential harm on the two sides is a delicate issue. However, drivers seem to have more to lose than riders if their reputation is damaged. This suggests that harmful behavior could be more likely on the riders' side. Drivers may thus have a harder time trusting riders than the other way around, which would make the drivers' UAC relatively larger. In the case of Bsit, the probabilities of harmful conduct might be hard to compare, but it is fair to say that the potential damages of any foul play are perceived as larger by parents than by sitters. In Chapter 6, we will have a deeper look at the trust issues that arise on platforms and we will describe various strategies that platforms can design to address these issues.

Comparing attraction powers

Consider now the beam part of the lever. In our analogy, the length of the beam refers to the AP of the group through which the effort is exerted; that is, the cross-side network effect that this group generates for the other. Other things equal (supposing that both groups have the same UAC), it is more efficient to focus on the group with the stronger AP since you will attract proportionally more new users as a result.

> **It is generally more efficient to focus on the group with the stronger AP since you will attract proportionally more new users as a result.**

To check if our intuition is correct, let us go through a simple numerical example. Suppose that one more user of group A attracts three more users of group B, while one more user of group B attracts only two more users of group A. This means that group A users exert stronger cross-side network effects than group B users. Our prediction is thus that we should better attract group A users first. The following back-of-the-envelope calculation, schematized in Figure 4.2, confirms that our instincts are right:

- *Scenario 1: Starting with group A.* (Stage 1) 1 more user in group A; (Stage 2) 1×3=3 more users in group B; (Stage 3) 3×2=6 more users in group A;

(Stage 4) 6×3=18 more users in group B. **Total**: 1+6=7 users in group A and 3+18=21 users in group B, that is, 28 users on the platform.

- *Scenario 2: Starting with group B.* (Stage 1) 1 more user in group B; (Stage 2) 1×2=2 more users in group A; (Stage 3) 2×3=6 more users in group B; (Stage 4) 6×2=12 more users in group A. **Total**: 1+6=7 users in group B and 2+12=14 users in group A, that is, 24 users on the platform.

Your task is thus to compare the APs of the two groups. That is, you want to estimate the relative value that users in one group create for users in the other group when they are active on your platform. We now identify various factors that allow you to perform such a comparison. To do so, we will borrow some criteria from the resource-based view (RBV) of the firm, a theory that aims at explaining the sources of competitive advantage. In 1991, Jay Barney proposed the VRIO model (previously called VRIN) to evaluate the extent to which a given resource makes it possible to build a competitive advantage.[4] According to this model, the attributes that a

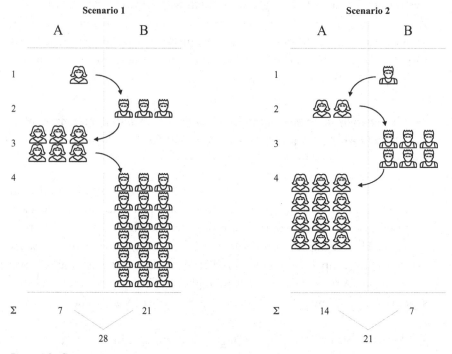

Figure 4.2 Comparing attraction powers.

firm resource must have to generate a competitive advantage are as follows: Valuable (a resource that can bring value), Rare (a resource that is not widely available), Imperfectly Imitable (a resource that is not easy to replicate), and Non-substitutable (a resource that cannot be substituted by any other resource). In the present context, we can see the two groups of users as two alternative resources, with different capacities to generate a 'competitive advantage', that is, to contribute to the platform's growth.

Scarcity of potential users

In the early days of a platform, any additional user plays an important part in co-creating value. But is one extra user in one group worth the same as one extra user in the other group? Probably not. When potential users are relatively scarce in one group, any extra user from this group tends to bring more additional value than one extra user from a more populated group. The question is then: Why are there fewer potential users in one group than in another? There are two reasons: Either the group has a smaller size to start with – meaning that in absolute terms, the size of one reference population is naturally smaller than another – or its members face entry barriers and experience difficulties to join the platform due to factors on which you have little control.

To illustrate the first reason, take the example of Parkbee, a digital platform (based in the Netherlands) that makes private parking places accessible to the general public. As urban constraints put a limit on parking space, there are naturally fewer owners of private parking places than there are commuters looking for a place to park their cars.

The second reason can be illustrated by any platform that links 'professionals' to 'consumers', insofar as becoming a professional supposes an initial investment of some sort (education, accreditation, assets, etc.), while being a consumer is open to anyone. Other things being equal, it is thus legitimate to expect fewer drivers than riders to join a ride-hailing platform, fewer restaurants than diners to join a food-delivery platform or fewer babysitters than parents to join a babysitting app. This applies quite generally to marketplaces that link providers to customers. For instance, the so-called 'provider-to-customer ratio' is estimated to be 1:70 on Airbnb, 1:50 on Uber, and 1:5 on eBay.[5] For another example of entry barriers being larger for one group of users, one might think of a platform that connects home care providers with seniors. Since the elderly are still relatively unfamiliar with the use of a smartphone, this could be seen as a natural hindrance to the broad acceptance among this target group, at least in comparison with the group of care providers.

There are thus many situations in which one group can be seen as the 'short side' of the platform and the other group as the 'long side'. On markets, we all know by experience that it is more comfortable to be on the short side than on the long side. By analogy, *on platforms, being the short side – that is, counting relatively fewer potential users – endows a group with a stronger AP.*

> **Being on the 'short side' of a platform endows a group with a stronger AP.**

Exclusivity and capacity to interact outside the platform

While the relative scarcity of potential users in two groups determines the relative AP of these two groups on any platform trying to link them, we look now at factors that are specific to a given platform. Our argument is the following. The AP of some group (say group A) *on a given platform* depends on how easy or difficult it is for users in the other group to interact with group A *outside the platform*. The more difficult it is to interact with group A outside the platform, the more the platform becomes an essential gateway for users in group B to interact with users in group A. As a result, the AP that group A exerts on group B on this platform grows stronger. In sum, *the harder it is to interact with a group outside your platform, the stronger the AP of that group on your platform.* Case 4.2 gives a nice illustration of this principle.

Case 4.2 APs on Glassdoor.com

Glassdoor is a platform that connects job seekers and employees. The idea is the following: Current and former employees submit, anonymously, information about their company (reviews, salaries, ...); the platform compiles this information and makes it available to job seekers; it also allows job seekers to directly apply for jobs listed on the platform.

There exist positive cross-side network effects between the two groups: The more employees join the platform, the more companies are reviewed and the more attractive the platform becomes for job seekers; also, the more job seekers join the platform, the more it becomes rewarding for employees to provide information about their company. The first effect, however, seems stronger than the second. Job seekers would need a wide network of personal contacts within companies to match the services that the platform offers to them. In contrast, employees can find a variety of ways to disseminate information about their company; they do not need to identify a particular job seeker to do so. That is to say, job seekers need to find a specific match while employees do not. The upshot is that job seekers are more in need of the platform than employees are. Applying our theory, we conclude thus that employees (that is, the providers of information) have a stronger AP; they should thus be attracted in priority (for equal UAC).

It seems that Glassdoor figured that out pretty well. As Schonfeld (2008) reports, the platform is indeed presented in its early days as a site that "collects company reviews and real salaries from employees of large companies and displays them anonymously for all members to see." In other words, given the importance of having employees – and more specifically, their information – on the platform, Glassdoor did not really operate as a platform initially: It provided the information using its own forces instead of relying on the voluntary contributions of employees.

> **The harder it is to interact with a group outside your platform, the stronger the AP exerted by that particular group on your platform.**

To ascertain the relative difficulty for different groups of interacting outside the platform, it is useful to compare the outside options that users have in each group if they want to interact with the other group. If these options are more limited for users in, say, group A, then these users will see your platform as the main gateway to interact with users in group B, meaning that group B exerts a stronger AP. Referring to the VRIO model evoked previously, the presence of group B is less imitable than the presence of group A and is, therefore, more conducive to generating a competitive advantage for the platform.

To assess the outside options of the different groups, you can find precious indications in the analyses that you performed in the previous two chapters. In Chapter 2, you were advised to phrase the value proposition of your platform as a coherent combination of related value propositions, one for each group of users that the platform connects. Doing so, you might have realized that the value you propose is perceived as higher by one group than by the other group(s). For instance, if your platform provides users in group A with a brand-new way to interact with users in group B, then the outside option in group A is almost non-existent, meaning that group B's AP is stronger (as illustrated by the launch of Glassdoor – see Case 4.2). In other words, *if involving a particular user group is key to making your value proposition unique and differentiating, then the AP of this group is likely to be very strong.*

Another important element to take into account when estimating the AP of different groups is whether their members are restricted to *singlehome* (that is, they cannot be active on more than one platform at the same time) or they have the freedom to *multihome* (that is, they can be active on several platforms offering similar services). In line with the previous discussion, we understand that *singlehomers exert a stronger AP for your platform than multihomers do.* The reason is obvious: To interact with a singlehomer, users of the other group have no other choice than to join your platform; in that sense, as you control the access to these users, your platform is essential to reach them. In contrast, it is possible to interact with a multihomer through different channels and platforms. So, for that reason, it may pay more to attract first the group of users that are more likely to remain singlehomers, not because they face the largest difficulties to multihome, but mainly because they are the ones who generate the greatest attraction to the other group.

> **The harder it is for a group of users to multihome, the stronger the AP of this group on your platform.**

Note that singlehoming may either result from the environment, in particular when affiliation to a platform is costly (for example, because some costly device – like a console or a smartphone – needs to be purchased) and users are reluctant to double their costs. But singlehoming may also result from exclusive contracts passed between platform and users (we analyze the ins and outs of signing exclusive contracts with users later in this chapter).

Substitutability and alternatives on the market

The intensity of the AP also clearly depends on the competitive environment, which you have assessed in Chapter 3. Imagine for instance that none of your potential competitors is satisfactorily meeting the needs of users in group A, whereas users in group B may find alternatives to the services that you propose. Having group B on board is thus essential to ensure the participation of group A, but the reverse is not true (as group B users do not necessarily need to interact with group A on your platform to have their needs answered). It follows that group B exerts a stronger AP than group A. Based on the Platform Value Net model, it is thus possible to identify arguments that are useful for the evaluation of the AP, specifically by considering the substitutes and rivals that you reported in the canvas proposed in Chapter 3. In short, *the larger the set of substitutes and rivals that a group of users has access to, the stronger the AP that this group exerts on your platform.*

Another way to look at substitutability is to analyze the specificity of a particular user group. The question can be asked whether there is another group of actors that could substitute for the one under consideration. For example, let us imagine a platform that connects language teachers with people who want to learn foreign languages. If it would be very difficult to attract teachers (for example because they are already very busy with their professional schedules), the platform could consider turning to retired teachers or native speakers of the language that is in demand. In other cases, the platform itself could temporarily replace a group to prime the pump (as will be discussed later in this chapter). In the end, the idea here is that *a group exerts a stronger AP, the more complicated it is to substitute this group with another group.* This is the same reasoning as for the multihoming and outside option risk described above, except that the reasons for the platform to be difficult to circumvent are different here.

> **If there exist more substitutes and rivals for a group of users or if it is harder to replace this group with another, then the AP of this group is relatively stronger.**

The Lever Selector

Combining the previous elements, we now propose a simple method to help you decide how best to allocate your efforts to kickstart your platform. We call it the 'Lever Selector' as the objective is to select the best lever to launch your platform. The method is divided into two phases. First, we ask you to go through a thought-provoking canvas to compare the UAC and the AP for the two groups of users. Second, we propose a simple matrix to translate the results of your comparisons into an appropriate course of action to launch your platform.

Step 1. Analysis (comparison of UACs and APs)

The proposed canvas (which you can download from www.platformstrate-gies.org) separates the comparison of the UACs (on the left) and the APs (on the right) of the two groups. Each column is divided into three spaces, which refer to the criteria described in the previous section. The goal is to list the relevant elements that can be used to decide which group has a lower UAC and a stronger AP according to the criterion under review (Figure 4.3).

Let us start by comparing the UAC for the two groups. Based on the various types of costs that we described previously, we suggest three categories

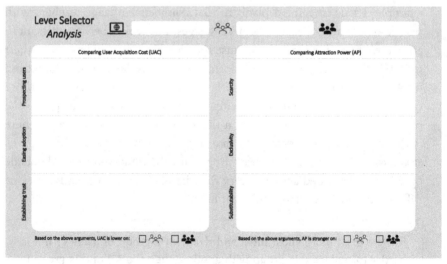

Figure 4.3 The Lever Selector: Analysis.

to help you decide for which user group UACs are lower in *relative terms*: 'Prospecting users', 'Easing adoption', and 'Establishing trust'. Table 4.1 reports the questions that we formulate for each of these categories to fuel the reflection.

It is important to stress that these lists are not meant to be exhaustive; in particular, you should feel free to add questions that you may find more appropriate to the specificities of your platform. Also, the questions we propose are likely to vary in importance and relevance depending on the nature of the platform being considered. To help your decision process, you may then want to associate a particular score with each element that you report. At the end of this thought process, you should draw one of three possible conclusions: Group A has a lower UAC than group B (check box A), Group B has a lower UAC than group A (check box B), or the two groups have similar UACs (check both boxes).

Table 4.1 Questions to compare UAC across user groups

Prospecting users

In which group is it cheaper to identify potential users?	The cheaper, the lower the UAC.
For which group does there exist directories or databases containing target users?	As they decrease search costs, they also decrease the UAC.
For which group is it cheaper to get in touch with potential users?	The cheaper, the lower the UAC.

Easing adoption

In which groups do users need to invest less in specific assets before joining the platform?	The lower the required investment, the lower the UAC.
For which group of users is it cheaper to offer stand-alone benefits?	The cheaper, the lower the UAC.
In which group are users already more familiar with the concept that the platform proposes?	The more familiar they are, the lower their UAC.
In which group are same-side network effects (if any) stronger?	The more positive the same-side network effects, the lower the UAC.

Establishing trust

In which group are users less fearful of misconduct by the other party?	The less fearful, the lower the UAC.
In case of misconduct, in which group would users be less harmed?	The lower the harm, the lower the UAC.
In which group are users less concerned with defending their reputation outside the platform?	The lower the concern, the lower the UAC.

You can now repeat the exercise to compare the AP of the two groups. As for the UAC, we invite you to think about three categories, which address the different factors determining the relative AP of the user groups: 'Scarcity', 'Exclusivity', and 'Substitutability'. Table 4.2 lists the main questions for each of these categories. Do not hesitate to phrase additional questions if appropriate and rank your answers by order of importance. As for the UAC, your analysis should lead you to conclude that either group A has a stronger AP than group B (check box A), the reverse applies (check box B), or the two groups have similar APs (check both boxes).

Step 2. Recommendation

Once you have compared UACs and APs across groups, you can use your analysis to figure out which type of launch strategy you should implement. As three answers are possible for each dimension (UAC and AP), we

Table 4.2 Questions to compare AP across user groups

Scarcity	
Which group counts naturally relatively fewer users?	The smaller the group, the stronger the AP.
In which group do users face higher entry barriers to join the platform?	The higher the barriers, the stronger the AP.
In which group can users interact more easily with multiple users of the other group?	The more easily, the stronger the AP.
Exclusivity	
Which users are harder to reach outside the platform?	The harder it is to reach users, the stronger their AP.
Which users have access to the broader set of outside options?	The more available outside options there are, the stronger the AP.
Which users are more constrained to singlehome?	Singlehoming users exert a stronger AP.
Which users contribute more to making your value proposition unique and differentiating?	Key contributors exert a stronger AP.
Substitutability	
Which group is less substitutable by another group?	The less substitutable, the stronger the AP.
Which group is less substitutable by the platform?	The less substitutable, the stronger the AP.
Which group has the less imitable contribution?	The less imitable the contribution, the stronger the AP.

propose a 3×3 matrix to determine the most adequate course of action to launch your platform (see Figure 4.4). Three typical strategies emerge from the results of the two comparisons:

1. *Pick a starter.* If one group emerges as a 'winner' both in terms of UAC and AP, then the recommendation is unambiguously to start with this group. Indeed, if users in this group are relatively less costly to attract and, at the same time, exert a relatively stronger AP, then they provide you with a more efficient lever without any ambiguity. By extension, this recommendation also applies to cases in which one user group is a winner in one dimension, while there is a tie in the other dimension.

2. *Go fifty/fifty.* If there is a tie in both dimensions (that is, if the two groups appear to have similar UACs and APs), then the recommendation differs. As there is no clear reason to start with one group or the other, the best course of action is to court both groups equally. This should not be taken as a sign of indecisiveness but as a well-thought strategy given the circumstances (as discussed later, eBay started in this way).

3. *Buy up or replace.* What should you do if each group is a winner in one dimension? These cases may seem problematic insofar as it is a priori impossible to decide which group gives you a more efficient lever. Should you extend the previous recommendation and go fifty-fifty? We do not believe so. Here, one group (call it group X) has a stronger AP but also a larger UAC than the other group (call it group Y). The stronger AP, on the one hand, means that what users in group X can provide is really key to attracting users of group Y and, thereby, for the very existence of your operations. The larger UAC, on the other hand, means that users of group X will not join the platform easily. In particular, it is not so much the prospect of interacting with group Y that attracts them to the platform: They need to receive more to be convinced to join. As you cannot do without users of group X – or without what they provide – you are left with two options: You can either *buy up* users in that group to guarantee their participation (as Epic did with game developers – see Case 4.1) or, more radically, you can *replace* that group altogether by producing its offering all by yourself (that is, to start as a pipeline, with the hope of turning into a true platform at a later stage).

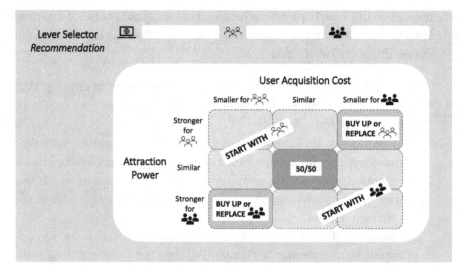

Figure 4.4 The Lever Selector: Recommendation.

To illustrate how valuable the Lever Selector can be, we apply it to our running example of Airbnb, going back to the early days of the platform, as described in Case 4.3.

Case 4.3 Airbnb started by replacing and then buying up hosts

The first version of Airbnb, created in 2017, was called 'Air Bed and Breakfast'. In a Knowledge at Wharton (2017) article, Leigh Gallagher – the author of the book *The Airbnb Story* – describes the difficulties that the co-founders encountered to raise funds to develop their idea:

> No one thought this was a good idea. (...) Investors wouldn't even meet with them, or if they did, they just said, "You guys are crazy. There's going to be a murder in one of these houses. There's going to be blood on your hands. I am not touching this with a 10-foot pole." And no one did. They almost didn't get off the ground. They almost had to close up shop because people thought it was that crazy.

Leigh Gallagher identifies two turning points that can explain how the venture eventually took off. The first moment is when two of the co-founders (Brian Chesky and Joe Gebbia) decided to rent out air mattresses in their apartment (adding a free breakfast and free Wi-Fi to the package). At that time, they were struggling to pay their rent and a big conference was taking place in their city (San Francisco). The second moment is when Y Combinator (a San Francisco start-up accelerator program) convinced the co-founders to meet their potential hosts. Gallagher explains:

> They didn't have many users, but the few that they had were in New York City, and [visiting them] hadn't occurred to them. They went to New York, and they really sat with their users and helped them dress up their properties with better language, better pricing, and just gussied up the listings—and that was enough to turn the numbers to where they then started to catch fire.

The previous elements suggest that the early version of Airbnb was launched by following the 'buy up or replace' strategy: The co-founders first replaced the hosts' side by proposing mattresses for rent in their own apartment; then, they bought up the first independent hosts in New York by accompanying them through the process of listing their property on the platform.

Can we make sense, retrospectively, of the decisions made by the co-founders of Airbnb? The Lever Selector tells us that replacing and buying up hosts was called for if, at the time, hosts had a larger UAC and a stronger AP than guests. We argue now that there are good reasons to believe that it was so when Airbnb started. Figure 4.5 summarizes our analysis.

Comparison of UACs

- *Prospecting users.* When Airbnb started, it seemed more difficult to identify and reach potential hosts than potential guests, for the simple reason that anyone could be a guest while only homeowners, in attractive enough locations, could become hosts. By the same token, it also

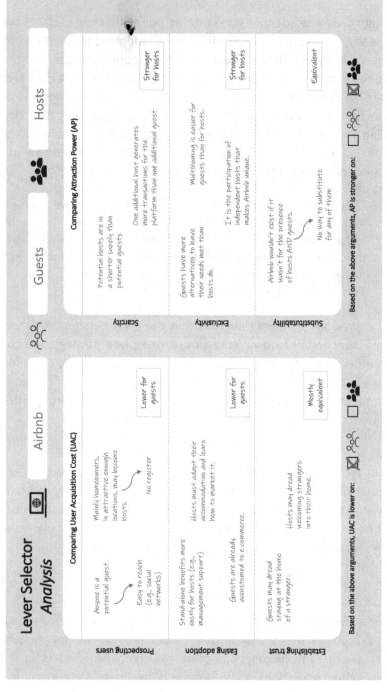

Figure 4.5 The Lever Selector applied to Airbnb.

seemed easier to reach a prospective guest – via social networks for example – than a prospective host, especially because of the relative lack of official recognition of the hosts (in contrast with hotels or vacation homes, for instance, for which there exist public registers).

- *Easing adoption.* Regarding stand-alone benefits, guests are less likely to expect sophisticated additional services that they would value aside from matching with hosts. For hosts, however, the platform can offer management and promotion tools that will help the owner to ensure the administrative and commercial management of the property. But developing this type of service is expensive and can only be profitable once a critical size is reached. Regarding investments in specific assets and operating costs related to service adoption, adoption barriers seem again to be higher for hosts, owing to the expenses they have to incur to adapt their flat for short-term location, to fill out their host profile, etc. As the first hosts were not professionals, they were less accustomed to using services of this type; guests, in contrast, were already familiar with e-commerce and online shopping.

- *Establishing trust.* Trust issues seemed to arise equally on both sides. First, guests may dread staying at the home of a stranger as much as hosts may dread welcoming strangers into their homes. Second, as the first hosts were not professionals, they did not have any reputation to defend outside the platform, which puts them on the same level as guests in this matter.

- *In aggregate*, the UAC was unambiguously lower for *guests*.

Comparison of APs

- *Scarcity.* We first note that potential hosts were in a shorter supply than potential guests, owing to natural limitations on the number of properties suitable for short-term rental and to the costs of making such properties attractive. By the same token, one additional host generated more transactions for the platform than one additional guest.[6]

- *Exclusivity.* Looking for a room or an entire flat on Airbnb was one among several options that guests could use to find short-term accommodations (they could search, for instance, for a hotel). In contrast, fewer alternatives existed at the time for private homeowners to put their house (or part of it) for rental. As far as homing is concerned, it was arguably easier for guests than for hosts to multihome. First, alternative platforms for listing properties existed for vacation spots but not for city centers. Second, even if hosts could list their accommodation on several platforms, a major challenge was (and still is) to keep an up-to-date availability calendar on several sites simultaneously (to prevent double bookings for instance). Finally, the uniqueness of Airbnb's value proposition relies on the availability of 'non-hotel accommodations'. Therefore, the participation of hosts is crucial and hardly imitable.

- *Substitutability.* When Airbnb started, neither hosts nor guests could easily be replaced by other groups of users or the platform itself (even if Airbnb enlisted hotels at a later stage as a way to complement the supply of hosts). Moreover, the same users could belong to both groups at different times (as the initial hosts were non-professionals). There was, therefore, no difference between the two groups in terms of substitutability.
- In *aggregate*, it is fair to say that hosts had a stronger AP than guests.

How to catch chickens or collect eggs?

We present now specific tactics that should allow you to implement whichever of the three strategies that the Lever Selector has indicated as being appropriate for launching your platform.

Pick a starter

If one of the groups that your platform aims to bring together has both a lower UAC and a stronger AP than the other group(s), then it is this group that you should attract first. We list here several tactics you can use to do so. Two comments are in order at this stage. First, the tactics that we describe are not exclusive: You can gain by cleverly combining them (you should not put all your eggs in one basket!). Second, we focus here on tactics that aim at using one group as leverage to attract the other group, as these tactics are particularly suited for platforms. We do not describe more common marketing tools, which any startup – platforms included – can resort to.

Partner with a chicken farm

A group of users may be relatively less costly to attract to your platform because this group is already active on some other – complementary – platform (probably to be found among the complementors that you identified while carrying out the analysis of your competitive environment – see Chapter 3). The idea is to partner with this platform, so that it will serve as a gateway through which you can access an entire group of users at once, instead of having to contact every user of this group separately. Naturally, the resources you will save in this way must be weighed against what you will have to give to the partner platform as compensation for its collaboration. We illustrate this point in Case 4.4.

Case 4.4 Three years of fame for Famest

In 2012, three former students of UCLouvain (Belgium) launched Famest, a platform linking fashionistas and fashion brands. The value proposition for fashionistas was: "Tag your style and get rewarded by your favorite brands." Users were invited to post pictures on which they tagged their outfits; pictures were then automatically shared on the platform and social networks (at the time, Facebook, Twitter, and Pinterest), and points were awarded per like received; finally, users could redeem their points for rewards. As for brands, the value came from the power of personalized recommendations compared to traditional ads: Famest reported click-through rates through their tags that were 25 times as large as those of classical ads.

Famest faced a severe chicken-and-egg problem, as all brands had to be on board from the outset: Fashionistas would only find the platform attractive if it gave them the possibility to tag any outfit from any brand. To remedy this problem, the founders decided to partner with Zalando, a large online retailer of fashion and lifestyle products. Even if Zalando claimed a share of the value created, the one-stop contact point with all brands that they were providing was much more efficient than the countless – and uncertain – bilateral deals that Famest would have had to negotiate otherwise. As part of the deal, Zalando also accepted to issue the discount vouchers that were used to reward the users recognized as 'influencers'.

Rewarding influencers was also a way to leverage positive same-side network effects among users. To increase their chances of obtaining rewards, users were indeed incentivized to invite their contacts to join the platform and like their style. This 'gamification' technique, coupled with sustained press coverage (via a deal with *OK!*, a British magazine specializing in lifestyle and celebrity news), allowed Famest to grow quickly its user base. Yet, this growth was not sufficient to convince investors of the future profitability of the business. The main problem was the poor retention rate, as users preferred to pursue their interaction on the well-established social networks, a sad illustration of the platform leakage issue that we address in Chapter 6. This story also demonstrates that solving the chicken-and-egg problem is a necessary – but, by no means, sufficient – condition for a platform to succeed.

As a result, the founders decided to sell their platform to a French group in 2015. They may now regret having taken the risky road of launching their own social network, instead of choosing the safer option of selling their tagging technology (their true innovative asset) to existing networks. The fact that Instagram started to offer this functionality in 2018 ('Shopping on Instagram') seems to prove them right. Of course, this is easy to say with hindsight...

Two variations of this strategy, which is also called 'piggybacking', aim at importing users from other platforms.[7] The first consists in offering a direct gateway to users from an external platform; this can be done, for example, through the social login possibilities proposed by large social media platforms (such as Facebook Connect or Google Sign-In). The second, which is arguably less noble, seeks to convert users from other platforms without any upfront agreement; a well-known example of this strategy is what Airbnb did in its early days with its 'publish on Craigslist' button.[8]

Offer chickens an eggless diet

Recall that a group of users may have a relatively lower UAC because they value stand-alone benefits relatively more than network benefits. These users are thus easier to attract because their participation is less dependent on the participation of users in the other group. The proposed tactics consist then in providing these users with sufficiently attractive stand-alone services, that is, services they can enjoy even in the absence of interaction with users of the other group; hence the name of this tactic.

This is, for example, the route followed by TikTok, the popular social media video app for creating and sharing videos. What partly explains the amazing growth of this platform is the fact that the app is also entertaining for users who are not following any other user.[9] OpenTable – a booking platform for restaurants – also adopted a similar tactic in its early days, as it provided restaurants with a booking management software that they could use for any customer (not just the ones they could access through the platform). In the same vein, many applications were first presented as a tool for their users to organize their data or content (a stand-alone benefit), and only later as a platform for sharing data or content with other users (a network benefit). Think, for instance, of Pinterest (pictures), Dropbox (files), or Strava (sport tracking).

Shelter runaway chickens

Another reason for which it may be relatively less costly to attract some users to your platform is that they are keener to leave some platform competing with you. We have in mind situations with the following two features. First, the market you try to enter is already occupied by a large platform (as you realized from your analysis of the competitive environment). Second, negative network effects are at work on this platform. The first feature is bad news for you, as the network effects at work on this existing platform raise entry barriers for potential competitors; this is the 'winner-takes-all' (or 'winner-takes-most') tendency that is observed in many markets with platforms. But good news comes from the second feature: Some users may perceive that the existing platform becomes so large that it ends up offering them poorer services.

This is especially true when users in a group are somehow competing with each other, which generates negative same-side network effects. Think of service providers on peer-to-peer marketplaces (such as Airbnb, TaskRabbit, or Etsy): The more numerous they are, the fiercer they compete for a given set of customers. Even if the set of customers grows larger when there are more service providers, there is a point where the benefit of such market expansion is offset by the negative impact of increased competition. Service providers may then be attracted by the alternative that you propose with your new – and for that matter, smaller – platform. Your selling point is that you can provide these users with an environment where they would face less intense competition. Hence, the larger your competitor, the stronger the negative same-side network effects among its users, and the easier it becomes for you to attract these users, or at least a small number of them. This can be seen as a form of 'judo strategy', as you use the size of your competitor against itself.[10]

> **Do judo against a big existing platform: Use its size (and the negative network effects it may cause) against itself.**

A similar strategy can be observed in the market for social media. Here, the dominant players in the market (Facebook, Twitter, or Instagram) have chosen to monetize their operations by collecting their users' personal data and selling them to advertisers, which has generated negative cross-side network effects for many users. Several alternative social media have then been launched with the promise to keep their users' data private (e.g., Vero, Mastodon, or Diaspora). As Newman (2018) reports: these 'privacy-first' social media "have tried to compete with Facebook and Twitter on ideological grounds. None have succeeded, but some are still alive and kicking."

As the previous example shows, applying this strategy may be a tough nut to crack, especially in markets in which positive cross-side network effects and switching costs are particularly strong. The strategy may succeed in other markets, though. But then, it should be used with care. As the proverb goes, one day chicken and the next day feathers: You could quickly lose your advantage if you do not keep the growth of your platform under control. The key here is to make sure that service providers can serve, on average, more customers on your platform than on the competing platform. This may force you to stay in a niche, but this might be the only effective way to compete sustainably with a powerful incumbent platform.

Incubate golden eggs

Within the group of users that you have decided to attract first, you may identify a subset of them who stand out because their AP is even larger than the average, in the sense that more users of the other group are willing to interact with them. In our jargon, these are users who generate stronger cross-side network effects, meaning that you can design an even more efficient lever by having them on the platform rather than other – more regular – users. These 'golden eggs' are also known as 'marquee users'. Well-known examples are popular games on a gaming console, opinion leaders on digital media, marquee shops in a shopping mall, important buyers on B2B platforms, or well-known restaurants in the food-delivery sector. It pays thus to court marquee users because, compared to regular users, they attract a larger number of users from the other group. Marquee users may also reassure the users of their own group, who see in their presence a convincing signal that the platform is likely to thrive. For instance, some crowdfunding platforms invite institutional investors to participate in funding campaigns because the crowd realizes that these investors are better equipped to identify projects with a higher chance of success; it is therefore reassuring for crowdfunders to follow the cue of these investors. Furthermore, in a competitive setting, it is tempting to make sure that these marquee users can be accessed through your platform only. Case 4.5 illustrates how competing food-delivery platforms are increasingly trying to secure exclusive deals with big chains of restaurants.

Case 4.5 Exclusivity in the food delivery sector

The home food delivery market is in constant expansion. For decades, the market was limited to a small set of restaurants (mainly pizzerias) using their own fleet of mopeds to deliver their meals to hungry customers living in city centers. Digital technologies have radically transformed this industry, with the emergence of platforms that act as intermediaries between restaurants, customers, and couriers.

Platforms have initially expanded the market by providing efficient delivery solutions to restaurants that did not have their own logistics. The second wave of expansion is currently taking place with big chains of restaurants turning to delivery platforms as substitutes for their own delivery operations. In the U.S., chains of fast-food restaurants are increasingly partnering with delivery platforms: McDonald's with Uber Eats, Wendy's with DoorDash, White Castle with Grubhub.

Generally, nothing prevents restaurants from multihoming, that is, using more than one delivery service. Yet, in practice, one observes that exclusive arrangements are becoming the rule rather than the exception. The benefit of exclusivity is obvious for platforms: Being the only service delivering meals from a well-known chain with national coverage is a strong asset to attract customers and couriers. This is the 'marquee user' argument that we developed above. As for restaurants, having a single delivery partner greatly simplifies the operations. For small restaurants, contracting with a unique partner may involve some risks of post-contractual opportunistic behavior. But large restaurant chains have a sufficiently strong bargaining power to transfer this risk to the delivery platform.

It is thus fair to say that the competition among home food delivery platforms is moving toward exclusivity with large national and international chains of restaurants.[11]

The downside of the 'golden eggs' tactic is that the UAC of marquee users is likely to rise in proportion to their AP. As you may not be the only platform trying to win them over, they may acquire a bargaining power that allows them to extract most, if not all, of the benefits that you would secure by having them affiliate exclusively with you. And if affiliation is not exclusive, you will have to share the marquee users with your competitors, which would not give you much of an advantage (apart from avoiding the disadvantage of not having them on board).

> **Like all golden eggs, 'marquee users' are valuable and ... expensive.**

As illustrated in Case 4.6, there is also a risk that marquee users might go away at some point – and even become your competitors. Retaining these particular users is thus more challenging compared to regular users. In sum, although attracting marquee users and signing exclusive deals with them brings many benefits, following such a strategy can quickly become expensive, and perhaps unaffordable in the case of a newly founded platform with limited resources.

Case 4.6 Marquee users in the video game industry

In the video game industry, not all games are equal, as some are much more popular than others. The video game business is hit-driven: The great bulk of cross-side network effects is exerted by a limited number of popular games. Hence, when choosing among consoles, gamers care less about the depth of the game catalog than about the presence of what they consider are the 'right' games. The fact that the Xbox One is (at the time of this writing) behind the PlayStation 4 in terms of sales is not surprising from that angle, as everyone in the industry – Microsoft included – acknowledges that Sony has a stronger line-up of exclusives.

Developers of highly coveted games represent marquee users because of the high cross-side network effects they generate. Their presence in a game catalog is so critical for console manufacturers that they have to pay developers to get the right to distribute their games. It also happens that platforms pay a premium for exclusive rights. For instance, *Bloodborne* (FromSoftware) is only available on PlayStation 4, *Pokemon Sun and Moon* (Game Freak) only on Nintendo 3DS, and *Sea of Thieves* (Rare) is exclusively available on Xbox One. It is not clear how much money is spent on such agreements, but a document presented in the lawsuit between Apple and Epic Games revealed that the latter paid a $146 million advance to secure exclusivity on *Borderlands 3*.

The same goes in the market for video game live streaming. Platforms are competing fiercely for signing exclusive deals with the most influential 'streamers'. In 2019, Mixer (operated by Microsoft) poached two top streamers (Ninja and Shroud) from its main competitor (Twitch, operated by Amazon.com) in a desperate attempt to gain a foothold in the market. According to Perez (2020), Ninja's contract with Microsoft was estimated to be $30 million. Yet, the strategy did not seem to work: In June 2020, Microsoft announced that Mixer would be shut down in the summer of 2022. Two months later, Shroud decided to make his return to Twitch. Given Shroud's 7 million followers, Twitch was happy to buy off his eight-figure Mixer contract.

When game developers become successful, they may feel like standing on their own two feet. This is what happened to Zynga, an American game developer founded in 2007. Two years later, the firm launched its social video game *FarmVille* on Facebook. It became the social network's most popular app with over 10 million daily active users. In 2012, Zynga decided to end its reliance on Facebook and set itself up as a standalone gaming social network, launching the *Zynga With Friends* platform that counted 80 million monthly active users and generated $861.4 million in revenues in 2017.

Beat egg whites

We also indicated previously that a group of users may have a lower UAC because positive same-side network effects exist within this group and act as a multiplier of the cross-side network effects. This drives us to make the analogy with egg whites, which – as you probably know – substantially increase in volume when beaten (as much as six to eight times). The tactic of beating egg whites amounts thus to igniting these positive same-side network effects, so that each time you attract one extra user in this group, you eventually attract several extra users. For instance, the possibility to play online with friends generates powerful same-side network effects among video game players, making them coordinate their decisions to adopt particular games or even a particular console.

Another example is Klaxit, a French carpooling platform that focuses on commuting to work. Klaxit wisely decided to partner with large companies, allowing employees of these companies to create 'communities' on the platform. As the members of these communities share many characteristics, the level of trust and, hence, the number of transactions is larger within communities than overall on the platform. Moreover, the existence of these communities is shown to contribute significantly to the growth of the platform.[12] One way to activate this tactic is to offer discounts to users if they join the platform in conjunction. Klaxit does so by partnering with companies and allowing their employees to benefit from cheaper rates. So does Bsit (the babysitting platform described previously in this chapter): With its service Bsit Care, the platform allows companies to set up the (co-branded) application internally for a subscription fee of about €1 per employee per month (see Charlot, 2018). Another well-known example is Spotify: They have long offered a family plan, which they complemented, in June 2020, with a 'Premium Duo' account targeted at couples.[13]

Go fifty/fifty

When groups of users show similar UAC and AP, they both generate levers of similar efficiency. As there is no reason to focus on one group in particular, roughly equivalent marketing efforts should then be made to attract both groups and exploit the leverages that they exert on one another. We describe two tactics for this purpose.

Chickens make eggs, which make chickens, which make eggs ...

Leveraging some users to attract other users remains a powerful way to launch a platform even when the different groups of users exert similar leverage. The idea is to build participation incrementally: Attract some users in whichever group; use their presence to persuade some users in the other group to join; use in turn these users to attract some more users in the first group; and so on. Through this step-by-step process – also known as the 'zigzag tactic' – you will exploit the cross-side network effects to slowly build your audience on both sides. For example, this is what e-Bay did in its early days. In an interview conducted by one of the authors in 2008, a representative from eBay explained that the platform was alternating its marketing campaigns, targeting buyers one month and sellers the next month.

Boost 'eggspectations'[14]

As explained in Chapter 1, network effects make the users' decisions about participating in the platform interdependent. As users can rarely observe other users' decisions before making their own, they have to form expectations about what other users will eventually do. What these expectations are and how they are formed is thus critical for the success of a platform. In particular, if most users have pessimistic expectations about the future platform's success, then it is very likely that the platform will flop. In contrast, if expectations are optimistic, users will be more eager to join, and the platform may then have higher chances of success. In both cases, the outcome that is initially expected may show to be true: one talks of 'self-fulfilling prophecies'.

> **Advertising growing participation numbers may convince users of the platform's future success, which may drive them to join – a self-fulfilling prophecy!**

Your goal as a platform manager is obviously to generate positive expectations among your potential users. The first step in this direction is the formulation of a clear and appealing value proposition (see Chapter 2), which should then be diffused through advertising and promotional efforts. Compared to other products and services, platforms have more incentives to advertise their penetration into a particular market (number of users, transactions, etc.); the objective is precisely to convince users that the platform is thriving and, therefore, worth joining. You may then succumb to the temptation of inflating participation numbers. After all, this looks like a temporary – and thus forgivable – lie, as it may turn true when it is believed hard enough (given the self-fulfilling nature of expectations). Yet, competitors or customers might call your bluff, which may damage your image and your business altogether, as illustrated in Case 4.7.

Case 4.7 Grubhub's 'growth hack'

Grubhub and Seamless are two American food-delivery platforms that connect diners with local takeout restaurants; they merged in 2013. In 2020, the *San Francisco Chronicle* reported the case of a restaurant owner who discovered, after receiving a phone call from a customer asking for delivery, that her restaurant was listed on both platforms, although she never agreed to it. To make things worse, the platforms mentioned a menu of dishes that she did not serve.

To the owner's complaint, the company replied that it

> recently started adding other restaurants to its sites without [an explicit] partnership, when it finds restaurants that are in high demand. In those cases, someone from the company orders the food ahead or at the restaurant, and a driver is sent to pick it up.
>
> (see Duggan, 2020)

Another article, published in *The Verge*, explains that this practice is widespread in the food-delivery sector, as many platforms list restaurants by default, leaving to those that do not want to appear the burden of asking to be removed (see Garun, 2020).

On top of creating costs for restaurants (especially small ones), this practice misleads diners about the number of restaurants that they can effectively interact with, which may end up in bad press and reputation losses.

Buy up or replace

As we explained in the previous section, you may face – like Airbnb did – the problematic situation in which one group of users has a stronger AP and, at the same time, a larger UAC than the other group. This means that the presence of that group – or what it can provide – is key for your value proposition, but is also quite costly to acquire. We present here three alternative tactics that you may use in this situation.

Offer chickens a deal they can't refuse

The first tactic consists in 'buying up' the participation of an entire group of users. The idea is to offer a group of users a subsidy that is equivalent to the value that they would get if the other group of users was present on the platform as well. With such a subsidy, users face no uncertainty (as they obtain the same value whether the other group joins the platform or not). In particular, they do not fear that the platform would remain a 'ghost town'. This group of users, therefore, decides to join the platform and, consequently, so does the other group (for which all uncertainty has disappeared as well). This strategy is often referred to as 'Divide-and-conquer': A negative price is set to convince one group to join the platform ('divide') and a positive price is then charged to the other group, whose willingness to pay has increased because of the (observed) presence of the first group ('conquer').

For instance, Benjamin Lauzier of Lyft explained the following: "We had an income floor for drivers, to guarantee some amount of money per hour. This helped us jump-start the marketplace from scratch" (see Rachitsky, 2019). Of course, this strategy can only be profitable if the gains obtained from the second group outweigh the losses incurred from the first group. This is why the 'divide' group is necessarily the one with the stronger AP.

Fake the chickens (or the eggs)

Because they find the previous tactic too expensive, some platforms may be tempted to choose an alternative method that is more questionable from an ethical viewpoint. This method consists in pretending that many users in one group have joined the platform to lure users of the other group to join as well. Case 4.8 gives two illustrations.

Case 4.8 'Fake it till you make it'

Reddit is a social news aggregation platform (launched in June 2005) that allows its users to share titles with their URL links, and to cast votes to influence the visibility of what has been posted. In 2012, as a contribution to an online course on Web development, Steve Huffman, the co-founder of Reddit, admitted that all the content submitted in the beginning was shared by him and his associate, Alexis Ohanian:[15]

> In the beginning, Alexis and I submitted all the content. You'd go to Reddit in the early days, the first couple of months, and there'd be

tons of content. I shouldn't say "fake content," but it was fake users. It was really all just Alexis and I.

Udemy, a MOOC (Massive Online Open Courses) platform, was launched similarly. One of its co-founders, Gagan Biyani, explained in a series of Tweets (Biyani, 2021) how they decided to 'fake the chicken' before they could actually 'make the chicken':

> We had o courses but a built-out product. Eren Bali [*another co-founder*] created a crawler that went on YouTube and built courses out of YouTube playlists. Now we had talks from Marissa Meyer & Mark Zuckerberg on our site so any users who came on had something to learn. Our product finally seemed presentable. Users would be more likely to sign up after looking through and seeing the depth and breadth of content provided. The launch announcement generated 10,000 users and allowed us to raise our seed round. However ... In the back of your mind, you're probably thinking that was a bit of a bullshit move. And you're right. Most users bounced, and the core issue was not resolved. Faking the chicken was only a temporary solution for making the chicken.

Like inflating participation numbers, generating artificial content, or creating fake user accounts is a deception to the users of a platform. Even if well-known platforms like Reddit and Udemy got away with it, this aggressive method goes against a key principle in building a platform – trust – and you cannot build trust on a lie. Therefore, we do not recommend you to go down that route.

Lay the first eggs yourself

If cross-side network effects are central for the participants in your platform and if you have few stand-alone benefits to offer them, there is a risk that none of the previous strategies will succeed in solving the chicken-and-egg problem. You may then want to postpone for a while operating as a true platform and start instead your business like a more traditional pipeline. That is, instead of relying on third-party service providers, you may decide to cater to the needs of the customers by yourself.

You should certainly not see this decision as an admission of failure. Many existing platforms (and not the least) followed this route. Think of the first gaming consoles, which came bundled with their own games. Think also of Apple which dominated the early years of personal computers with an integrated approach. Amazon is an even clearer example, as it started as a pure reseller before managing same-side network effects on the buyer side (by implementing rating, review, and recommendation systems), and finally leveraging cross-side network effects (by letting third-party sellers use the infrastructure of its marketplace).

> **Sometimes, the only way to become a platform is to start by not being one...**

The idea behind this strategy is simple: You attract end customers more easily by offering yourself the service or goods that they wish to consume. They will indeed feel reassured to find what they are looking for, without having to second-guess whether participants on the other side of the market will also jump on board or not. In a sense, the chicken-and-egg problem disappears because there is no longer any ambiguity as to which comes first – the chicken (or the egg) is already there!

Once an installed base of customers has been built, you may think of opening up your business to third-party providers and, thereby, start operating as a platform. The advantage of this strategy is clear: You will not only expand the supply of services or products for your customers but also save on costs (as long as coordination costs are lower than production costs). Yet, a downside could be that external service providers feel uncomfortable with the presence of your own in-house offering. To reduce this risk, you should make sure that your offering does not compete directly with the third-party products or services; even better, you should try to exploit complementarities or synergies between the various offerings (we return to this issue in Chapter 6).

To close this section, we provide you with a strategic guide to address the chicken-and-egg conundrum and, thereby, launch your platform most efficiently. Figure 4.6 summarizes the ten tactics that we have described and organizes them according to the three typical strategies that the Lever Selector might advise you to follow. If one group of users has a stronger

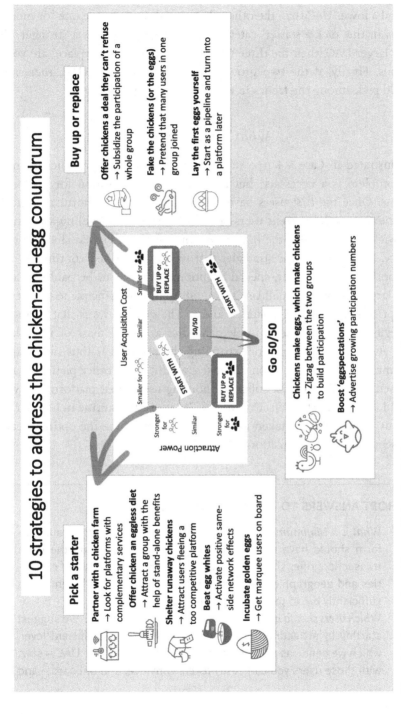

Figure 4.6 A strategic guide to address the chicken-and-egg conundrum.

AP and a lower UAC than the other, then you should choose one (or more) tactics in the 'pick a starter' category. If the group that has a stronger AP has a larger UAC, then the three tactics in the 'buy up or replace' are your options. Finally, if the two groups have similar AP and UAC, then you should pick among the tactics in the 'Go 50/50' category.

What comes next?

As illustrated in Case 4.4 (the story of Famest), solving the chicken-and-egg problem is a necessary, but not a sufficient, condition for platform success. Once the first users have been attracted, the platform must still strive to retain the current users and attract new ones. Fueling a positive feedback loop is indeed the best recipe for a platform's sustainable performance. By and large, the strategies that we just described continue to be appropriate. In particular, special attention still needs to be paid to users with large APs and/or small UACs; we will apply this principle to price and non-price strategies in Chapters 5 and 6. The good news is that all these strategies become easier to implement after a critical mass of users has been attracted to each group. Expanding the platform is thus important, as it makes further expansion easier (especially when other platforms are competing for the same set of single-homing users). Yet, platform growth should not become an objective in itself. As we will examine in Chapter 6, various factors must be taken into account to determine the optimal scale and scope at which the platform should operate.

> **SHORT ANSWERS TO THE KEY QUESTIONS**
> - *What is a Minimum Viable Platform?* At the launch stage, your platform should have a minimum scope (that is, focus on the main transaction, offer simple features, and cover a limited set of categories and geographies) to avoid wasting resources, while remaining sufficiently broad to grow a large enough audience.
> - *Which users should be attracted first to launch a platform?* We suggest starting by attracting the user group with the most efficient lever, which we define as a combination of two elements: The UAC – start with those users you can easily reach, convince, and onboard – and

the AP – start with those users who exert the strongest cross-side network effects.

- *How costly is it to attract a particular group of users?* Unlike the typical 'CAC' formula, we invite you to reflect on three different types of costs that are relevant for platforms: (i) The cost of reaching out to particular users, (ii) the efforts you have to exert to ease users' adoption, and (iii) the efforts to create a trusted environment on the platform.
- *Which launching tactics should be deployed in practice?* Using the 'Lever Selector', we suggest three typical launching strategies. In the 'Pick a starter' strategy, leveraging one group is clearly more efficient than leveraging the other; corresponding tactics exploit either the low UAC or the large AP of this group. The 'Go 50/50' strategy corresponds to cases in which the groups are relatively equivalent both in terms of UAC and AP; the recommendation is then to build the platform incrementally by attracting users in each group in turn. Finally, the 'Buy up or replace' strategy is recommended when users in one group have both a larger AP and UAC; the corresponding tactics amount to integrate with that group, that is, either buy out their participation or replace them altogether with your own offering.
- *When is 'not being a platform' the best way to (eventually) 'be a platform'?* As just explained, if the platform does not manage to attract enough users in its early stages, then it should be possible to consider priming the pump by substituting oneself for one of the sides of the market. The idea is, for example, to play the role of the supplier to attract the first customers. When enough customers have joined, it is then possible to open to independent providers and become, eventually, a true platform.

FURTHER READINGS

For some practical tips about the design of a Minimum Viable Platform, read Gracia (2022). To know more about the lean startup methodology and the VRIN framework, read Ries (2011) and Barney (1991) respectively. For a fully-fledged case study of the initial success and then failure of a platform active in the home-food delivery sector, see Belleflamme and Neysen (2017).

Notes

1. The numbers reported in Case 4.1 appeared in a document that surfaced in the wake of the legal battle between Epic Games and Apple (see, e.g., Porter, 2021).
2. See Sharetribe (2020).
3. End of 2019, Uber released its first comprehensive safety report about its rides in the US over 2017–2018 (see Uber, 2019). It indicates that riders and drivers report assaults at roughly the same rate. In total, about 3,000 sexual assaults were reported during the period, which suggests that although ride-hailing platforms are now widely accepted, and despite all Uber's efforts to screen its users, trust (or the lack of it) remains a major issue.
4. See Barney (1991).
5. See Makkonen (2022).
6. Back-of-the-envelope computations suggest that a 'host-to-guest ratio' of 1:70 should suffice to clear the market (if you divide 365 – that is, the number of days that a given accommodation is available per year – by 70, you get 5.2, which looks like a reasonable estimation of the average number of days that a guest would be willing to spend in an Airbnb accommodation per year).
7. See Dou and Wu (2021).
8. Teixeira (2016) explains that by clicking on this button, Airbnb hosts were able to publish their Airbnb listings on Craigslist at no cost, while still being able to be reached by guests on Airbnb.
9. See, e.g., Newton (2019).
10. Gelman and Salop (1983) introduce 'judo economics', while Yoffie and Kwak (2001) describe 'judo business strategies'.
11. For more, see Hawley (2018).
12. See Malardé (2019).
13. Wicklow, Belleflamme, and Peitz (2020) explain how the family plan aims at leveraging network effects: "Spotify is willing to use lower tariffs to increase traffic on the platform, as traffic rhymes with data and data are precious to improve the service."
14. We borrow this pun from a Canadian chain of restaurants (see https://www.eggspectation.com/#our-story, last accessed on 08/10/2021).
15. 'Growing Reddit – Web Development' by Udacity. YouTube video submitted on May 27, 2012. Webpage consulted on May 10, 2021. https://www.youtube.com/watch?v=zmeDzx4SUME.

Bibliography

Barney, J. (1991). Firm resources and sustained competitive advantage. *Journal of Management* 17(1), 99–120. https://doi.org/10.1177/014920639101700108.

Belleflamme, P. and N. Neysen (2017). The rise and fall of Take Eat Easy, or why markets are not easy to take in the sharing economy. *Digiworld Economic Journal (Communications & Strategies)* 108, 59–76.

Biyani, G. (2021). Before Udemy could succeed…, Thread on Twitter (January 22). https://twitter.com/gaganbiyani/status/1352714283323437057?ref_src= twsrc%5Etfw.

Charlot, C. (2018). Quand le babysitting devient un business numérique. Trends-Tendances (February 8). https://trends.levif.be/economie/high-tech/numerik/quand-le-babysitting-devient-un-business-numerique/ article-normal-792279.html.

Choudary, S. (2014). Platform design: The three elements for designing platforms. Platform Revolution. https://platformthinkinglabs.com/materials/the-three-design-elements-for-designing-platforms/.

De Boose, D. (2018). A chaque palier de croissance son mode de financement. Blog post (April 23). https://www.ing.be/fr/business/my-business/growth/ financing-growth.

Dou, Y. and Wu, D.J. (2021). Platform competition under network effects: Piggybacking and optimal subsidization. *Information Systems Research* 32(3), 820–835. https://doi.org/10.1287/isre.2021.1017.

Duggan, T. (2020). Seamless, Grubhub deliver confusion with mistaken restaurant listings. *San Francisco Chronicle* (January 26). https://www.sfchronicle. com/food/article/SF-restaurant-Kin-Khao-doesn-t-offer-delivery-15005797.php.

Garun, N. (2020). Grubhub's new growth hack is listing restaurants that didn't agree to be listed. The latest in its string of shady practices. *The Verge* (January 30). https://www.theverge.com/2020/1/29/21113876/grubhub-seamless-fake-restaurant-listings-no-permission-postmates-doordash.

Gelman J.R. and S.C. Salop (1983). Judo economics: Capacity limitation and coupon competition. *The Bell Journal of Economics* 14, 315–325. https://doi. org/10.2307/3003635.

Gracia, C. (2022). Your marketplace MVP – How to build a Minimum Viable Platform. Marketplace Academy – Sharetribe (January 5). https://www. sharetribe.com/academy/how-to-build-a-minimum-viable-platform/.

Hawley, K. (2018). White Castle partners with Grubhub as delivery moves toward exclusivity. Skift.Table (January 10). https://table.skift.

com/2018/01/10/white-castle-partners-with-grubhub-as-delivery-moves-toward-exclusivity/.

Knowledge at Wharton (2017). The inside story behind the unlikely rise of Airbnb (April 26). https://knowledge.wharton.upenn.edu/article/the-inside-story-behind-the-unlikely-rise-of-airbnb/.

Makkonen, J. (2022). 11 marketplace metrics you should be tracking your measure your success. Sharetribe. https://www.sharetribe.com/academy/measure-your-success-key-marketplace-metrics/.

Malardé, V. (2019). Economie collaborative et régulation des plateformes numériques. PhD Dissertation, Université de Rennes 1.

Newman, J. (2018). The dream of a privacy-first social network: 6 alternatives to Facebook. FastCompany (April 19). https://www.fastcompany.com/40559106/the-privacy-first-social-network-a-great-idea-that-never-works.

Newton, C. (2019). How TikTok could fail. *The Verge* (August 7). https://www.theverge.com/interface/2019/8/7/20757855/tiktok-growth-monetization-influencers-regulation.

Perez, M. (2020). Shroud signs a streaming deal with Twitch after a stint on Microsoft's defunct Mixer. *Forbes* (August 11). https://www.forbes.com/sites/mattperez/2020/08/11/shroud-signs-a-streaming-deal-with-twitch-after-a-stint-on-microsofts-defunct-mixer/.

Porter, J. (2021). Epic spent at least $11.6 million on free games and gained 5 million new users in return. *The Verge* (May 4). https://www.theverge.com/2021/5/4/22418782/epic-games-store-free-games-cost-apple-trial-arkham-subnautica-mutant-year-zero.

Rachitsky, L. (2019). How to kickstart and scale a marketplace business – Phase 1: Crackthechicken-and-eggproblem. *Lenny'sNewsletter* (November 20). https://www.lennysnewsletter.com/p/how-to-kickstart-and-scale-a-marketplace.

Ries, E. (2011). *The lean startup: How today's entrepreneurs use continuous innovation to create radically successful businesses.* New York: Crown Business.

Schonfeld, E. (2008). At Glassdoor, find out how much people really make at Google, Microsoft, Yahoo, and everywhere else. *TechCrunch* (June 11). https://techcrunch.com/2008/06/10/at-glassdoor-find-out-how-much-people-really-make-at-google-microsoft-yahoo-and-everywhere-else/.

Sharetribe (2020). Talk to your users before building anything with Charles Armitage (Florence). Transcript of *Two-Sided: The Marketplace Podcast* (Season 1, Episode 4, June 17). https://www.sharetribe.com/twosided/ep4-charles-armitage-florence-talk-users-before-building/.

Teixeira, T. (2016). How Uber, Airbnb, and Etsy attracted their first 1,000 customers. *Harvard Business School Working Knowledge* (July 13). http://hbswk.hbs.edu/item/how-uber-airbnb-and-etsyattracted-their-first-1-000-customers.

Uber (2019). US safety report 2017–2018. https://www.uber-assets.com/image/upload/v1575580686/Documents/Safety/UberUSSafetyReport_201718_FullReport.pdf.

Wicklow, M., Belleflamme, P., and Peitz, M. (2020). Who pays what on Spotify? IPdigIT (May 18). http://www.ipdigit.eu/2020/05/who-pays-what-on-spotify/.

Yoffie, D.B. and Kwak, M. (2001). Judo strategy. Turning your competitors' strength to your advantage. Boston MA: Harvard Business School Press.

Part III

VALUE CAPTURE

5

MONETIZING A PLATFORM

KEY QUESTIONS

- Should all platform users be charged the same price?
- Should users be charged to access the platform or to use it (or both)?
- Why is it complex to determine how much platform users can be charged?
- Apart from charging users, are there other ways to monetize a platform?
- Should the platform regulate how sellers set prices for buyers?

In the previous stage, your goal was to solve the chicken-and-egg problem. As getting users onboard was the paramount objective, the absence of profits (or the build-up of losses) was the least of your concerns. Now that you have successfully managed to launch your platform, it is time to find ways to monetize the services that you offer to your users. That is, you need to find ways to capture the value that you are creating. The objective

DOI: 10.4324/9780429490873-9

is, at the very least, to cover your costs sustainably. On top of that, you may want to make a profit (which you will redistribute as you see fit if you run a for-profit company or which you will reinvest in the platform itself if you manage a not-for-profit organization).

The first monetization strategy that comes to mind is pricing: Let users pay for the value they get on the platform. This seems self-evident but it is quite tricky to achieve in practice, mainly because the value that users get on a platform is conditional on the participation of other users. It is then of primary importance to take the users' interdependence into account when setting prices. We discuss pricing in the first section by addressing the following three questions: Whom to charge? How to charge? How much to charge? We propose an organizing tool – the Platform Pricing Matrix – to help you collect your answers to the first two questions and, thereby, address the third one more efficiently.

As it is sometimes challenging to make users pay for the services of the platform, it may be useful to look for alternative monetization strategies. One route is to onboard other groups of users on the platform for the sake of raising revenues; we think here of advertisers, who are willing to pay for the attention (and, potentially, the personal data) of the primary users of the platform. Another possibility consists in entering into revenue-sharing agreements with complementors; a platform may, for instance, refer its users to another platform for some extra services and get, as a quid pro quo, a commission on the revenues that these users generate on this other platform. We describe these other monetization strategies in the second section.

Finally, we end this chapter by examining whether platforms should leave some pricing decisions to their users (typically sellers or service providers) and if so, to which extent they should control these decisions.

Pricing strategies for platforms

It is common for platforms to practice differential pricing, that is to set different prices for different users. On a multisided platform, users belong to different groups and have different roles; it is then relatively easy for the platform to tell users apart and charge them different prices. On a ride-hailing platform like BlaBlaCar for instance, drivers pay nothing for the use of the platform, while travelers pay a fee for each ride, on which the platform takes a commission of up to 30%. Even on platforms that cater to a unique group of users (like social networks), it is often possible (and sensible) to adjust prices according to user profiles; for instance, discounts may be offered to early or heavy users.

In parallel, the same user may be charged different prices for different uses they make of the platform. For example, they may have to pay first for registering on the platform (membership price) and, next, for each transaction they make (transaction price).

Compared to 'pipeline pricing', 'platform pricing' is more complex but also more powerful. In a pipeline business, you largely set the prices of your products or services independently of one another. Hence, prices are relatively simple to set but their effects are also limited: Changing the price of a product affects the quantity demanded of that product in the opposite direction and that's about it. In contrast, on a platform, you must choose a price *structure* and a price mix. The *price structure* is the coordination of prices across the various groups of users that interact on the platform. Because of the strong complementarity between the different groups (in terms of participation in and usage of the platform), the prices for one group are inevitably linked to the prices for the other groups. The *price mix* has to do with the combination of different types of prices, namely membership and transaction prices, which play different roles.

> **Platforms must choose the right price structure and price mix.**

As the effects of all these prices are intertwined, finding the right price structure and price mix is not a piece of cake. Yet, you can take comfort from two facts. First, because prices can be combined in so many ways, you can take several routes to reach the same destination and fine-tune your pricing flexibly. Second, we provide you in this section with several guiding principles that should help you make the right pricing decisions at the right time. We first claim that cost-based and value-based pricing must give way to *leverage-based pricing* when it comes to determining the price structure. We then turn to the price mix by comparing the merits of different types of prices and by explaining that the right price must be chosen for the right purpose. Finally, we address the delicate question of how much to charge. You could think that we should have started there but, as we will argue, what you can charge your users heavily depends on the price structure and price mix that you have chosen.

Who to charge? A leverage-based price structure

When businesses try to figure out how to price their products or services, they usually think of the following two methods – cost-based pricing and value-based pricing. As the names indicate, the idea is to base the price either on the cost of manufacturing the product (or of providing the service) or on the value that the product or service may bring to its consumers. In the first case, a percentage is added on top of the cost to secure a margin; this may be seen as a 'bottom-up' approach, as the starting point is the minimum price that is needed to cover the cost. In the second case, the objective is to adapt the price to the consumers' willingness to pay; we have here a 'top-down' approach, as the reference point is the maximum price that a consumer is willing to pay (also called the 'pain point').[1]

In the context of platform businesses, it is difficult to apply either cost-based or value-based pricing as such. The problem is that costs and value are intrinsically linked. To see this, suppose that to accommodate one extra user in group A, the platform must incur a cost of €10. But, at the same time, the participation of this extra user allows the platform to raise an extra revenue of €3 from users in group B (because of cross-side network effects). Then the 'true' cost of this extra user is not €10 but €10 − €3 = €7, that is, the 'accommodation cost' minus the value that this user contributes to generating on the other side of the platform. In general, *the costs incurred for users on one side of the platform must be adjusted downward to account for the additional revenues that these users generate on the other side of the platform.*

It follows that cost-based and value-based considerations must somehow be mixed when setting prices on a platform. We, therefore, propose an alternative method for setting prices on platforms, which we call *leverage-based pricing*. The idea is to base prices on the leverage that users exert when being active on a platform. We now examine how to do so.

Choosing prices jointly to leverage network effects

Because users co-create value on the platform, prices for different groups are necessarily interdependent. This is so because by changing the price on, say, side B, the platform affects the leverage conditions on which it bases the price for side A. More precisely, when changing the price on side B, the platform modifies the participation on side B and, thereby, the value that it can generate on side A by attracting users on side B; but if the latter value changes, so do the platform's incentives to change the price on side A.

Prices for different users must then be chosen in a coordinated way. In other words, platform operators are bound for serious mistakes if they set prices separately for the different sides of the platform. The platform's task is thus to choose a price *structure*, that is a set of articulated – and not distinct – prices. A related reason to think in terms of price structure is that users do also think in this way: They are not only influenced by the prices they have to pay but also (at least indirectly) by the prices users of other groups have to pay.

> **Platforms must choose a leveraged-based structure of interconnected prices because changing the price for one group affects the revenues that can be collected from the other group.**

To grasp the importance of choosing prices jointly rather than separately, let us walk you through a slightly more complex numerical example (see Case 5.1). If numbers are not your forte, you may want to skip that box and jump to the next section, where we summarize the main insights.

Case 5.1 A toy model to understand leveraged-based pricing

Imagine that the platform is a marketplace that links buyers and sellers. To keep things simple, we make the following assumptions:

- There is one potential buyer – Bree – and two potential sellers – Sue and Sean;
- A transaction between a buyer and seller yields a gross benefit of €100 to each of them;
- On this value, the platform takes a commission, which can either be equal to 20%, 10%, or 4% (the commission can differ across sides);
- The buyer and the sellers incur specific costs for each transaction they conduct on the platform: €75 for Bree, €85 for Sue, and €95 for Sean.

We see that Bree is willing to participate even if the platform charges her a high commission of 20%. She would indeed receive, for each transaction, a benefit of €80 (that is, €100 minus a commission of €20), which is higher than her cost (€75). So, pricing on this side is a no-brainer: The platform can safely set a commission of 20%, meaning that it will earn €20 per transaction that Bree conducts.

Things are a bit more involved on the seller side. Clearly, none of the sellers would accept to pay a commission of 20% (as they would be left with €80, which is below their respective costs, that is, €85 for Sue and €95 for Sean). To attract Sue, the platform must lower the commission to at least 10% (leaving her with at least €90), and to attract Sean, the platform must set the lowest commission of 4% (leaving him with €96). *So, which commission should the platform set on the seller side?*

Scenario 1: Narrow-minded manager. Suppose first that the manager considers only the revenues that can be raised on the seller side. As Bree joins the platform, each seller will transact with her. There are thus two possibilities:

- **Set a commission of 10%.** In this case, only Sue joins the platform and one transaction takes place (Bree & Sue); the platform collects thus one time €10 from Sue, meaning that revenues on the seller side are then equal to €10.
- **Set a commission of 4%.** Now, both Sue and Sean join the platform, meaning that *two* transactions take place (on top of Bree & Sue, we also have Bree & Sean); this allows the platform to collect €4 from both Sue and Sean, which makes revenues on the seller side equal to 2 × €4 = €8.

According to this logic, the preferred commission should be 10%. Reducing the commission to 4% is not worth it in terms of revenues on the seller side: The extra revenue that could be gained from Sean (€4) is lower than the revenue that would be lost from Sue (€10 − €4 = €6).

Scenario 2: Platform-minded manager. A 'platform-minded' manager should realize that more participation on the seller side generates more value on the buyer side because it increases the number of transactions. Let us reconsider the two options under this broader perspective:

- **Set a commission of 10%.** The transaction between Bree and Sue is the only one to take place. The platform collects €10 from Sue and €20 from Bree, leading to total revenues (on the seller *and* the buyer side) of €10 + €20 = €30;
- **Set a commission of 4%.** There is now one more transaction (between Bree and Sean), allowing the platform to collect €4 from Sue *and Sean*, and *two* times €20 from Bree; total revenues are then equal to €4 + €4 + 2 × €20 = €48.

It appears now clear that the best course of action is to set a commission of 20% on the buyer side and 4% on the seller side. It is still true that €2 of revenues are lost on the seller side when reducing the commission from 10% to 4%. But this loss is more than compensated by the extra revenues raised on the buyer side: Having Sean on board allows the platform to collect an extra €20 from the second transaction that Bree conducts. The net gain is thus €20 − €2 = €18.

Scenario 3: Optimal subsidies. To push this logic one step further, let us show that it might even be profit-maximizing for the platform to *subsidize* the participation of sellers, that is, to pay them to participate! To see this, assume that Sean's cost per transaction is now equal to €102 (instead of €95). This means that to convince Sean to join the platform, the seller commission must become *negative*; for instance, a subsidy of 3% per transaction would work. Note that if Sean is subsidized, so must be Sue (as we assume that both sellers must be charged the same commission). Clearly, no narrow-minded manager would set such a price as, in their view, this would entail losses. But a platform-minded manager would consider it. And in the present case, they would choose to set that negative commission. Indeed, total revenues are now computed as: 2 × €20 (collected from Bree) − €3 (paid to Sue) − €3 (paid to Sean) = €34, which is still larger than the €30 the platform would obtain if it was charging a commission of 10% on the seller side. Table 5.1 summarizes the computations we made so far.

Table 5.1 Platform's revenues in Scenarios 1 to 3

	(A) Bree	(B) Sue	(C) Sean	(D) = (B) + (C) Sellers	(E) = (A) + (D) Total
(1) 20%/10%	20	10	0	10	30
(2) 20%/4%	40	4	4	8	48
(3) 20%/-3%	40	-3	-3	-6	34

Scenario 4: Pricing for not-for-profit platforms. Let us continue assuming that Sean's cost is equal to €102. But we assume now that the platform is a not-for-profit platform; that is, its objective is to maximize the total value generated for users, with the constraint of not making losses. At first glance, we could think that free access (that is, zero commission on both sides) maximizes value for users but, actually, it is not so. Let us show why. With zero commissions, Bree joins on the buyer side and Sue joins on the seller side. Bree gets a net value of €100 − €75 = €25 (as she conducts one transaction) and Sue gets a net value of €100 − €85 = €15. The total value for users is thus equal to €25 + €15 = €40.

Suppose now that the platform subsidizes sellers by paying them a 'commission' of 3% per transaction to attract Sean as well. To avoid making losses (and profits), the platform has to set a corresponding commission of 3% on the buyer side (so that the total commission per transaction remains equal to zero). What is the total value generated for users under this scenario? Bree now conducts two transactions but pays €3 instead of €0 on each transaction, meaning that her net value is equal to 2 × (€100 − €3 − €75) = €44; Sue gets a net value of €100 + €3 − €85 = €18, while Sean gest a net value of €100 + €3 − €102 = €1. The total value generated for the users of the platform is thus equal to: €44 + €18 + €1 = €63 (see Table 5.2 for a summary). This is way larger than what free access

Table 5.2 Users' value in the two options of Scenario 4

	Bree	Sue	Sean	Total
(1) 0%/0%	25	15	0	40
(2) 3%/−3%	44	18	1	63

would generate. So, a not-for-profit platform must also follow a leverage-based pricing approach and factor in the interdependence between the two groups of users. One group of users may be asked to subsidize the participation of the other group, but it would gladly agree to do so as it generates a larger value for them.

A skewed price structure

Let us take stock of what we have learned from the previous discussions and examples. First, to optimize their pricing, platforms must factor in the interdependence that exists between the prices set for different groups of users; that is, they choose a *price structure* instead of a set of separate prices. Second, the price structure is *leverage-based* insofar as prices are used to operate levers, that is, to activate the network effects that users exert on one another. Third, as far as network effects differ in strength across groups of users, the price structure is *skewed*, that is, different groups of users are charged different prices. Fourth, platforms may find it optimal to *subsidize* a group of users whenever the losses incurred on this group are recouped by the extra gains made on the other group. Finally, the previous principles apply equally to for-profit and not-for-profit platforms.

> **The leveraged-based price structure on a platform is generally skewed: Some users pay more, while other users pay less (or are even subsidized).**

Regarding the third principle, you may wonder what subsidizing users exactly means. As just explained, a platform that subsidizes users accepts to make losses on them, that is, to charge a price that is below the cost that the platform faces to accommodate these users. For instance, in the video game market, it is customary to sell consoles below cost (meaning that gamers are subsidized). Similarly, in the ride-hailing industry, platforms like Uber and Lyft initially guaranteed some minimum earnings to their drivers, thereby offering them better conditions than they would get otherwise. When the cost of accommodating users is negligible, then below-cost prices are 'negative', in the sense that users are charged nothing and receive some positive compensation on top. This compensation can be monetary (like promotional codes or discounts) or in-kind (like gifts or freebies). It can also take the form of a cost avoidance; for instance, at the early stage of Android, Google provided application developers with a free-to-use software development kit (free parking slots in shopping malls follow the same idea).

Subsidies are often offered to early users who sponsor a new user. One talks then of *seeding prices*, because the underlying objective is to 'seed the platform', that is, to grow its user base. The logic of leverage-based pricing is applied here to the relationship between current and future prices. As bigger platforms generate more benefits for their users, future users are more likely to join a platform that has already attracted a large number of users. The group of current users can then be seen as exerting positive cross-side network effects on the group of future users. In less technical terms, the first users can serve as leverage for the future growth of the platform. It makes thus full sense for a platform to lower the price for early users. This will allow the platform not only to attract more users later on but also to charge those users larger prices (as the value would have been increased). As a result, the platform will be able to recoup the revenues that it forewent initially (or even the losses if it chose to subsidize the first users). The leverage is even more direct if being charged the low price (or subsidy) is conditional on sponsoring new users.

Picking the 'money side'

It should be clear by now that having all users pay the same price on a platform is the exception rather than the rule: What we expect is that the platform charges a group of users more than the other. It is customary to call the first group the 'money side' and the second, the 'subsidy side' (even if users in this group are not actually subsidized but just pay a lower price). The question that naturally arises is which group should be the money side and which group, the subsidy side. To answer this question, we need to compare the two groups in terms of *attraction power* (AP) and *price sensitivity* (PS). There are indeed two reasons that drive a platform to charge one group of users less than the other: This group exerts a relatively larger AP and/or this group is relatively more sensitive to price changes. To understand these two logics, let us use a simple example and distinguish between two scenarios to isolate the impacts of differences in AP and PS.

- *Scenario 1: Same PS/Larger AP for group A.* Suppose that the two groups have the same PS; in particular, suppose that, in both groups, a price reduction of 1€ induces an increase in the participation of one user. Suppose, in contrast, that users in group A exert a larger AP than users in group B; in particular, one extra user in group A allows the platform to collect twice as much extra revenues on side B than what an extra user in group B allows it to collect on side A. Under these conditions, reducing the price by 1€ is twice as efficient if it is done on side A than on side B. Group A is thus clearly the subsidy side and group B, the money side.
- *Scenario 2: Larger PS/Same AP for group A.* Suppose now that both groups have the same attraction power: One extra user on any side allows the platform to collect the same extra revenues on the other side. Yet, the groups differ in terms of PS; in particular, a price reduction of €1 leads to an increase in participation of two users in group A but only of 1 user in group B. Again, reducing the price by 1€ is twice as efficient when done on side A, meaning that group A should be the subsidy side and group B, the money side.

We separated the two scenarios for the sake of the illustration. Yet, in reality, there is little point in doing so, because the ranking of the two groups should not change whether we compare their attraction powers or their price sensitivities. That is, if one group has a relatively larger AP, it should also have a relatively larger PS. To understand this, we need to go back to the analyses that we carried out in the previous two chapters. Recall first from Chapter 4 that the relative AP of your groups of users depends on your competitive environment. For instance, if none of your potential competitors is meeting the needs of users in group B, whereas users in group A may find alternatives to the services that you propose, then having group A on board is essential to ensure the participation of group B, but the reverse is not true (as group A users do not necessarily need to interact with group B on your platform to have their needs answered). In other words, group A has a relatively larger AP because it has access to more alternative options than group B. Now, recall from Chapter 3 how 'substitutes' are defined in the specific case of platforms: The substitutes are the various ways by which users in one group manage to have their needs answered without interacting with users in the other group (in that sense, substitutes pose a threat to the platform on a single side, in contrast with rivals that pose a threat on both sides).

So, if a group of users has access to more and/or stronger substitutes, then this group has a relatively larger AP on your platform. And, by the same token, users in this group are also more sensitive to price changes: If you raise the price for these users, they will leave the platform in greater numbers, as they can turn easily to attractive alternatives (or, conversely, you will have to lower your price relatively more if you want to drive a given number of them away from these alternatives).

In a nutshell, the decision process to choose which group of users should be your money or subsidy side is fairly straightforward:

1. Refer to the Platform Value Net to compare the threat of substitutes on the two sides.
2. Pick as your money side the group where the threat of substitutes is relatively weaker because lowering prices for this group is less necessary − this group is less price-sensitive − and less profitable − this group exerts a lower attraction power.

> **Your money side is the group of users who have fewer alternatives to using your platform.**

Let us apply this intuition to Airbnb. Referring to the Platform Value Net that we quickly filled in for Airbnb in Chapter 3, we could be left with the impression that the threat of substitutes is always stronger for guests than for hosts. Yet, a distinction must be made between non-professional and professional hosts (like hotels). As far as non-professional hosts are concerned, it is fair to say that Airbnb has become so dominant nowadays that guests can hardly reach such hosts through other ways; then, the threat of substitutes is arguably lower for guests than for non-professional hosts (who can, alternatively, rent their property on the long-term market). Arguably, the opposite prevails for professional hosts, as guests can easily find similar offerings outside Airbnb; here, the threat of substitutes is relatively larger on the guests' side. We should, therefore, observe that for transactions with non-professional hosts, Airbnb charges more on the guests' side, while the reverse applies for transactions with professional hosts. Cicero (2021) reports numbers that match this prediction:

> For non-professional hosts, the take rate [that is, commission] is around 3% on the hosts' side (or little more, up to 6% in some cases) and circa 14% on the guest's side, while for professional hosts (like hotels and some other hosts) the guest doesn't get any visible "service fee" and the host is charged around 14–16%.

How to charge? A multipurpose price mix

Platforms set several different prices, not only because it makes sense to target different prices to different groups of users (as we just explained) but also because different prices can achieve different objectives. Typically, there are two main objectives that you pursue as a platform operator when using prices (on top of monetizing your activities, of course): You want to regulate the *access to* and the *activities on* the platform. That is, you want to control (1) how many – and potentially which – users join the platform and (2) who does what on the platform. In general, platforms use membership prices to achieve the first objective and transaction prices to achieve the second. We discuss these two types of prices in turn. We then explain why it may be a good idea to charge different prices to users *within* a given group. Finally, we discuss how these various pricing tactics can be combined.

Membership prices

Membership (or subscription) prices are well-suited to control participation in the platform. Users pay them once or regularly, *independently of their actual usage of the platform*. Examples are the price of a game console, the monthly subscription to Spotify, or the listing fee for making a product available on Etsy. Membership prices are key for users to determine whether they want to join the platform or not. This is why these prices shape the *size of* the groups of users (*how many?*) that will interact on the platform during a given period. As is the case in any market, price and users' participation (that is 'demand') are inversely related: The larger the price, the smaller the participation, as only those users who are willing (and can afford) to pay the price will participate. In that sense, membership prices also determine the *composition* of a group of users (*who?*) and thereby, can be a useful *signal* for other users. For instance, a high price tends to limit demand by creaming off a small subset of the total population within a particular user group. This strategy is notably applied in situations where the sense of exclusiveness is extremely valued by users. This is so if 'elite people' do not want to get mixed with 'common people'. The example of dating services targeting successful and wealthy individuals is particularly relevant here, as Case 5.2 illustrates. Similarly, a large enough listing fee on trading platforms increases the average quality of listings on the platform, as sellers put more effort into proposing a listing and spammers get discouraged.

Displaying a high entry price will have the consequence of limiting strongly the participating candidates... which can be a profitable strategy if the platform targets a high-end niche.

Case 5.2 'Please, don't get us mixed with the riff-raff!'

Rich Kids is the self-proclaimed 'world's most exclusive social network'. Downloading the app is free but if you want to post pictures, preferably of your lavish possessions, you have to pay a membership fee of $1,000 per month. Why this form of differential pricing? The high price for posting pictures is meant to select only (very) wealthy providers of content; to be sure that the selection operates, Rich Kids gives the following advice: "If it's too much for you, it's not for you." As for letting people download the app for free, the objective is to constitute an audience of viewers who, supposedly, will watch enviously the posted pictures. This audience exerts a positive cross-side network effect on the paying consumers because, as the website states, "being rich is boring when nobody sees you."

Similarly, in a matching context, when Berkeley International describes themselves on their website with the words "In the world of singles clubs we are the haute couture label," it is rather clear that price is not the main factor in user affiliation decision. Another example is probably the World Economic Forum, which brings together political, business, and other leaders of society each year in Davos. For business participants, the annual membership fees range from CHF60,000 to CHF600,000 (see Cann, 2017). In these cases, a price is much more a filtering tool than the result of a calculation based on the costs of the underlying mediating infrastructure.

Conversely, reducing the membership fee for users in a given group tells users in the other group that they can expect more interaction possibilities on the platform. For instance, a consumer may be more eager to use Etsy if they learn that sellers will be charged a lower listing fee; they will indeed expect that this price reduction will raise the participation of sellers, which will make the platform more attractive. It might then be useful to advertise any price change on both sides of the platform and not just to the users directly affected by that change. Even if this can help, nothing is ever certain about users' participation on a platform: The chicken-and-egg quandary is always looming. This is why setting membership fees may be tricky: If users have pessimistic expectations about the participation of other users, the value they will anticipate from joining the platform will be low and, as a result, they may not be willing to pay the membership fee that you ask.

One way to circumvent this problem is to offer sufficiently attractive stand-alone services. As explained in the previous chapter, stand-alone services reduce the interdependence between the different groups of users (see the 'eggless diet' launching strategy). Another way to make participation less risky is to charge users only for their actual usage of the platform; then, a user will pay nothing in the worst-case scenario in which she does not find any counterpart on the platform. This brings us to the second category of prices that you can think of using.

Transaction prices

Transaction (or usage) prices are paid *per effective transaction*. There are two main ways to achieve this: You can charge users either a fixed fee per transaction they conduct (or per unit they exchange) or a share (percentage) of the transaction price (a.k.a. a 'commission' or 'take rate'). Many major platforms – like eBay, Booking.com, Deliveroo, or Alibaba – charge commissions as a percentage of the transaction value of goods or services sold. Transaction prices are meant to regulate the activity on the platform, as the total bill that users end up paying depends on the number and value of the transactions that they conduct. Therefore, transaction prices address your second objective – controlling who does what. Transaction prices also indirectly address the first objective: When forward-looking users decide whether or not to join the platform, they estimate how much value they will gain from transacting on the platform, which depends on the transaction prices.

> **Lower transaction prices increase the volume of transactions and so, the value that users co-create on the platform.**

The main difficulty with transaction prices is that they may hurt the users' activities, both on and off the platform. First, users may have an incentive to cheat on the volume or number of transactions that they report to the platform, in an attempt to minimize their payments. Facing this risk, you may have to monitor closely the transactions that take place on the platform; you may also have to impose penalties on those who do not play by the rules. Yet, beware that such measures could be counterproductive, as they may alienate right-minded sellers, who would feel under suspicion. Second, users may choose to use your platform just to find counterparts and, once they have found them, complete the transaction outside the platform. If transaction prices are paid only for effective transactions, this would translate into a serious loss of earnings for you. To address this phenomenon – known as 'bypass' or 'leakage', you will have to deploy appropriate alternative strategies (which we describe in the next chapter).

Another obvious disadvantage of transaction prices is that they generate revenues only if a transaction takes place. Hence, there is no interest whatsoever in charging a transaction price for items that never attract any consumer. In that respect, listing fees are a much better option as sellers have to pay them irrespective of the sales they make (if any).

Same-side differential pricing

When discussing the price structure, we understood that platforms should charge different prices *across* different groups of users. We note here that differential pricing may also prove profitable *within* a given group of users. This is true, in particular, when negative same-side network effects exist in a group. Think, typically, of sellers competing on the platform for the custom of a group of buyers. The more sellers there are, the harder it is for each of them to get noticed by the customers. The platform may then want to sell some form of prominence to those sellers that accept to pay more. That is, against a larger commission or listing fee, sellers gain more exposure, obtain a better placement, or benefit from marketing activities whereby the platform increases the success rate of transactions. What makes this strategy tricky to implement is that the prominence that the platform can offer is inversely related to the number of sellers that pay to be prominent. Prominence must therefore be sufficiently expensive so that only a few sellers pay for it, which guarantees that each of them obtains the visibility they are looking for.

Differential pricing may also prove profitable *within* a given group of users.

This is just one example of menu pricing (or versioning), whereby users self-select into a menu of options that are priced differently according to the quality of service they involve. One can think of many other 'premium' services that platforms can offer at 'premium' prices. For instance, the food-delivery platform Takeaway.com charges an extra fee to users for the possibility to pay online. When 'basic' services are offered for free, we have then the well-known 'freemium' monetization strategy. This strategy is particularly efficient in the presence of positive network effects as free services are a powerful instrument to attract a critical mass of users and, thereby, increase what other users are willing to pay for premium services. The challenge of course is to set the prices and the versions right to convert enough free users into premium ones, without compromising revenue generation. As Case 5.3 shows, this may not be an easy task.

Case 5.3 Low conversion rate at Quibi

Quibi was a US-based streaming platform designed for users who consume short-form entertainment on mobile devices. The platform shut down in December 2020, barely ten months after it launched. Although the COVID-19 pandemic and the fierce competition from existing platforms did not help, a major reason for Quibi's failure was its inability to convert a sufficient share of the users it attracted through its free offering. As Statt (2020) reports:

> Streaming service Quibi only managed to convert a little under 10 percent of its early wave of users into paying subscribers, says mobile analytics firm Sensor Tower. According to the firm's new report on Quibi's early growth, the short-form video platform signed up about 910,000 users in its first few days back in April. Of those users, only about 72,000 stuck around after the three-month free trial, indicating the app had about an 8 percent conversion rate.

Even if these numbers caused controversy (conversion rates are notoriously hard to estimate), it was pretty clear that users did not find Quibi's premium version attractive enough because of the lack of exciting content.

Another useful form of differential pricing is to offer group discounts, that is, lower the price for users who join or use the platform as a group. Many platforms propose specific price schemes for companies and often use company size as a proxy for willingness to pay (for example, this is customary practice for SaaS – Software as a Service – platforms). As we discussed in the previous chapter, this tactic proves useful when launching the platform, as it instrumentalizes the 'Beat egg whites' strategy.

Mixing different types of prices

As we hinted above, membership and transaction prices are complementary to one another: Lowering one type of price gives more room to raise the other type. For instance, if you decrease transaction prices, users will be incentivized to conduct more transactions and the platform will become more attractive for everyone; as a result, you will be able to increase the membership prices without putting off too many (if any) participants. Similarly, if you prefer to lower membership prices (or even make them negative) to make participation less risky, you will guarantee a larger volume of transactions, which you can monetize through larger transaction prices. Your job is thus to find the right balance between the two types of prices, given their complementarity and given the environment in which you operate (which conditions, for instance, the feasibility of monitoring transactions on and off the platform, as well as the provision of stand-alone services). As Case 5.4 illustrates, platforms do combine different types of prices.[2]

Case 5.4 Store selling fees on eBay

Here is how eBay described its 'Store selling fees':

> For a monthly subscription, you can run your own eBay Store. The fees and benefits vary depending on the type of Store subscription you choose. When you have an eBay Store, you get more listings with zero insertion fees and pay lower final value fees, compared to selling without a Store. You also get access to additional tools to manage and promote your business. The rest of the fee structure is the same as non-Store subscribers. We charge an insertion fee when you create a listing and a final value fee when your item sells. The amount we charge for Store subscribers depends on the item's price, the format and category you choose for your listing, any optional listing upgrades you add, your Store subscription package, and your seller conduct and performance.

As you can see, there is a mix of transaction and subscription prices, with a menu of different options.

Platforms may also choose different types of prices at different stages of their development. For instance, as illustrated in Case 5.5, transaction prices, which are often the only prices that users would accept to pay when the platform is small, might be replaced by subscription prices once the platform has grown a solid base of regular users.

Case 5.5 Why Bsit changed its price mix

Bsit is a Belgian-based platform, launched in 2015, that facilitates the interaction between parents and babysitters. In its early years, the platform mostly relied on transaction prices: It was taking a commission of 25% on the hourly rate paid by parents. Even if this strategy was generating little and uncertain revenues (the volume of transactions was still low and parents were induced to bypass the platform once they had found a suitable babysitter), it had the advantage of letting parents test the service at a relatively low cost. This seemed to pay off as trust in the platform built up and the user base grew steadily. The time was then ripe to change gear. In October 2017, the platform decided to switch to a subscription model: Parents were now asked to pay a monthly subscription to use the services of the platform (the price was roughly equivalent to the cost of one hour of babysitting under the previous scheme). The CEO, Dimitri De Boose explains (see Charlot, 2018) that the change was meant not only to increase revenues but also to make them more predictable. And it worked! Total monthly revenues in the Belgian market more than trebled over the next year, despite a short-term reduction in parents' participation over the three months that followed the change (it took time for some parents to accept paying a subscription).

Before moving to the last question (*How much to charge?*), we propose an organizing tool – the *Platform Pricing Matrix* – that you can use to reflect upon (and record) the pricing decisions that you deem appropriate for your platform. To guide you, we placed in Figure 5.1 some reminders of the main lessons drawn so far (you can download a blank version from www. platformstrategies.org).

How much to charge? A moving target

Here comes the last and delicate question: How much should you charge for your services? We first explain that this question is even trickier for platforms than for other startups because the target that you are aiming at is moving. We provide you, nevertheless, with some practical tips to improve your aim.

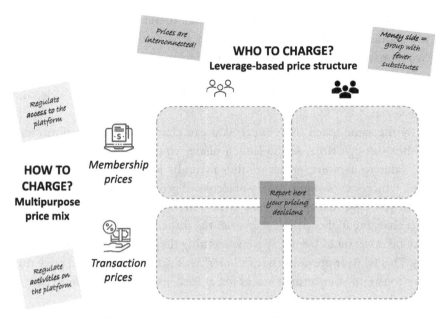

Figure 5.1 The Platform Pricing Matrix (commented).

The 'who' and the 'how' condition the 'how much'

What makes setting prices more complex for platforms is that the 'how much' is conditioned by the 'who' and the 'how' (this explains why we started our analysis with the latter two questions). The reasoning goes as follows: How much you can charge your users is proportional to the value that you create for them; but this value essentially depends on the participation of your users (recall that value is co-created on a platform), which depends itself, as we just discussed, on whom (which users) you decide to charge (the price structure) and how you charge them (the price mix). As a result, the 'how much' is a moving target: Your objective moves as you try to hit it!

These are issues that you do not face if you are selling, say, washing machines. First, you only have one group of users, which removes the 'whom to charge' question. Second, and more importantly, even if your price determines the quantity that you can sell, this quantity has no impact whatsoever on the consumers' willingness to pay. That is, the form of your demand function – which tells you how your sales increase when you decrease your price – does not change with the quantity that you sell. So, by estimating what this demand function looks like, you can figure out the implications of changing your price and, thereby, evaluate which price you should optimally set. In contrast, on a two-sided platform, there are two demand functions to estimate (the demand for participation on each side) and these functions depend on one another (because the price you can set on one side depends on the participation on the other side, and vice versa).

By the same token, how much you can charge on your platform also evolves through time. At the launch phase, your platform brings little (if no) value to its users; prices are thus naturally low (and potentially negative), which serves your primary objective of growing your audience. Later, when you have managed to get a critical mass of users on board, you can start charging higher prices. However, the difficulty here is that your users may be reluctant to pay today for something they could get for free yesterday. That is, your previous choices in terms of price structure and price mix may constrain your future choices (or, at least, expose you to some risks, as illustrated in Case 5.5).[3]

> **How much you can charge depends on which users your charge and how (and when) you charge them.**

How to improve your aim?

As we just explained, the value that you can generate for your users is a moving target. It is thus vain to try and evaluate it as such. What can be estimated more easily, however, is the value that your users will have to renounce if they join your platform, that is, the value of their best alternative to using your platform. You can identify this value for your different groups of users by referring to the analysis you carried out in the Platform Value Net (in which you listed all the alternatives that your users can resort to, either rival platforms or substitutable solutions). You can see this value as a benchmark against which you can evaluate how much you can charge. To see how, let us formalize the reasoning a little bit.

- Call V_0 the gross value that a user obtains if they stick to their best alternative and p_0, the price they pay for this alternative (the difference, $V_0 - p_0$, is thus their net value).

- Similarly, call V_1 the gross value that a user would obtain if they join your platform and p_1, the price that you plan to charge them.
- Finally, let C denote the cost that you must incur to deliver a value V_1 to this user.

There are two conditions that you must satisfy if you want to attract a user profitably. First, you must offer this user a larger net value than what they get in the best alternative; using the above notation, you need to make sure that $V_1 - p_1 > V_0 - p_0$. Second, your costs cannot exceed your price: $C < p_1$. By combining the two inequalities, you can define the feasible range in which your price should fall:

$$C < p_1 < p_0 + (V_1 - V_0)$$

What this equation tells you is that your price is bounded below by your cost (C) and above by the price that a user pays for their best alternative (p_0), potentially augmented by the extra value that your platform brings on top of this best alternative ($V_1 - V_0$). Your objective is, of course, to set the price as close as possible to the upper bound, while hoping that it is above the lower bound. So, on top of indicating how much you can charge a given user, this equation also suggests the two generic strategies that you can follow to improve value capture. Referring to Porter (1980), the two main ways to increase your margin ($p_1 - C$) are cost leadership (you reduce the lower bound) and differentiation (you raise the upper bound by adding value compared to your competitors).

We refer you to your favorite strategy textbook for a description of these two generic strategies (which apply to any type of business). Let us just stress here how positive network effects affect the implementation of these strategies. We know that the value generated by your platform during the launch phase is pretty low. Chances are thus high that the equation above cannot be satisfied: If V_1 is close to zero, then the 'upper bound' is likely to be negative and thus, below your cost. You will have to set prices below cost to attract users. Yet, as explained above, you can see these early losses as a form of investment: By growing your user base, you increase the value generated on your platform and, thereby, your capacity to raise prices in the future. Imagine now that you managed to attract a critical mass of users and so, initiate a positive feedback loop. This means that the value that you generate (V_1) increases in an autonomous and costless way (as you no longer have to subsidize users). Moreover, if the best alternative for your users is a rival platform, then the value generated there (V_0) may *decrease* as more users leave this platform for yours, meaning that the gap $V_1 - V_0$ is constantly widening.

> **Network effects affect the two generic strategies of cost leadership and differentiation.**

Although positive network effects allow you to amplify differentiation without sacrificing cost leadership, the above example illustrates how the window of opportunity is rather small for a young platform. A cost-minimizing strategy may even result in significant losses in the hope of gaining users. On the other hand, setting the price too high will prevent the platform from reaching critical mass and will require strong commercial arguments to highlight the value of the intermediation service and justify the expense. And all this takes place in a context often marked by uncertainty about the short-term survival of the nascent platform.

Complementary sources of revenue

The monetization strategies described so far consists in charging the platform users for the services that the platform offers and for the resulting positive network benefits that users enjoy. Other strategies aim at leveraging the activities taking place on the platform to extract revenues from agents that operate *outside* the platform. That is, instead (or on top) of charging users for access to your platform, you can charge third parties for granting them access to your users. We describe three such strategies in this section: advertising, data exploitation, and affiliate marketing. For each strategy, the logic of leverage-based pricing still applies: As the platform sells access to its users' attention or data to third parties, revenues increase with the number of active users, which drives the platform to lower its membership and transaction prices (if any).

> **Instead (or on top) of charging users for your services, you can charge third parties for accessing your users' attention (advertising), personal data (data exploitation), or potential custom (affiliate marketing).**

Advertising

One well-known strategy to complement the revenues you get directly from your users is to let advertisers promote their products or services on your platform (through graphics, banners, text, or any other means). This is another way to leverage network effects as advertisers are keener to pay for ads on platforms that attract a larger base of users. That is, platform users – or more precisely their 'eyeballs' – exert a positive cross-side network effect on advertisers. Advertisers can thus be seen as a new group that is added to the platform. Yet, by capturing value from advertisers, you may compromise the value created for other groups of users. Think, for instance, of online video-sharing platforms (such as YouTube or Vimeo). On the one hand, some viewers may see ads as a nuisance (because it damages their viewing experience); advertisers exert then negative cross-side network effects on those viewers. On the other hand, as some advertisers fear being associated with content that may endanger their brand image, the platform may want to police content more closely, which is likely to displease some content providers. In sum, you must be aware that including ads on your website or app is equivalent to charging a 'shadow price' to your users (or at least to some of them), with potential negative impacts on the level of participation on the platform.

One way to alleviate this problem is to combine advertising with a freemium strategy: The free version comes bundled with ads, while the premium (paying) version ensures an ad-free experience. That is, you let your users choose between two forms of payment: Either they pay with their attention to ads or they pay a monetary sum. In the first case, advertisers pay for the ads that are shown, whereas in the second case, users pay for having ads not shown to them.

Another solution is to use your knowledge of the users and their behavior on the platform to allow advertisers to target their ads to specific segments of users. This has, potentially, the combined advantage of increasing the advertisers' willingness to pay (as ads are more efficient) and of decreasing the users' ad annoyance (as they are shown ads that fit better their needs or tastes). However, as we discuss in the next point, improving targeting may raise privacy concerns.

Data monetization

As Meglena Kuneva, European Consumer Commissioner from 2007 to 2010, once declared: "Personal data is the new oil of the internet and the new currency of the digital world."[4] In this respect, your platform can be turned into an oil field that you can profitably exploit. You can indeed collect an appreciable amount of data about your users – from the profile that they fill in when registering and from the usage that they make of the platform.

These data are certainly of great use internally. On the one hand, knowing your users better allows you to customize your offering to their needs and, as explained above, charge them prices closer to their willingness to pay. On the other hand, data can also help you optimize your operations; for instance, algorithms for matching or logistics become more efficient as you feed them with more and richer data.

You can also think of monetizing your data externally. Other organizations may indeed value the data you collect from your users and from the transactions they conduct on your platform. You may then want to sell direct access to your data to these organizations, either in raw form or in a transformed form (that is, data analytics or insights). Case 5.6 gives an example of this practice.

Case 5.6 Uber Movement: Uber's move toward data monetization

In 2017, Uber unveiled its software 'Uber Movement', which "provides data and tools for cities to more deeply understand and address urban transportation challenges"; the targeted 'clients' are transportation planners, academics, elected officials, and non-profits (movement.uber.com, last consulted March 18, 2021). Even if data are shared for free, it can be argued that Uber monetizes them indirectly: As Ong (2018) explains, "Uber Movement is part of the company's wider plan to mollify regulators by sharing valuable data with them after years of abrasive business tactics." It is also important to stress that Uber carefully states in its FAQs that this initiative does not compromise rider and driver privacy: "All data is anonymized and aggregated to ensure no personally identifiable information or user behavior can be surfaced through the Movement tool. (...) At no point will Movement provide a means for users to access individual user details."

As Case 5.6 suggests, you need to be careful when using this strategy. First and foremost, you must make sure that you do not run afoul of data protection legislation, such as the European General Data Protection Regulation (GDPR) or the California Consumer Privacy Act (CCPA). Second, even if you comply with the legislation, you may still lose the confidence of users who are concerned about their online privacy. You could thus face the same dilemma as with advertising: What you gain by selling your users' personal data must be balanced against what you lose by driving some users away.

> **Advertising or data exploitation might alienate some users. The revenues you earn on one side might then constrain the value you can create on another side.**

Affiliate marketing

Arguably, the previous two strategies are more meaningful for platforms operating at a sufficiently large scale, because they attract a large mass of users and/or because their users spend a lot of time or conduct recurrent transactions on the platform. In contrast, becoming an affiliate marketer is well within the reach of smaller platforms. Affiliate marketing is a strategy by which a business enlists other businesses, called 'affiliates' or 'affiliate marketers', to redirect traffic to its website (or application). In contrast with traditional (direct) advertising, which mainly aims at creating brand awareness, affiliate marketing seeks to increase sales more directly by spreading the word about products and services.

If you become an affiliate marketer for merchant partners, you will earn a commission for each sale that the partners make as a result of referrals coming from your platform. Although any business (or individual) with an online presence can become an affiliate marketer, platforms have two strong points: They link well-identified groups of users and generate recurrent traffic. Your platform is thus likely to be a sought-after affiliate for merchants that want to reach your audience. You should, however, select carefully the merchants you affiliate with. You must refer only to products and services that are likely to appeal to your users. This will increase your expected commissions and make sure that you keep your users' trust.

Otherwise, you may lose the custom of users who resent the merchants you recommend. You would then face the same dilemma as with advertising and data monetization: Capturing value on one side implies destroying value on another. In consequence, the crucial question is: How can I find the right merchants to partner with (or how can they find me)? As you might guess, there are platforms for that! Affiliate marketing platforms (or networks), like ShareASale, Awin, or CJ Affiliate, connect merchants with affiliate marketers; they may also offer additional services, such as tracking sales, managing payments, or resolving disputes.

Regulating prices on the platform

We focused so far on the prices that the platform sets itself to regulate access and usage, and we argued that these prices must be adjusted in accordance with the various network effects that are at play on the platform. Now, we focus on platforms that facilitate various forms of buying and selling (known as 'marketplaces' or 'transaction platforms') and on which sellers are also setting prices. Such platforms may want to administer the way sellers set their prices. One objective could be to avoid displaying too great a disparity in prices, as this could harm the credibility of the platform. Another objective could be to promote the transparency of prices to protect consumers. After describing how platforms can do so, we examine the implications of such strategies. As we will see, platforms also need to take network effects carefully into account when they decide to interfere with pricing by sellers.

Options to administer seller pricing

As a platform operator, how can you administer pricing on the platform? At one extreme, you can do nothing and leave complete freedom to your sellers, as BlaBlaCar did in its early days.[5] At the other extreme, you can set the price of all transactions yourself, like ride-hailing platforms Uber and Lyft do through their surge-pricing algorithm. Between the two extremes, you can think of a wide array of possibilities.

Some marketplaces organize auctions, which are typically more to the advantage of sellers (as they drive buyers to reveal their willingness to pay); eBay proposes auctions, as did Prosper (a crowdlending platform) before moving to pre-set rates in 2010 (which demonstrates that these choices are not set in stone).

Other platforms use various devices to recommend prices to their sellers. Big platforms take advantage of the huge amount of data that they collect to feed algorithms that help sellers choose their prices (like the Smart Pricing tool proposed by Airbnb).[6] Platforms can also help their sellers implement differential pricing, that is, charge different prices for the same good in different markets. Steiner (2019) explains that Etsy did so after it started to penalize sellers who did not offer free shipping in the US (see Case 5.7 for more). As this policy put international sellers at a disadvantage (due to their higher shipping costs), Etsy proposed them a tool to charge different prices in the US than in their domestic market.

Platforms may also adopt measures that are more favorable to buyers than to sellers. Imposing price transparency is one such measure. This can be done by preventing sellers from shrouding additional fees (such as shipping and handling fees on trading platforms, or resort fees and upgrades on hotel booking platforms). For example, Ellison and Ellison (2009, p. 432) report that Pricewatch (a price search engine for electronics products based in the US) prevented firms from setting their shipping charges above some preset amount and warned customers against buying from firms not reporting their shipping charges. Etsy's imposition of free shipping (which we discuss in Case 5.7) goes in the same direction.

Purpose and impacts

To understand the effects of such policies, platforms must realize that the prices that sellers set affect the strength of the cross-side network effects between buyers and sellers. To see this, take again the example of Etsy. Because the sellers' offerings are unique and because buyers usually have a vague idea of what they are looking for when they arrive on the platform, the value that a buyer attaches to the platform can be approximated by the number of sellers on the platform (which measures the probability that this buyer will find an item of their liking) multiplied by the buyer's net benefit of a transaction (that is, the difference between what the buyer is willing to pay and what they actually pay). Similarly, the value of the platform for sellers can be approximated by the number of buyers on the platform (which measures the probability of a sale) multiplied by the profit from a transaction. Now, the split between buyers' net benefit and sellers' profit depends on the price that sellers set: Higher prices make sellers better off and buyers worse off (as long as transactions take place). Hence, sellers value each transaction more, which is to say that buyers exert a stronger cross-side network effect on them (as they become more valuable). Conversely, buyers value each transaction less, meaning that sellers exert a weaker cross-side network effect on them. The exact reverse applies if sellers set lower prices.

> **Interfering in the pricing policy of sellers for the benefit of one user group can backfire if it creates too much resistance from the other user group.**

Such changes in the intensity of the cross-side network effects crucially matter for the platform: If, for instance, buyers earn more per transaction, the platform can attract them more easily (and may choose, for instance, to charge them a larger membership price) but the exact opposite happens for sellers, who earn less per transaction and become thus harder to attract. Facing situations of this type, the platform may decide, on top of adjusting its own prices, to interfere with the price-setting behavior of the independent sellers. However, for the reasons that we just explained, strategies of this type must be implemented with great care. The following case illustrates that a policy aimed at attracting more users in one group (here, buyers) may well reduce users' participation in the other group (here, sellers). To gauge the net impact of such policy, it is thus crucial to estimate, as precisely as possible, the resulting changes in the intensity of cross-side network effects.

Case 5.7 Etsy pushes sellers to offer free shipping

In July 2019, Etsy announced its decision to give more prominence in US search results to items and sellers that offer free shipping. This decision was based on the observation that free shipping increases by 20% buyers' propensity to buy items on the platform. Meanwhile, Etsy advised its sellers to include shipping costs in their prices and offered a tool to help them do so. As evidenced by the number of messages posted on Etsy forums and social networks, the decision outraged many sellers. Small shops feared being unable to raise their prices and/or absorb the shipping costs. Larger shops complained as well. As Swanson (2020) explains:

> Many sellers shared a mutual complaint that if an Etsy store offers a diverse array of items varying in height and weight then it is impossible to offer the consumer free shipping only keeping in mind a medium-sized package. Although Etsy offered to pay for the shipping cost for both the buyer and the seller, the seller ended up having to pay out of pocket for any item that exceeded the shipping limit.

Lee (2019) also notes that "[i]mplementing flat shipping fees in prices can pose a challenge to international sellers who ship worldwide."

SHORT ANSWERS TO THE KEY QUESTIONS

- *Should all platform users be charged the same price?* It is short-sighted to think that all users should be charged the same price because they all benefit from a common intermediation service. Instead, the platform can exploit the fact that users belong to distinct groups and differ in the value they attach to interacting with the other group. Then, it makes sense to set lower prices (sometimes, below cost) for the group that exerts stronger cross-side network effects and/or is more sensitive to price. In general, this is the group for which the threat of substitutes is relatively stronger.
- *Should users be charged to access the platform or to use it (or both)?* The more the platform imposes conditions on access and use, the more it reduces the willingness of users to join the platform. But charging users for the platform's services remains the main monetization source. The question is thus how best to charge users. If it is difficult to control the usage of the platform *a posteriori* (observing the number of transactions, for example), then it is preferable to opt for a flat (membership) price. If, on the other hand, the principle of the platform is based on a high frequency of use that is also easily measurable, then paying for each transaction may be the solution. The two types of prices can also be combined.

- *Why is it complex to determine how much platform users can be charged?* What makes setting prices more complex for platforms is that you must first answer the questions 'Whom to charge?' and 'How to charge?' before addressing the question 'How much to charge?' This is because what you can charge is proportional to the value that you create for your users; but this value depends on the participation of other users, which depends itself on which users you decide to charge and how you charge them. What you can charge is thus a moving target.

- *Apart from charging users, are there other ways to monetize a platform?* When it is complicated (or insufficient) to charge users, there are other possibilities to make the platform viable. The general idea is to charge third parties for gaining access to your users' attention (advertising), personal data (data exploitation), or potential custom (affiliate marketing). The risk, however, is to alienate your main users if they object to the use of these alternative monetization methods (for example because they are annoyed by advertising or reluctant to share personal data).

- *Should the platform regulate how sellers set prices for buyers?* The response to this question depends on the circumstances. Some platforms take direct control of the pricing of the goods or services exchanged on their marketplace, other platforms leave complete freedom to their third-party sellers or providers, and a range of other possibilities exist between these two options. What must be understood is that the decisions platforms make in this matter determine how buyers and sellers divide the value of a transaction among themselves and, thereby, the strength of the cross-side network effects that they exert on one another.

FURTHER READINGS

Following the seminal papers of Rochet and Tirole (2003, 2006) and Armstrong (2006), abundant literature in economics considers pricing by two-sided platforms and formalizes the principles of what we call 'leverage-based pricing'. As this literature heavily relies on (sometimes complex) game-theoretical models, there is little point in advising you to dive into it. However, for those of you in search of a slightly more formalized approach than ours, you can have a look at Evans and Schmalensee (2007).

Notes

1. To apply value-based pricing, the seller must have a sufficiently good knowledge of the profiles of its consumers. In that respect, cost-based pricing seems easier to apply.
2. See www.ebay.com (last consulted on March 10, 2021).
3. You can also reverse the argument: If users are somewhat forward-looking, they will see through your game and anticipate that they will be charged tomorrow for the service that they receive for free today. You may then face difficulties in convincing your first users to join. In this respect, Lehr (2020) gives a useful practical tip as to how seeding prices should be designed:

   Instead of lowering your price or giving the product away for free, however, consider using early adopter discounts. This way you still have the original price as an anchor and you clearly communicate the real value of your product offering.

4. See https://ec.europa.eu/commission/presscorner/detail/en/SPEECH_09_156 (last consulted March 18, 2021).
5. Nowadays, BlaBlaCar recommends prices to its drivers: "We recommend a contribution per passenger on your rides. These suggestions help you set fair contributions for your rides (those most likely to get your seats filled!), but can still be adjusted within a margin of our recommendation" (www.blablacar.co.uk/faq/question/how-do-i-set-my-price; last consulted on October 2, 2020).
6. "Smart Pricing lets you set your prices to automatically go up or down based on changes in demand for listings like yours. You're always responsible for your price, so Smart Pricing is controlled by other pricing settings you choose, and you can adjust nightly prices any time (www.airbnb.com/help/)."

Bibliography

Armstrong, M. (2006). Competition in two-sided markets. *Rand Journal of Economics* 37, 668–691. https://doi.org/10.1111/j.1756-2171.2006.tb00037.x.

Cann, O. (2017). Who pays for Davos? *World Economic Forum* (January 16). https://www.weforum.org/agenda/2017/01/who-pays-for-davos.

Charlot, C. (2018). Quand le babysitting devient un business numérique. Trends-Tendances (February 8). https://trends.levif.be/economie/high-tech/

numerik/quand-le-babysitting-devient-un-business-numerique/article-normal-792279.html.

Cicero, S. (2021). Pricing in platforms and marketplaces. https://stories. platformdesigntoolkit.com/pricing-platforms-marketplaces-151ab67b130a.

Ellison, G. and S. F. Ellison (2009). Search, obfuscation, and price elasticities. *Econometrica* 77, 427–452. https://doi.org/10.3982/ECTA5708.

Evans, D.S. and R. Schmalensee (2007). The industrial organization of markets with two-sided platforms. *Competition Policy International* 3, 150–179. https://www.competitionpolicyinternational.com/assets/0d358061e11f27 08ad9d62634c6c40ad/EvansSchmalensee.pdf.

Lee, D. (2019). Etsy sellers aren't happy with the platform pushing them to offer free shipping. *The Verge* (July 9). https://www.theverge.com/2019/7/9/ 20687821/etsy-free-shipping-policy-seller-us-uk.

Lehr J. (2020). 9 tricks to experiment with your pricing strategy. Medium (July 2). https://medium.com/point-nine-news/9-tricks-to-experiment-with-your-pricing-strategy-329b07a5b171.

Ong, T. (2018). Uber is bringing its urban planning tool Uber Movement to London. *The Verge* (March 15, 2018). https://www.theverge.com/2018/3/15/17123372/ uber-movement-urban-planning-tool-anonymized-ride-data-london.

Porter, M.E. (1980). *Competitive strategy*. New York: Free Press.

Rochet, J.-C. and J. Tirole (2003). Platform competition in two-sided markets. *Journal of the European Economic Association* 1, 990–1029. https://doi. org/10.1162/154247603322493212.

Rochet, J.-C. and J. Tirole (2006). Two-sided markets: A progress report. *Rand Journal of Economics* 37, 645–667. https://doi.org/10.1111/j.1756-2171.2006. tb00036.x.

Statt, N. (2020). Quibi reportedly lost 90 percent of early users after their free trial expired. *The Verge* (July 8). https://www.theverge.com/2020/7/8/21318060/ quibi-subscriber-count-free-trial-paying-users-conversion-rate.

Steiner, I. (2019). Etsy helps UK sellers compete in the US with new pricing tools. eCommerceBytes (August 14). https://www.ecommercebytes.com/C/ abblog/blog.pl?/pl/2019/8/1565819902.html.

Swanson, S. (2020). Etsy's "Free Shipping" controversy. Emenator. https:// www.emenator.com/news/Etsy-s-Free-Shipping-Controversy/45/.

6

CONSOLIDATING AND GROWING A PLATFORM

KEY QUESTIONS

- How can a platform raise the overall level of trust between users?
- What is 'platform leakage' and how can it be curbed?
- Should rapid growth be an absolute goal?
- What are the options to grow a platform?
- How can the performance of a platform be measured?

Now that you have understood how to activate and leverage network effects to implement your unique value proposition and launch your platform, you may think that the hard part is over. You may be tempted to sit back and let positive feedback loops work their 'snowballing magic' for you. But – sorry to break the bad news – it is way too early to rest on your laurels: There is still some serious work ahead! If you can get a positive feedback loop running, so can your competitors. Your next challenge is thus to consolidate

DOI: 10.4324/9780429490873-10

your platform by retaining your users. This is key to ensuring the success of your platform in the long run and this is what this last chapter is about.

Our goal here is to shed light on the most common risks and opportunities related to choices that must be made once the platform is already up and running. First, we summarize the major arguments around the central question of trust, whereby we understand trusting the value proposition, trusting the platform itself, and finally trusting other users and participants in the platform. Second, we examine how to design appropriate retention strategies to counter the risk of platform leakage. Third, we explore the ins and outs of platform growth. On the one hand, the so-called exponential growth of digital platforms – often extolled in the business press – comes with significant perils, which you should be aware of. On the other hand, adding new user groups, reinforcing network effects, and expanding the ecosystem are sound ways to grow a platform, while stabilizing its competitive position. We conclude by highlighting the importance of monitoring the activity taking place on the platform. Collecting and processing meaningful information will indeed help you make informed choices and consolidate your value proposition.

Trust – a vital building block

Because platforms enable transactions instead of controlling them (like pipelines do), they rely on external and independent service providers to deliver goods and services to customers. Similarly, when the platform facilitates matchmaking, it does not provide a service by itself but offers an infrastructure allowing users from different groups to co-create this service. In any case, a prerequisite for transactions to take place on the platform is that users sufficiently trust one another. It is thus the platform's foremost responsibility to establish a climate of trust among participants, a daunting task given that transactions are largely anonymous and one-off (users rarely meet before or after the transaction). Let us understand why, before looking for possible remedies.[1]

> **A platform's foremost responsibility is to establish a climate of trust among its users.**

Problems of asymmetric information

In the parlance of economics, platforms are prone to problems of asymmetric information. These problems arise in two typical situations. First, the parties to a transaction may differ in their access to the information relevant to that transaction. One talks of problems of *hidden information*, as some information is not accessible to one party. For instance, buyers have often a harder time than sellers ascertaining the quality of products or services (which are then called 'experience goods', as their quality can only be learned by 'experiencing' them). Similarly, job seekers have information about their competencies that is largely unknown to employers. In such cases, the price that buyers are willing to pay is proportional to what they believe is the average quality offered to them. But this price may not be large enough to convince sellers of high-quality goods (who face higher costs) to offer their items for sale. Realizing that, buyers will revise downward their estimate of the average quality for sale, which will scare away even medium-quality sellers. At the end of this unraveling process, only low-quality goods or services will be for sale, which is inefficient.

The second typical situation of asymmetric information has to do with *hidden actions*. Problems may arise here because the quality of the good or service depends on actions taken by one and/or the other party and because such actions cannot be observed or controlled. If the transaction price is decided before actions are taken, the parties may not invest enough time and energy in improving the quality of the good or service. For instance, the quality of carpooling depends on the level of effort, attention, and care exerted mostly by the driver, but also by the traveler. As chances are high that the two parties will not meet again in the future, they may both consider that any misbehavior will be of little consequence for them. Anticipating such opportunistic behavior and the resulting poor quality of the transaction, the parties may just refrain from engaging in this transaction altogether, another source of inefficiency.

Inefficiencies due to opportunistic behaviors and high information costs represent obstacles to the smooth and optimal progress of a transaction between parties. At the same time, this is exactly where market intermediaries like platforms should see an opportunity to fix the problem by creating a trusted environment. Various mechanisms exist and have already demonstrated their importance and effectiveness. We separate these mechanisms

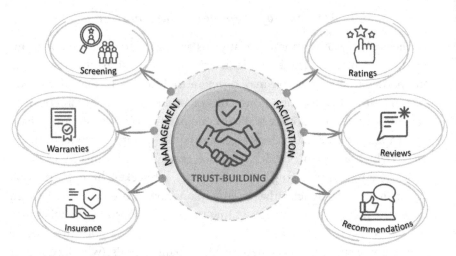

Figure 6.1 Trust-building mechanisms.

according to whether the platform takes active measures to build trust itself or provides users with tools that allow them to build trust on their own (see Figure 6.1 for a schematic representation).

Active trust-building by the platform

Screening and certification

The first way to prevent hidden information and hidden action problems is to actively screen would-be participants on the platform. Take the example of a platform linking producers (product and service providers) to consumers. As just explained, producers not only have more information about the intrinsic quality of their service but are also likely to take unobservable actions to improve relevant aspects of the transaction. The platform may then condition the participation of producers to obtain – and retain – some form of certification. The objective is to ensure a minimum quality standard for the services provided on the platform. How? By operating a selection *ex ante* to keep lower-quality providers off and by exerting controls *ex post* to expel worse-performing producers. Note that some platforms make certification mandatory (such as Uber, which checks whether its drivers are eligible to drive), while others propose it voluntarily (such as Airbnb, which offers hosts the option to have the authenticity of the pictures of their property certified).

> By operating a selection beforehand to keep lower-quality providers off and by exerting controls afterward to expel worse-performing providers, you can ensure that transactions on the platform stay above some minimum quality standard.

Warranties, guarantees, and insurance

Another traditional way to reassure customers in transactions fraught with asymmetric information problems is to offer them warranties, guarantees, or insurances. The objective is to convince customers that quality will be preserved in any circumstances because the product will be repaired (warranty) or replaced (guarantee) in case of failure or breakdown, or because the buyer will be compensated if some specific event occurs (insurance). For instance, Airbnb ensures hosts against vandalism by guests.

Note that sellers can, to a large extent, attenuate (if not solve) asymmetric information problems by themselves. Indeed, they can seek certification from third parties, provide their own warranties and guarantees, or even subscribe to specific insurance policies. Yet, it is important to understand that a platform is in a better position than individual sellers to offer these services. On the one hand, the platform interacts more frequently and directly with users and, on the other hand, the large volume managed by the platform gives access to cheaper offers. Recall that those third-party players offering certification and other trust-consolidating solutions may be seen as complementors (as defined in Chapter 3) since they contribute to increasing the consumers' perceived value of the transacted product or service.

As a result, a platform can become the bearer of the collective reputation of the sellers that it takes on board. This is so because a seller selected by the platform is believed to be of high quality by a buyer unless they previously experienced the low quality of some other seller met through the platform. Hence, to avoid any stain on its reputation, the platform will directly discontinue the operation of low-quality sellers. Understanding that, sellers do not find it profitable to provide low-quality services, implying that only high-quality services are eventually provided on the platform. In a nutshell, buyers do not really have to trust each seller separately; they can simply trust the platform because they realize that the platform has much more to lose from a stain on its reputation than any separate seller does (one rotten apple is enough to spoil the rest of the bag). The same reasoning applies more generally to any two-sided platform (not just to marketplaces linking buyers and sellers).

The previous idea relates to the 'trust stack model' proposed by Botsman (2017): Once users have accepted the idea of using a platform rather than a pipeline (first layer of trust), they eventually trust other participants (third layer) because they already placed their trust into the platform (second layer). Let us apply the model to ride-hailing platforms for an illustration. From the point of view of riders, the first layer of trust is in the idea of being picked up by an unknown individual instead of a registered taxi driver. The second layer of trust is in the company (Uber, Lyft, or Didi), which is supposed to manage the transactions between riders and drivers and alleviate asymmetric information problems. Finally, the third layer of trust is in the driver with whom the rider is eventually interacting.

The 3Rs: ratings, reviews, and recommendation systems

Digital platforms are increasingly relying on ratings, reviews, and recommendations systems (referred to as '3R systems') as a way to build trust among participants and promote the transparency of transactions. Compared to hands-on approaches like screening, certification, or insurance, 3R systems can be seen as indirect trust-building mechanisms. The platform's role is limited to establishing and administering an infrastructure. It is then the users' task to take advantage of this infrastructure to build trust among them. That is, 3R systems nudge users toward keeping the digital platform a safe and trustworthy place.

Recent studies suggest that 3R systems are more efficient trust-builders than active instruments. For instance, Farronato et al. (2020) collected evidence from a large US online platform for residential home services. They show that a platform-verified certification mechanism – here, a professional's licensing status which is only granted after the platform has independently verified the licensure – plays a little role in consumer choices and satisfaction, compared to ratings and peer reviews (a result that they confirm in an independent consumer survey). It is thus important to understand how 3R systems work and to weigh their pros and cons for trust-building on platforms.

What 3R systems are and do

Ratings and reviews are part of a platform's information-pull strategy, whereby users are invited to provide information about the transactions that they conducted and/or their counterparty to these transactions. In parallel, platforms often pursue an information-push strategy by making specific recommendations to users, based on these users' characteristics or observed behavior, and/or on the characteristics, reliability, or popularity of the proposed match. Importantly, many platforms exploit the interdependence between information-pull and information-push strategies by using ratings and reviews as inputs for their recommendation algorithms. Case 6.1 shows how Amazon implements these tools.

Case 6.1 Some examples of Amazon's use of 3R systems

Amazon provides sellers with a 'Request a Review' button on their personal interface called *Seller Central*. When the seller clicks the button for a given transaction, Amazon sends a standardized feedback request which is automatically translated into the buyer's chosen language. This is what the message looks like in the buyer's inbox:

> Your opinion matters! Seller <the seller's pseudonym> requests you to share your experience regarding your recent order with other Amazon shoppers. Please take a moment to review your recent Amazon purchase. Rate this item <picture of the item followed by 5 grey stars on which the buyer can click>. Rate your experience with seller <the seller's pseudonym followed by a second line of 5 grey stars>.

Amazon extensively relies on recommendations in both marketing emails and on most of its website pages. For example, the 'frequently bought together' list of items aims to make customers buy more by providing suggestions based on items they already have in their shopping basket or they are currently looking at. Amazon's recommendation algorithm is therefore an effective way of increasing the average order value. According to Morgan (2018),

35% of the total company's revenue is generated thanks to its recommendation engine.

Digital platforms exploit the interdependence between information-
pull and information-push strategies by using ratings and reviews as
inputs for their recommendation algorithms.

Informativeness of 3R systems

Once 3R systems are implemented, the main challenge of the platform is
to make sure that these systems – ratings and reviews in particular – are
informative, in the sense that they help users make more informed decisions.
Otherwise, these systems will just add noise to the users' decision process,
meaning that they will hinder trust-building instead of enabling it. The
problem is that the informativeness of 3R systems partly depends on decisions made by the users who provide the information in the first place.

The first issue is that users may leave ratings and reviews of little relevance if they fail to understand what they are asked or if they have idiosyn-
cratic tastes. For instance, we hope that if you leave a good review about this
book on some e-commerce platform, it will be because you like its content
and not because you appreciated the smile of the person who delivered the
book to your door or because you are, on principle, fond of anything that
comes out of Belgium. Although, as a platform operator, you may have little
impact on the latter point, you can certainly act upon the former by tracing
clearly the contours of what your users are asked to evaluate.

The second and more serious issue is that some (true or pretended) users
may have strategic motives to distort their evaluation and publish 'fake
reviews'. In particular, service providers may manipulate reviews to promote their own business (and/or hurt the business of rival providers). If the
platform does not take serious actions against such fake reviews, the whole
system may collapse, as users will lose faith in the usefulness of the reviews
and will, consequently, stop providing them. Case 6.2 describes Amazon's
stand on this matter. Besides the actions that a platform can take by itself,
other players, such as ReviewMeta or Fakespot, provide users with analyti-
cal tools to qualify product reviews. Since these companies help platforms

Case 6.2 Some examples of Amazon's use of 3R systems (continued)

Over the last few years, Amazon has taken actions to fight fake reviews, banning incentivized and paid reviews. Now, to post a product review on Amazon along with the 'Verified purchase' label, a buyer must strictly meet three criteria: Buying the product at Amazon, paying at least 80% of the original price (that is, 'Verified purchase' badges do not show up for reviews on items discounted more than 20%), and spending at least $50 on their Amazon account (newly created accounts with a one-shot purchase are thus excluded from the scope).

(and consumers) to fight against disinformation, they clearly can be assimilated into complementors, in the way we defined them in Chapter 3.

The third threat to the informativeness of ratings and reviews is specific to *two-sided rating systems*, whereby both parties to a transaction leave feedback on one another. Such systems may be desirable when both parties have hidden information or make hidden actions. That is, both parties have a hard time trusting the other. For instance, a host on Airbnb may worry about whether a guest will create a mess or damage some furniture, while the guest may fear that the accommodation will be less pleasant than described. The main risks with two-sided rating systems in terms of informativeness are *collusion* – parties, caring for their own reputation, agree beforehand on leaving each other positive feedback – and *retaliation* – parties leaving negative feedback fear receiving negative feedback as well in return. In both cases, ratings and reviews tend to be distorted upward. The fact that parties interact socially on some platforms may further prevent them from leaving bad reviews. As these problems may seriously reduce the relevance of your rating and review system, you may want to experiment with different design options before rolling out the final version. Options concern, among others, the anonymity of the feedback, the possibility to read the other party's feedback before leaving one's own, and the type of feedback (If a score, on which scale? If a text, of which length?).

Finally, there exist other 'behavioral' reasons for which users may not leave feedback that entirely reflect their true opinion. First, users are often influenced by previous feedback when leaving their own. This would not be a serious issue if it had not been documented that positive ratings tend to propagate more quickly than negative ones. That is, this form of 'herding' behavior would further distort ratings upward. Another behavioral bias may hamper users' ability to learn from ratings and reviews by leading them to treat correlated information as if it was coming from independent sources. In simpler words, platform users may fail to acknowledge that the ratings they observe depend on information retrieved from earlier ratings, thereby putting too large a weight on earlier ratings.

Given the issues that we have just raised, what attitude should you have, as a platform operator, regarding the informativeness of 3R systems? A priori, more informative ratings and reviews tend to make the platform more trustworthy and thus, more attractive. You should thus endeavor, for instance, to fight errors and manipulations. You should also design the systems in the most effective way to induce users to reveal their true evaluations and to aggregate properly this information. One solution that many platforms implement is to invite users to leave 'reviews of reviews', that is, to evaluate the relevance of other users' comments (for instance by responding to questions like "Did you find this review useful?").

Yet, you may sometimes be tempted to sacrifice informativeness for other motives. In particular, you may achieve larger revenues by distorting your 3R systems in favor of certain users that are relatively more profitable for your operations. For instance, some 'marquee' service providers may attract more customers; you may also have higher margins on some products or services. You may then have an incentive to give them more visibility by affecting the aggregate rankings, varying the ordering and display of reviews, or biasing the recommendation algorithm. This is, however, a dangerous game to play, as the overall trust on the platform may be jeopardized and regulatory authorities may cry foul.

Additional benefits of 3R systems

On top of facilitating trust-building, 3R systems are also powerful tools to generate positive feedback loops and retain users. We examine these two additional benefits in turn.

Recall first from Chapter 1 that positive feedback loops are self-reinforcing mechanisms whereby a platform becomes more attractive as it grows bigger. Here is how 3R systems can be instrumental in this process. The more users a platform attracts and the more transactions it facilitates, the larger the volume, variety, velocity, and veracity of the data that the platform can collect. And data is precisely the fuel on which 3R systems are running! With more fuel, the engines of 3R systems (typically machine-learning algorithms and artificial intelligence) become more efficient, which allows the platform to improve its services and attract more users. For instance, buyers prefer larger marketplaces because they expect to find more relevant reviews for the products they are looking for.

Second, 3R systems help retain users by making it costly for users to switch platforms. Transactions conducted outside the platform will not help users to strengthen their reputation on the platform. Also, because recommendations are generated by machine-learning algorithms, users receive more relevant recommendations the more they interact on the platform, which encourages them to stick with a given platform instead of switching or multihoming.

In sum, 3R systems can help you retain existing users and attract new ones in three complementary ways. First, their main function is to help users establish trust among themselves. Second, as their quality increases with the volume and variety of data that the platform can collect (about users and transactions), 3R systems allow the platform to fuel a positive feedback loop. Finally, 3R systems raise users' switching costs, which dissuades them from bypassing the platform.

> Ratings, reviews, and recommendations are the Swiss Army Knife of digital platforms, as they serve as a trust builder, a generator of network effects, and an anti-leakage tool.

Retention: when a platform leaks, everybody sinks

In Chapter 4, we discussed the way a platform can solve the chicken-and-egg problem by attracting the right users at the right time. Nevertheless, attracting users is not enough. The real challenge is to keep them active – and repeatedly so – on the platform. The danger is that users take advantage of the platform in an opportunistic way or leave it altogether after a while.

If you fail to prevent such *leakage* (or disintermediation), you will not be able to capture much of the value that your platform creates for your users and you will soon be forced out of business. To help you out, we first identify factors that may aggravate the risk of leakage. We then propose several 'anti-leakage tactics'.

Factors aggravating leakage

The main source of platform leakage is the users' perception that they get insufficient value for money when interacting on the platform. This is either because the pricing is badly designed or because transactions on the platform are, by nature, of little value.

Inadequate pricing

As we explained in Chapter 5, choosing the right price mix for your platform is a tricky decision, insofar as the different types of prices affect users' incentives in contrasting ways. Recall that when it comes to motivating users' participation, transaction fees (commissions) fare better than membership fees (subscriptions), as they make users pay only if they effectively transact on the platform (instead of making them pay upfront). Yet, you also recall that, for the very same reason, transaction fees induce users to bypass the platform; that is, users may be tempted to leave the platform once the initial contact is made and avoid payment by completing the transaction through some other means.

Your immediate reaction might be to reduce transaction fees and compensate by inflating membership fees. The risk, then, is to put many users off, as they will form pessimistic expectations about the participation of other users. Leakage would be avoided ... but simply because there is not much to leak. As we discuss later, the trick to escape this quandary is to maintain a good value-for-money perception for your users.

Long-term matches

It is not because users agree, initially, to take out a subscription and/or to pay a commission on their transactions that they will refrain from bypassing the platform at a later stage. If the value of repeatedly using the platform dwindles, there will be a point at which users will no longer be willing to pay the price. This is especially true when the platform focuses on matchmaking, without offering many additional services. Once users have found a successful match and developed a working relationship, there is little value for them to continue using the platform. For instance, TaskRabbit helps you find local taskers who can provide small services, like putting together furniture, moving heavy items, or painting walls. One can easily imagine that once you have found the right handyperson living nearby, you would call them directly the next time instead of using the platform. Another example is online dating: If you have found a person you like, you will continue to build this nascent relationship outside the platform.

The root of the problem is that users value long-term matches. That is, they place a high value on repeated interaction with the same counterparty. One reason is that users find switching counterparties unnecessary. Think of a carpooling platform like BlaBlaCar. Users with convergent needs – for instance, users making the exact same journey every weekend – will quickly find a private agreement outside the platform. Switching counterparties may also be deemed too costly. This is especially true when trust-building requires repeated and personal interaction (think of babysitting, for example). Large variability in the quality of interaction across users can also heighten the (expected) switching costs.

These transactions that occur repeatedly between the same pair of platform users are sometimes called 'monogamous' transactions.[2] A general lesson is thus that the more users favor monogamous transactions, the higher the risk of leakage. Another way to put it is that monogamous transactions limit the strength of network effects: Users value the participation of other users mainly *before* joining the platform but not so much *after*. That is, users find larger platforms more attractive beforehand because they increase their chances to find a match; in contrast, once a match is found, the number of active users becomes of secondary importance. In such situations, one understands that membership fees are more appropriate than transaction fees: A one-off fee will capture the value that users attach – before joining the platform – to the prospect of establishing a fruitful long-term relationship with another user. As illustrated in Case 6.3, this is exactly how Thumbtack designed its fee structure.

Case 6.3 'Anti-leakage' pricing by Thumbtack

Thumbtack is a platform connecting local customers and professionals providing specific services, such as landscapers, painters, personal trainers, or even dance teachers. Professionals are charged only once per new customer, at the time of the first contact. This is so irrespective of what happens afterward, meaning that even when a customer does not end up hiring the professional, the latter will be charged anyway. Thumbtack decides thus to charge professionals ahead of a possible transaction, that is, whether the match is successful or not. As a result, professionals must bear the risk of an unsuccessful match, which incentivizes them to adjust their offering to the customer's needs.

Here is how the platform justifies its model:

> You'll only pay the first time a customer reaches out. [...] the cost of each contact depends on the size of the job. [...] Once a customer gets in touch, the ball is in your court and it's up to you to close the deal. Which is what you do best.[3]

Apparently, such a model works as the platform has been constantly expanding since its creation in 2009.

Transactions that are monogamous, require personal contacts, or cause little friction are more prone to leakage.

'Leakable' transactions

By their nature, some transactions are more 'leakable' than others, in the sense that users find it more profitable, effective, or convenient to conduct these transactions outside of the platform rather than through it. First, in the same vein as the long-term matches that we just mentioned, transactions that are conducted in person are more prone to leakage. The reason is that personal contacts facilitate the coordination between users regarding various aspects relevant to the transaction (sharing information, agreeing on a price, and making the payment). In contrast, when transactions are completed online, the platform plays a more active role in providing the parties with a secure and controlled environment for their interaction. Yet, even when transactions can be completed remotely through the platform, users may still need to meet and communicate beforehand to define the scope of the transaction (for instance, a handyperson on TaskRabbit needs to evaluate the work required to give a quote). Again, such prior communication may pave the way for the completion of the transaction outside the platform.

Users are also more likely to bypass the platform when transactions involve little asymmetric information. If the parties can easily assess the quality and reliability of one another, then they do not really need the services of an intermediary. In contrast, when one party is uncertain about the trustworthiness of the other, then transacting directly is riskier and the platform has more room to add value, for example by building its own reputation, offering insurance, or vetting participants.

Finally, the incentives to stay on the platform are low for simple transactions that cause little friction between the parties. This is so if little coordination is needed and if users in each group are relatively similar or easily interchangeable. Conversely, if there is more variability in the sellers' qualifications or the buyers' needs, transactions become more complicated and users find it less convenient to bypass the platform.

Design decisions to curb leakage

As the operator of a platform, you must strive to curb leakage (eliminating it completely is probably illusory). To help you do so, we propose a carrot and stick approach. The carrots are *proactive actions* that aim at enhancing the value-for-money perception of your users. The sticks are *reactive actions* that intend to make leakage less attractive for users. In simpler words, you can either reward users if they stay or penalize them if they leave. We start with the former option, as we believe it is more likely to pay off.

> **Find ways to curb platform leakage, either proactively (by increasing the platform's value for users) or reactively (by raising users' costs when they bypass the platform).**

Proactive 'anti-leakage' actions

One of the first recommendations one can make is to focus on user experience. Whether users pay or not for using your platform, it should always be easier and more convenient for them to act 'inside' rather than 'outside' the platform. To make sure this is so, we advise you to describe all the micro-steps of a typical transaction between users from various groups and to see how you can best reduce frictions along the user journey. This is what some C2C (consumer-to-consumer) platforms do through the clever use of cutting-edge technologies, as described in Case 6.4.[4]

Case 6.4 How image recognition and AI can oil the wheels for sellers on C2C platforms

Imagine that you move houses and that you want to resell some of your furniture. Your first thought is probably to use an online C2C platform. These platforms, which allow individuals to conduct business with one another, have gained a lot in popularity lately. The main reason for their success is that they have succeeded in smoothing the user journey for buyers. By providing a clear categorization of products, detailed product descriptions, and loads of photos, these platforms make it very easy for buyers to find what they want. Yet, the burden of providing this information rests upon the sellers, which makes their user journey a lot bumpier. As it is costly to take photos, find the appropriate categories, or write appealing descriptions, some sellers may prefer alternative ways to sell their items, such as contacting friends and family to see if anyone is interested, posting an ad on their social network news feed, or participating in some local flea market.

To address this issue, PriceMinister (a French C2C platform) partnered in 2016 with Rakuten Institute of Technology to develop a solution – called Quicksell – that allows sellers to use the PriceMinister app on their smartphone to identify and register their products simply by taking a photo of them. This feature, which combines image recognition and artificial intelligence (AI) technology, greatly speeds up the process of selling an item and, thereby, contributes to retaining users on the seller side of the platform.

To increase the value for its users, the platform can also play the role of a trusted third party, as we explained in the previous section. By providing users with a safe transactional environment, platforms can make them less hesitant about dealing with strangers. What matters for curbing leakage is that users find it easier to establish trust inside rather than outside the platform. For instance, the car-sharing platform RelayRides (now called Turo) automatically provides vehicle owners with insurance that offers $1,000,000 in liability coverage when the person renting their car is in an accident. This discourages car owners to bypass the platform, as contracting with renters outside the platform would force them to extend their existing insurance policy and pay a higher premium.

Rating and review systems are other tools to build a trustworthy environment. Users care about receiving positive evaluations from their counterparties because it helps them build a reputation and secure more profitable deals in the future. For example, it has been shown that sellers on eBay with top ratings can charge higher prices than sellers with lower reputation scores or no reviews.[5] We argued previously that rating and review systems are instrumental in retaining users on a platform, as transactions taking place outside the platform are missed opportunities to consolidate a user's reputation. Yet, it may be counterproductive for a platform to make the environment too secure: If trust among users grows strong enough, the need for the platform may decrease and leakage may return. Gu and Zhu (2021) provide some evidence along these lines. Their study of an online freelance marketplace suggests that leakage increased after the platform improved its reputation system. More precisely, the authors noticed that high-quality freelancers tended to contract more with clients outside the platform, which was evidenced by "significantly lower charges, fewer hours reported, and the stronger intention to disintermediate expressed in chat messages between them" (p. 795).

Besides improving trust, one can think of complementing the platform's offering with other value-added features. The global goal remains the same: Encourage users to stay on the platform by making their life easier. In this spirit, marketplaces can give sellers (or service providers) access to management tools that facilitate the integration between the sellers' transactions on the platform and their other operations outside the platform. This can concern invoicing, payment, scheduling, dashboard, reporting, training, workflow management, etc. For instance, *Opentable* developed, for its affiliated restaurants, a guest management software that automates several mundane tasks. By allowing restaurants to save precious time, this software contributed to retaining them on the platform despite the commission they had to pay on each transaction.

Finally, a more radical move consists in making users directly interested in the platform's performance. Instead of funding your platform through venture capital, you can opt for a cooperative model, whereby the platform is owned – and potentially governed – by its users. For instance, Eva is a Canadian ride-sharing platform that is organized as a cooperative.[6] In contrast with competitors like Uber, Lyft, or Didi, Eva brings riders and drivers as members, relies on democratic and participative governance, and commits to a better redistribution of wealth across stakeholders (typically, rides are cheaper for rider members and wages are higher for driver members). Clearly, when the interests of the platform are aligned with those of its users, leakage is no longer an issue.

> **To curb leakage proactively, you can improve the user experience, add features, act as a trusted third party, or interest users in the platform's performance.**

Reactive 'anti-leakage' actions

If carrots are not effective, you may think of using the stick instead, that is, penalizing users if you catch them circumventing the platform. The ultimate penalty consists in banning such users. With such a rule, you assume that users will remain on the platform because of the threat that weighs on them. Airbnb, for example, applies this tactic by stating clearly the following:

> Any reservations that are made outside of Airbnb violate our Terms of Service. If we identify that a reservation was made through a third-party service, we may cancel the reservation and deactivate the accounts of the person who made the reservation and the guest.[7]

To avoid reaching such extremes, Airbnb prevents guests from seeing a host's exact location and phone number until payment is made. For the same reason, other platforms block their users from exchanging contact information.

A less aggressive and more preventive tactic consists in detecting leakage temptations before leakage materializes. This can be achieved by using diverse smart IT tools (such as screen crawlers running while platform users chat) or by sending messages via the platform's mailing system. Behavior and text analysis software applications can indeed create automated alerts based on pre-defined suspicious actions or terms (like 'phone' or 'email'). As the operator of the platform, your role is then to check compliance with the terms of use and, when appropriate, send warnings to dubious users.

The obvious downside of such strategies is that they degrade the user experience by making the platform more cumbersome to use or by invading users' privacy. As these strategies increase both the cost and the willingness to bypass the platform, their net effect on leakage remains unclear.

Dormant leakage

Platform leakage can be dormant in the sense that users stop using the platform instead of leaving it altogether; that is, although they do not delete their account, they do not interact with any other user nor conduct any transaction. At first glance, these situations are two sides of the same coin: Whether users stop interacting or leave for good, they no longer generate any revenue for the platform. However, dormant leakage has a hidden cost that platforms must be aware of. The presence of inactive users can indeed negatively impact the experience of active users. Active users might well try to interact with non-responsive users, as they are hard to identify a priori. Take for instance the case of outdated CVs staying on a job search platform. Since few people unsubscribe after their status has changed, companies looking for the ideal candidate might waste time reviewing CVs and contacting people who are no longer on the job market. The immediate consequence for active users is thus an increase in their search cost (as they must search for another match).[8] Disappointed users might then blame the platform for displaying a deceptive degree of variety, which might eventually prompt them to leave the platform. In other words, the presence of inactive users is a form of pollution that may drive active users away from the platform.

> **Beware of the potential pollution generated by inactive users, who remain on the platform but stop interacting with anyone. This dormant form of leakage might trigger real leakage.**

What can be done to limit dormant leakage? Obviously, dormant users must be somehow woken up; that is, you must find ways to encourage your users to keep on using the platform and interacting with other users. This can be achieved through a continuous improvement of the user's experience. As maintaining a high rate of active users is key for long-run success, you must see user engagement as the lifeblood of your platform. User engagement starts with the correct perception of what users enjoy most. Do not make too many assumptions about what users appreciate and what they do not. Reach out to users and let them define your strategic agenda on how to improve the level of service on your platform. Entering in contact with less active users (that is, the at-risk population) may help you reduce the sticking points and, as a result, enhance the user experience for everyone. Beyond the qualitative aspects, it is also possible to measure engagement. Choosing the right KPIs to track active users' behavior is therefore very important too. This last remark leads us naturally to the crucial question of monitoring the progress made by the platform, which we address in the last section of this chapter.

If your attempts to reactivate dormant users fail, it seems wiser to let these users go for good. As these users have slim chances to be active again, the revenue you can expect from them is way smaller than the pollution cost that their inactivity imposes on other users. It is then counterproductive to

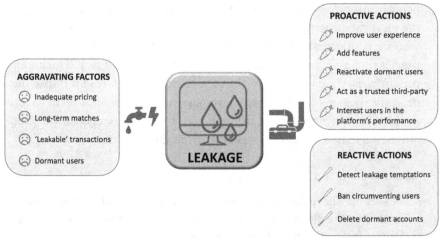

Figure 6.2 Leakage: Sources and remedies.

make it complex for users to unsubscribe or delete their accounts (as too many platforms do).

Figure 6.2 recaps the main elements of this section.

Growth: densify or diversify

We explained in Chapter 4 that a sound strategy for platforms at the launch stage is to constrain their operations, by operating initially within a bounded geographical location and/or a well-defined category of products or services. Starting small appears like a safer way to grow big. The key is thus to design a Minimum Viable Platform (MVP) that meets the main needs of your users while reaching a sufficient audience to generate a positive feedback loop. It is only once your MVP is up and running that you can start thinking of growing your platform.

We see two main routes to growth: You can either *densify* your value proposition (by expanding your activities within your initial market) or *diversify* your value proposition (by entering other markets). We study these two strategies in this section, after warning you about the perils of growing too fast and without a clear plan.

Grow wisely!

We know that in the case of platforms, growth begets growth: Expanding now makes it easier to expand later thanks to the positive feedback loop generated by network effects. Yet, platform growth should not become an objective in itself. Firstly, growth may be very costly to set in motion. Secondly, there may be some value in waiting. We examine these two reasons in turn.

Do not dig yourself into a hole too deep

We know from Chapter 4 that strategies aimed at solving the chicken-and-egg problem come with hefty costs. As the first users are typically hard to attract, you will have to subsidize their participation in one way or another. It is thus very likely that you will have to sustain losses (or, at best, an absence of revenues) in the early stages of your platform. As the proverb says, he that would have eggs must endure the cackling of hens, meaning that, to get what you want, you must be prepared to endure unpleasant things. Take the launch of the Xbox gaming platform as an illustration. To convince gamers of adopting it in the absence of a sufficiently large catalog of games, Microsoft decided to sell the console at a price below its manufacturing cost; in other words, Microsoft subsidized the first users, which was the main source of a total loss of $4 billion for the four years after the launch. Yet, the Xbox eventually became a success, which made Ed Fries, former head of Microsoft Game Studios, declare: "I wouldn't say we lost $4 billion. I'd say we spent $4 billion building the Xbox brand and business."[9]

You could thus see these initial 'chicken-and-egg losses' as an investment. But like any investment, it has to pay eventually; otherwise, it may be wiser not to undertake it. The problem is that returns are highly uncertain, as they hinge on the expectations that your potential users form: The more optimistic they are, the higher your chances of reaping the benefits of your investment. As a matter of fact, it is not only users that you need to convince of your future success: Funders constitute another important group that you must win over (and this is usually an enduring and exhausting battle). They are the ones who will accept to cover your initial losses, provided that they believe that you will eventually turn a profit. If they do believe it, you may actually succeed – another self-fulfilling prophecy! We see that important cross-side network effects are at work here as well: On the one hand, funders must expect sufficient future activity on the platform to agree to fund it; on the other hand, users are more likely to join the platform the more funding it can raise, as they can anticipate a larger value for money.

Funders must expect sufficient future activity on the platform to agree to fund it and users are more likely to join the platform the more funding it can raise.

The value of waiting

There are three pitfalls of growing too fast too early.[10] The first pitfall is that markets with platforms may reward second-movers more than first-movers. A platform that rushes to enter the market first may neglect the quality of the intermediation service that it provides. It may then run the risk of being superseded by an entrant platform. This second-mover would have an advantage because it would have learned from the mistakes of its predecessor and, thereby, would be able to build a more compelling value proposition. This may partly explain how Facebook supplanted MySpace in the social networks arena or how Google unseated early search engines like Yahoo! and Altavista.

Second, some growth strategies are more dangerous than others. In particular, the *Incubate Golden Eggs* strategy, which relies on marquee users to solve the chicken-and-egg problem, might unduly strengthen the bargaining power of these users (who may then capture an increasing share of the platform's value) or jeopardize diversity on the platform (as smaller users may get scared away).

Finally, the danger of hurried growth is the stress that it puts both on the platform's organization and cash flow. Nascent platforms are in general small companies, with limited human resources. If managers are too busy trying to expand the business, they may fail to correct – or even notice – the inevitable flaws of their initial business model. Instead, they may persist with the wrong course of action and quickly reach a point of no return because of the self-reinforcing nature of network effects. It will then be too late to rectify the initial miscalculations. This is what happened to the startup Take Eat Easy in the food delivery sector, as described in Case 6.5.[11]

Case 6.5 It wasn't easy-peasy for Take Eat Easy

Launched in Brussels in the summer of 2013, Take Eat Easy was among the first companies to enter the home food delivery market in Belgium (which is a small playground compared to other European countries like the UK or Germany). Very quickly, the start-up expanded to other cities. The entry into the international market started in 2014 with Paris, followed one year later by Berlin, London, and Madrid. At that time, the goal was clearly to become the leading platform in the European home food delivery market. To fuel its rapid growth, Take Eat Easy raised €6 million in a first venture capital funding round in April 2015 and a second one in August 2015, which brought an additional €10 million investment to sustain growth. Between August 2015 and July 2016, the young company increased the size of its team from 10 to 160 employees, grew its community from 30,000 to 350,000 customers, and concluded partnerships with 3,200 restaurants across 20 cities in Europe. Just after having reached a landmark in its history by achieving 1 million deliveries, Take Eat Easy abruptly announced in July 2016 its intention to apply for judicial restructuring and to cease trading. The reason behind this decision was that despite rapid growth, the start-up was making no profits, as announced on social media in 2016: "Contribution margin has been steadily improving and is now positive across the group, though not yet high enough to cover our fixed costs." It seems that the management did not pay enough attention to the local market conditions to drive international expansion. As noted by Adrien Roose, co-founder of the startup (cited in Belleflamme and Neysen, 2017),

we should have adopted a more military strategy, which means going into battle only where we knew we could end up as the market leader. From the start, it should have been clear to us that cities like London or Paris were no more within reach. So, one advice that I would give is not to make growth an end in itself.

Densify your value proposition

Once you have attracted a critical mass of users on your platform and met their basic needs, you can start expanding your activities to improve the experience of your existing users and to serve additional users. The first natural route is to *densify* your value proposition within the market segment that you have been serving so far. You can do so in three ways. First, you can add features, functionalities, or geographies. Second, you can onboard an additional group of users. Finally, you can think of selling your own products or services, alongside those that are already proposed on your platform.

Adding features, categories, geographies

Natural ways for platforms to grow consist in enriching the users' experience or catering to a larger set of users. In the former case, the idea is to complement the initial offering with features or functionalities that increase the value of using the platform. The objective here is to retain existing users and, if possible, drive them to raise their activity level on the platform (for instance, by increasing the size and/or frequency of their transactions). For example, Uber Eats added two new features in 2002 to make it more convenient for groups of friends or families to place a common order and, if they want, to split the bill.[12]

Alternatively, the platform can keep its current offering but make it available to a larger set of users. One example is the geographical expansion of services that require local interaction (like ride-hailing or food delivery). This is, for instance, what Take Eat Easy tried to achieve when it started to operate in Paris or Madrid (see Case 6.5). The experience gained in the original geography should make it cheaper for the platform to acquire users in the new geography. This cost-saving should compensate for the fact that new users do not generate any network effects for existing users (in Take Eat Easy example, a restaurant in Paris does not bring any additional value to diners in Brussels). Marketplaces (like Etsy or eBay) provide another example of this strategy: They enrich their offering to buyers by attracting sellers or service providers from other categories than the ones initially presented. For instance, Vinted started in 2008 as a marketplace for buying, selling, and exchanging clothing; now, the platform also makes it possible for its users to trade textiles, home accessories, tableware, and even books.

As Case 6.6 illustrates, suggestions as to which expansion path a platform should follow often come from the initial users. It is thus essential to engage with your users and understand what they want from you.

> **Let your current users suggest ways to densify your value proposition.**

Case 6.6 Let your users show you the way

Bumble is a dating and social networking app that was launched in the U.S. in 2014. It is often presented as a feminist alternative to Tinder because its policy is to let women make the first move and send the first message when there is a heterosexual match. At the launch stage, the app constrained its services to dating and its audience to women in their twenties. The first expansion was in terms of audience, as people of any gender, orientation, or age were quickly invited to join. The second – and more radical – expansion concerned the set of services offered by the app. As Clare O'Connor, head of editorial content at Bumble, explains (as reported in Joy, 2021, p. 47):

> A year or two after Bumble's launch, we noticed that some people were using the app to look for non-romantic relationships. Some wanted gym or yoga buddies. Others had business ideas and were looking for help with startups. So we launched two new modes: Bumble BFF [*Beft Friends Forever*] for platonic-friend-finding and Bumble Bizz for careers and networking. Folks might get on Bumble BFF because they're suddenly empty nesters and want to find new friends. Someone might use Bumble Bizz to look for a new board member for their company.

TempStars is a Canadian-based platform that connects dental offices to hygienists and dental assistants. The initial focus was on short-term or short-notice shifts of dental hygienists but James Younger – TempStars' founder and CEO – gradually densified the value proposition at the request of early users, as he explained in an interview[13]:

> Dental officers saying: "Oh, great work with finding us a hygienist. Do you have any dental assistants?" And then I would say: "No, we only do hygienists." And then finally, I got tired of saying no. So, then we added dental assistants and at this point, we had some word of mouth, so it wasn't as hard to get on initial dental assistants as it was for hygienists. But then the assistants come on and now we're just doing temping – hygienists and assistants. But then, of course, dental officers are saying: "Oh, those are great hygienists and assistants. Thank you. But now we need to hire someone. Can you tell us a good hygienist?" And I would say: "No, we just do temping." And so, I get tired of saying no about that. And then, we had to build a job board because people really wanted that. So then we build out essentially a job board for permanent and contract hiring, as opposed to the temping.

Adding a group of users

We explained in Chapter 4 that when the chicken-and-egg problem is too acute, operating as a platform might not be possible from the outset. To onboard the first users, it is necessary to operate first as a pipeline, by providing services in an integrated way (*Lay the first eggs yourself*, as we called this strategy). It is only at a later stage that in-house production can make way for third-party providers. That is, the initial pipeline becomes a true platform by attracting a group of independent service providers. Well-known examples are the opening of the Amazon marketplace to third-party sellers or game consoles to third-party game developers.

While moving from a one-sided pipeline to a two-sided platform looks like a natural step, adding a third side to a two-sided platform requires a careful evaluation of the expected benefits and costs. Let us start with the *expected benefits*. First, adding an extra side to your business expands the scope of potential interactions and broadens your footprint in the ecosystem. Reaching out to other sides and integrating them into your platform adds new sources of positive cross-side network effects and, thereby, increases the potential for igniting positive feedback loops. Take the example of operating systems for smartphones. Google's Android platform can be seen as a three-sided platform, which links end-users, application developers, and handset manufacturers (like Huawei or Samsung). In contrast, the competing Apple iOS platform has one side fewer since Apple fully controls the production of the iPhone, which is the only handset running on iOS. Arguably, Android's ecosystem is richer than Apple iOS's one, which may partly explain why Android phones dominate the market.

Another benefit of adding an extra side to your platform is that it often represents a new stream of revenues. Indeed, if you already control the access to large numbers of users in two different groups, users in a third group might have a large willingness to pay to get access to these users and to the transactions they conduct on your platform. Such an additional source of revenue might be particularly welcome when it is challenging to charge existing users. As an illustration, Case 6.7 describes how LinkedIn successfully implemented this step-by-step multi-sided approach.

Case 6.7 The progressive multi-sided strategy of LinkedIn

In its early days in 2003, LinkedIn was not a two-sided platform yet. Indeed, all users were part of the same group, that is, professionals connecting online with one another as if they were exchanging business cards offline. It only became a true two-sided platform two years later when LinkedIn launched its *Jobs* business line next to the *Subscriptions* one. The idea was to open the platform to a new group of users: recruiters looking for hiring people. This user group had a much higher willingness to pay to get access to the platform, which allowed LinkedIn to become profitable in 2006. In 2008, the platform launched *DirectAds*, a sponsored advertising service. It followed the example of other social media platforms in an attempt to increase its revenues. Advertising (called 'Marketing Solutions' by LinkedIn) nowadays represents about one-fifth of the platform's total revenues. The biggest part is still coming from the original business line (Talent Solutions), accounting for 65% of total revenues and the rest coming from premium subscriptions.

A last positive impact we see in onboarding new sides is the potential value that complementors can bring to the platform. Recall that complementors offer products and services that add value to your own offering when they are consumed in combination with it. In Chapter 3, we considered the option of contracting directly with one or a few pre-identified complementors. Alternatively, you can think of opening your platform to the whole group of complementors; they will then decide to join or not depending on how much you charge (or subsidize) them. Circumstances will determine which option is the most appropriate. The first option is sensible when the number of suitable complementors is limited and/or your existing users place little value on variety. For instance, if you want to build trust in your platform by offering insurance services, it makes more sense to negotiate a deal with a single insurance company instead of letting your users compare the policies of a large set of companies. In contrast, Case 6.8 illustrates a situation in which the second option makes more sense.

Case 6.8 How Spreds successfully spread

Spreds (formerly known as MyMicroInvest) is a Belgian equity-based crowdfunding platform. The majority of crowdfunding platforms are two-sided: They link entrepreneurs on one side to backers (the *crowd*) on the other side. Spreds decided to add a third side, made of professional investors, who are particularly knowledgeable of the financial sector and generally experts in private equity. These users are invited to consider investment opportunities in the same startups as anyone else on the platform. The difference here is that members of this specific group are much better equipped to conduct due diligence and business case analyses. As a result, their decisions to back a particular project are interpreted by the non-sophisticated backers in the crowd as a sign of the entrepreneur's reliability and solvability. Non-sophisticated backers can thus make more informed investment decisions, which increases the value that Spreds creates for them. In other words, the group of professional investors exerts a positive cross-side network effect on non-sophisticated backers, which justifies the platform's decision to attract this group in the first place.

Naturally, onboarding an additional user group also comes with extra *costs*. First, the new side adds an extra layer of complexity for the management of the platform; the corresponding costs should not be underestimated. Another risk is that the additional group may exert negative cross-side network effects on an existing group (or some members of this group). Referring to Case 6.8, the participation of professional investors on a crowdfunding platform may drive away those backers who have chosen to invest in crowdfunded projects precisely because they dislike or distrust the traditional financial sector. Another example can be found in Spotify's addition of podcasts to its traditional music offering. In early 2022, Neil Young urged Spotify to remove its music because he could not accept sharing the platform with a podcaster who was accused of spreading misinformation about Covid-19 vaccination; other artists, like Jonnie Mitchell, quickly followed suit.[14] This is evidence that podcasters can exert negative cross-side network effects on other content providers on Spotify, namely artists and record companies. In such cases, the additional revenues obtained from onboarding the new group of users must be balanced against the reduced attractiveness of the platform for other groups of users. This is reminiscent of the alternative monetization strategies that we discussed in Chapter 5: Selling your users' attention or personal data to third parties can bring additional revenues but can also alienate some users.

> **Adding a group of users is a sensible strategy if the benefits (increased revenues, additional positive cross-side network effects, complementary offerings) outweigh the costs (potential negative cross-side network effects, increased management complexity).**

Selling your own products/services

As we just recalled, direct – pipeline-like – production is often an unavoidable step for nascent platforms. Interestingly, in-house production may also be appealing to established platforms at later stages of their development. To increase their control over the transactions that they facilitate, platforms may want to enter the area of activity of their third-party providers. One motivation to do so can be seen as virtuous but a second motivation quite less so.[15]

The 'virtuous' reason for platforms to introduce their own offering alongside the offering of their providers is to enhance overall quality. Platforms may, for instance, identify a category of products or services valued by buyers but poorly served by independent providers. It seems then sensible to step in and fill the gap. The same argument applies to underserved geographies. For instance, to reach customers in locations with a short supply of restaurants, Deliveroo decided to build its own network of so-called 'Editions kitchens' (these kitchens are also dubbed 'dark', 'ghost', or 'cloud' because they prepare food for delivery-only customers, without a storefront). Platforms can also substitute their own offering for what is proposed by poorly performing providers. Finally, buyers may find it more convenient to consume a bundled service proposed by the same platform than to combine the services of several third-party providers. In all these cases, the strengthening of in-house production by the platform should benefit all parties – buyers, sellers, and the platform itself (only poorly performing sellers should pay the price if they do not manage to step up their game).

Platforms can also use in-house production to capture value directly from performant providers. If a platform identifies products or services that generate a lot of transactions and revenues, it may be tempted to propose its own version of these products or services and, possibly, drive buyers toward them by biasing its search or recommendation algorithms. Although this strategy can be quite profitable, it also involves serious risks. First, competition watchdogs may find the practice illegal (especially if search algorithms are twisted).[16] Second, the platform must take into account the potential reaction of the third-party sellers it has decided to compete with. As these sellers will see their revenues dwindle, they might reduce their activities on the platform or simply abandon ship. Other sellers may follow suit for fear of seeing the platform entering their turf as well. As sellers leave or reduce their involvement, buyers will benefit from weaker cross-side network effects, which may induce some of them to leave the platform as well. That is, a negative feedback loop may start unless buyers value sufficiently the alternative in-house production proposed by the platform.

Diversify your value proposition

Another growth strategy for platforms is to expand *outside* their initial market with the aim to diversify their initial value proposition. Roughly speaking, the platform proposes new value in an adjacent market. Naturally, the value and the market in question must be chosen with care. The idea is to leverage the platform's existing operations to facilitate entry into the new market, either by providing more value to users or by operating at lower costs. If so, this so-called 'platform envelopment strategy' can generate a competitive advantage with respect to organizations that would start from scratch in this market.[17]

If you want to grow by entering new markets, use your existing operations as leverage to outperform your competitors through increased value and/or lower costs.

Envelopment through increased value

It is often costly for users to mix and match the separate offerings of several platforms. A platform that can combine several complementary products and services into a single bundle is then able to create significant value for the users and, thereby, gain a competitive advantage over pure players. An envelopment strategy can allow a platform to build such a bundle of services. For example, Uber partnered in 2020 with Thames Clippers to allow the users of the Uber app to book a ride on the boats operated by this company on the Thames in London.[18] As users enjoy the ability to combine different modes of transportation through a single app, they are willing to pay more for Uber's joint offering. Here, the enveloper exploits the increased willingness to pay generated by one-stop shopping and convenience.

The enveloper can also enhance the users' willingness to pay because it is in a better position than its competitors to win the users' trust. Users will indeed form more optimistic expectations about the future success of a platform that has already proved successful in another market segment, compared to an unknown newcomer. Coming back to the previous example, you do not need a business degree to understand why Thames Clippers accepted to have its fleet of boats rebranded 'Uber boats by Thames Clippers'. The Uber brand name is indeed more powerful than theirs in attracting users.

Envelopment through lower costs

The cost of operating in market Y can be lower for a platform that already operates in market X than for a platform that only operates in market Y. This is so if the enveloper has some spare capacities in market X that it can deploy in market Y in some productive way. First, the enveloper can exploit the *data* collected on its users in market X to improve its offering in market Y; in our current example, Uber could leverage its knowledge of the demand for rides to adjust the schedule or the routes of the boats. Second, the algorithms and software used to match users or to streamline logistics can be deployed in adjacent markets at low costs; sticking with Uber, this explains why the company has invested in delivery services (Uber Eats for food or Uber Freight for parcels). Case 6.9 provides other illustrations of this strategy.

Case 6.9 Meituan's data envelopment strategies

Meituan is a Chinese e-commerce platform. It started in Beijing in 2010 as a group-discount website but quickly expanded both geographically and in terms of services. Meituan is now presented as "China's largest provider for local services with (...) over 130 million annual active purchasers."[19] Liu (2019) describes how Meituan managed to conquer adjacent markets by leveraging the data collected in the markets in which the company was already operating. For example, Meituan exploited its knowledge of the food delivery market (delivery route optimization, data from recommender systems) to deliver other foodstuffs and groceries. Meituan also entered the ride-sharing sector by taking advantage of its data on the locations of consumers (private and professional), restaurants, and shops, as well as its ability to determine the fastest way between any two points.

To conclude this section, note that the two growth paths that we have described – densifying and diversifying the value proposition – can both be pursued internally or externally. That is, you can rely on resources and capabilities that either you develop within your organization (internal growth) or obtain from outside (external growth). In the latter case, you can use M&A (Mergers and Acquisitions) or strategic alliances (like joint ventures). The examples that we gave throughout this section illustrate these different possibilities. Figure 6.3 summarizes what we learned in this section.

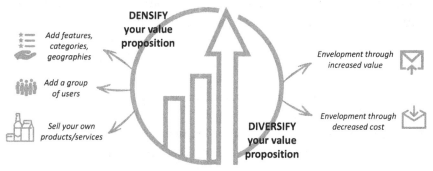

Figure 6.3 Growth strategies for platforms.

Monitoring: measure and improve

"If you can't measure it, you can't improve it." This famous quote from the consultant and founding father of modern management theory, Peter Drucker, will serve here as an anchor point. The sustainability of a platform largely depends on its ability to maintain a high level of interaction between user groups over time. This depends in turn on the platform's ability to innovate to offer ever more efficient services. Continuous improvement must therefore be a central goal, ideally guided by information on current performance.

The desire to measure the progress made by the platform has multiple advantages and can be used in different ways. First of all, in a context where the platform is being launched or is still at an early stage, using figures, for example on the evolution of the number of users, makes it possible to objectify the situation, better defend one's hypotheses regarding future growth and, eventually, reassure and convince investors. Also, making use of various relevant metrics will help you build and implement your strategy. This is done by basing decisions on a more solid foundation, setting realistic and tailored objectives, and then verifying the impact of the strategic choices on both the organization's financial and operational results.

What precedes applies to any organization and is not limited to platforms. However, the volatility of users and the fragile balance of interdependencies between different user groups make the monitoring function even more essential in the case of platforms. Indeed, too many platforms fail to attract or retain users although they seem to provide good value for money according to the usual indicators (they meet a need, are easy and inexpensive to use, etc.). The reason is probably, as we know it by now, that users in different user groups fear that they will not find an interesting counterparty with whom to conclude a transaction. Alternative indicators or metrics are then necessary to understand what is lacking in such a situation and act accordingly to solve the problem.

Some tools – such as the famous *Balanced Scorecard* (BSC) – offer a useful compass to navigate in this quest for improved quality and performance. As we did repeatedly in this book, we seek here to redefine the contours of the tool so that it best fits the reality of platforms.

The Balanced Scorecard

When it comes to assessing an organization's performance or evaluating its growth through objective indicators, the tool that tends to impose itself naturally is the BSC, which was first proposed by Kaplan and Norton (1992). It is a performance management tool that is articulated around four different key areas for which it is expected to find relevant metrics or Key Performance Indicators (KPIs) to look at. KPIs are indicators of the ongoing progress toward an intended result. As such, they provide a clear framework for the decision-making process by focusing on what matters most.

The BSC induces managers to consider their business from four perspectives:

- *Financial perspective:* "How do we look to shareholders?"
- *Internal business perspective:* "What must we excel at?"
- *Learning and growth perspective:* "Can we continue to improve and create value?"
- *Customer perspective:* "How do customers see us?"

Information about each perspective is collected through an appropriate set of KPIs. Examples of those for the four perspectives are, respectively, net profit margin, time to market, employee engagement, and customer satisfaction.

> **"Think of the balanced scorecard as the dials and indicators in an airplane cockpit. For the complex task of navigating and flying an airplane, pilots need detailed information about many aspects of the flight."**
> **(Kaplan and Norton, 1992)**

These four families of indicators revolve around the organization's vision and strategy. The *vision* is a relatively concise and abstract statement about the long-term ambition of the organization. For instance, Amazon's corporate vision is "to be Earth's most customer-centric company, where customers can find and discover anything they might want to buy online." Of course, vision alone is not sufficient to establish a strategic roadmap. This is why it must be broken down into strategic goals, that is, more precise statements of ambition that point out the priority areas on which the company wishes to act. Based on Amazon's vision, we could consider that the priority axes are: (1) Increase global reach ("to be Earth's..."); (2) Enhance customer experience ("most customer-centric company"); (3) Increase the number of products available for sale ("where customers can find and discover anything"); (4) Improve the efficiency of operations facilitating online sales ("they might want to buy online").

However, even after breaking down the vision into strategic goals, the terms used are still too general to measure performance. This is where the BSC comes in. Indeed, it is recommended to list several objectives to break the strategic goals further down. For instance, behind the goal of 'increasing global reach', one could imagine the more concrete *objective* of entering a dozen new geographic markets within three years. This is a quantified objective, very precise, and whose success is easy to measure in the end. The associated KPI would be 'number of new markets', the *target* '15', the time horizon '3 years', and the *initiatives* would for instance be the names of very concrete projects aimed at achieving the underlying objective.

In our previous example, we could consider that the first three goals belong to the *Customer* perspective, while the last one belongs to the *internal business* perspective. It goes without saying that Amazon also has internal objectives relating to innovation and talent management among its staff, as well as more financial objectives on the other hand. Yet, our purpose here is not to describe in detail the use of the BSC, but rather to see how it can be adapted to the specific case of platforms.

A change of perspective: the Multisided Balanced Scorecard

As the BSC was designed three decades ago, it catered to pipeline businesses. We have amply emphasized throughout this book the many ways in which platforms differ from pipelines. These differences call for a change

Original BSC		Multisided BSC	
Level	Perspective	Perspective	Level
1	Financial	*User*	*1*
2	Customer	*Interaction*	*2*
2	Internal business	*Network effects*	*2*
2	Learning & growth	*Financial*	*3*

Figure 6.4 Change of perspective in the Multisided BSC.

of perspective when evaluating the performance of platforms.[20] As we now explain, the four perspectives that underlie the original BSC must be reinterpreted and reordered, as summarized in Figure 6.4.

> To adapt the BSC to platform businesses, take the 'user' instead of the 'customer' perspective, the 'interaction' instead of the 'internal business' perspective, and the 'network effect' instead of the 'learning and growth' perspective.

User perspective

We immediately amend the original BSC in two major ways. First, we consider users instead of customers. Second, we place this perspective at the top of the list. Let us explain these two changes in turn.

As we argued earlier, talking of *users* instead of *customers* is not a semantic eccentricity. A customer is defined as a person who buys goods or services from a business. In a pipeline, customers are at the end of the linear value-creation process. On a platform, this is not so clear because it is ambiguous which goods or services and which business we are talking about. Take Etsy as an example and imagine that Ana is buying a handmade necklace from Bob. If we focus on this trading relationship, Ana is the customer and Bob is the seller. Yet, this trade would not have taken place without Etsy's intermediation services. From that perspective, both Ana and Bob are customers of Etsy's services. This is why we prefer to consider the likes of Ana and Bob as users of the platform and to divide these users into distinct user groups whenever they play different roles on the platform. For the matter at hand, distinguishing between different user groups is essential. To assess and optimize its performance, a platform must set different objectives, indicators, targets, and initiatives for the different types of users. For instance, Etsy needs distinct indicators to evaluate the degree of satisfaction of a buyer like Ana or a seller like Bob. Similarly, the objectives that a platform can set for raising participation in its different user groups should reflect the differences in attraction power that exist across these groups (as we discussed in Chapter 4).

The user perspective must also be seen as the primary one. Attracting and retaining users are a platform's priorities, as users co-create value with the platform. Kaplan and Norton (1992) consider customer satisfaction as a 'driver of future financial performance'. In the case of platforms, user satisfaction is not just a driver – it is a prerequisite for financial performance. The equation is indeed extremely simple: No user = No value.

Interaction perspective

Kaplan and Norton view the internal business perspective as 'what the company must do internally to meet its customers' expectations'. The authors add: "After all, excellent customer performance derives from processes, decisions, and actions occurring throughout an organization." On a platform, users essentially expect to be able to interact with other users. So, to meet its users' expectations, a platform must find ways to bring users together and facilitate interaction among them. These are the critical internal operations that a platform manager needs to focus on. Consequently, this perspective is renamed the *interaction perspective*.

Network effects perspective

In the original BSC, Kaplan and Norton (1992) clarify what they mean by the Learning & Growth perspective by asking this question: "Can we continue to improve and create value?". This question is as relevant for platforms as it is for pipelines. However, what differs across the two types of organizations is the source of value creation. On platforms, value is co-created by the users and it grows organically as more users join the platform and/or existing users increase their level of activity on the platform. The performance of this self-reinforcing process hinges on the network effects that the platform manages. It is thus natural to rename this perspective *the network effects perspective* for the case of platforms.

Financial perspective

The financial perspective remains essentially the same. For platforms and pipelines alike, "[f]inancial performance measures indicate whether the company's strategy, implementation, and execution are contributing to bottom-line improvement" (Kaplan and Norton, 1992). Yet, financial performance is often regarded as a secondary objective for a platform, at least in the first period of its existence. As explained in the previous two chapters, launching a platform is a very uncertain and costly process. This means that growth needs to be put before bottom-line improvement for a reasonable period.

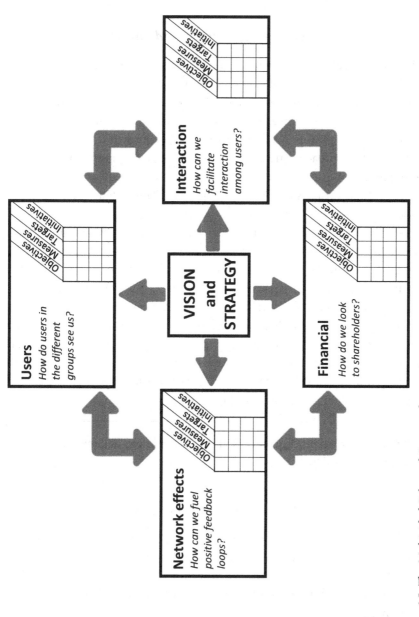

Figure 6.5 The Multisided Balanced Scorecard.

Based on these modifications, we delineate in Figure 6.5 the Multisided Balanced Scorecard (MBSC) as an adaptation of the original BSC that fits the reality of platforms.[21]

Selecting appropriate indicators

Like the original BSC, the MBSC is not just a scorecard: It is a methodology helping a platform implement its vision. It starts by identifying a small number of financial and non-financial objectives related to strategic priorities. It then looks at measures, sets targets for the measures, and finally strategic initiatives (often called projects or programs). It is in this latter stage that the approach differs from other strategic methodologies. It forces an organization to think about how objectives can be measured and only then identifies projects to drive the objectives. This avoids creating costly projects that have no impact on the strategy.

We discuss here a selection of the most useful and relevant KPIs for measuring the performance of a platform (we turn to objectives, targets, and initiatives in the next section). We organize KPIs along the four perspectives of the MBSC (that is, user, interaction, network effects, and financial). Of course, many other interesting indicators exist, which are relevant to any type of business. The idea here is not to present an exhaustive list, but to emphasize that some existing indicators must be adapted to the reality of platforms and some new indicators must be designed. We also limit our selection because it is generally accepted that it is better to focus on a few key indicators rather than multiplying them.

> **The MBSC is not just a scorecard: It is a methodology helping a platform implement its vision.**

KPIs for the user perspective

To measure the level of activity on the platform, the first indicator that comes to mind is the total number of **registered users**. It is important to track its evolution to understand whether you are on track to reach a critical mass of users (and get a positive feedback loop in motion) or whether you are moving away from the goal (the number of users stagnates or dwindles).

However, attracting new users is useless if they do not remain active on the platform. For this reason, the indicator that tends to prevail is the number of 'monthly active users' (MAU), defined as the number of unique users who visited the platform within the past month. The goal is obviously to increase the proportion of MAU in the mass of users because the difference between the two corresponds to the so-called inactive accounts that may pollute the platform, as we explained previously in this chapter.

It should be noted that there is no clear and shared definition of what is meant by an active user. Therefore, each platform can freely determine its own computation method; for example, Twitter takes into account users who logged on at least once in the past month, while Facebook goes further, requiring the user to interact by posting, liking, sharing, or commenting on content. This relative opacity behind the concept hinders the comparison of MAU across platforms. This is certainly a problem for analysts but it may come in handy for marketers. If you recall the 'Boost eggspectations' strategy depicted in Chapter 4, advertising a large number of users may be an effective way to attract a large number of users (by virtue of a self-fulfilling prophecy). Obviously, this strategy is better served by a broad interpretation of the MAU concept.

> **The number of MAUs is a KPI of user engagement that is largely referred to (although it lacks a shared computation method).**

To refine the analysis, it might be useful to understand how assiduously users are active and what exactly they are doing. Useful indicators at this level include the time spent on the platform (or on a web page) or the percentage of visitors leaving the platform site (or a specific web page) without having clicked on a link or an action button (known as the **bounce rate**). Nowadays, Customer Relationship Management (CRM) tools and inbound marketing software are indispensable tools for automating this kind of analysis and generating clear and reliable usage statistics.

In the same line of thought, another useful indicator is the **churn rate**, that is, the rate of active users who decide to discontinue their consumption of a service.[22] In the case of a platform, users may close their account altogether or become dormant users. Tracking the churn rate is helpful, but more important is the ability to gain insights into the reasons why users stop using the platform. These users have been convinced once to join the platform. If they leave, it means that something has changed in the meantime (new competitor, negative experience, …) and you should be concerned about this before the wave of departures intensifies. Apart from the failure to interact with someone else (which we discuss within the next perspective), another cause can be the lack of attractive stand-alone services. Here, tracking the usage of such services can be very informative.

KPIs for the interaction perspective

As the previous indicators focus on users taken individually, they convey little information about the level and quality of interaction among users, which are key elements of any platform's performance. Having more users on board may smooth the matching process but is no guarantee for successful and valuable matches. So, beyond the number of participants, you need to look at metrics that relate specifically to interaction and transactions among users on the platform. Moreover, these metrics must be actionable: They must inform you about the necessary changes for improving performance.

Finding a match. For interaction and transactions to materialize on a platform, users must first be able to find their desired match at a reasonable cost. On two-sided platforms, users in one group are willing to interact with specific users in the other group. So, a crude indicator of the likelihood to find one's match is the **ratio between the numbers of MAU** in the two groups. For instance, on marketplaces (that is, platforms connecting sellers and buyers of products and services, like Etsy), the **buyer-to-seller ratio** tells you how many buyers a seller would be asked to serve on average (assuming that each seller is equally attractive to each buyer). This number should then be compared to a lower and an upper bound. The lower bound is the number of buyers that a seller needs to serve to make their participation in the platform profitable (profitability threshold). The upper bound is the number of buyers that a seller is able to serve (capacity threshold). You should make sure that the observed ratio stays comfortably between these two bounds at any time. If the ratio comes close to any bound, the probability for buyers to be served becomes dangerously low. This is so either because there are too few sellers for a given number of buyers (when the profitability threshold is barely crossed) or because there are too many buyers for a given number of sellers (when the capacity threshold is nearly reached). In such cases, the marked imbalance between the two groups causes congestion or bottlenecks on the platform, which may hinder the interaction process. However, as described in Case 6.10, this type of situation may also have some unexpected positive effects.

On a marketplace, measure the buyer-to-seller ratio and make sure that it ensures profitability for sellers and convenience for buyers.

Case 6.10 Congestion on dating platforms

Using data from 12,900 members of a heterosexual dating platform, Lehmann et al. (2022) analyze platform congestion to understand its consequences. Congestion is materialized here by a double reality: On the one hand, the overrepresentation of men on the platform (67% of men against only 33% of women); on the other hand, the higher activity of men (men like on average 53% of the profiles they see, against only 11% for women). The bottleneck is thus, unsurprisingly, located on the men's side, which affects men negatively. However, it is interesting to note that positive effects arise on the women's side. For men, competition (modeled here by 100 extra likes for the same female profile) leads to a negative effect since it reduces by 23% the probability of being seen by the woman behind this profile, and it increases by two days the time needed before getting a match. For women, on the other hand, congestion has a beneficial effect since they have a larger pool of 'waiting' male profiles who have already expressed their willingness to get in touch with them. The probability of obtaining a match is therefore much higher and the time required is much shorter. The researchers, therefore, draw attention to the fact that while reducing the level of congestion on one side of a platform may seem like a laudable objective, it may also compromise monetization on the other side of the platform.

In the event of expected congestion, it must be possible to adjust its objectives and the target values of the indicators accordingly, for each of the groups in a relatively independent manner. For example, knowing that a dating platform attracts men much more easily than women (see Case 6.10), it will make sense to differentiate the growth targets in these two groups and probably focus more effort on the women's group. Also, as the size of the population can vary greatly from one group to another, it is normal to adjust the objectives accordingly. If the objectives relate to participation in a marketplace, the appropriate unit of measure should, for instance, be of the order of hundreds of users on the providers' side, but of hundreds of thousands on the buyers' side. KPIs also need to be defined carefully for platforms on which users can be active on both sides (as is common for sharing economy platforms, like Vinted or BlaBlaCar). Here, counting users is not terribly informative; it is preferable to measure the frequency at which users take on one or the other role on the platform.

If you have put in place a search engine on your platform, you can also gauge the cost that users face to find their match. Useful **search effectiveness metrics** are the number of searches performed and the number of results per search for an average user. In the same spirit, you can measure the **time to match** as the time needed before a match can be achieved. Note that a larger number of users on both sides should help to reduce this time but you can achieve the same goals with other tools, such as filters, categories, advanced search criteria, etc. These tools should contribute to reducing both the search costs and the time to match.

Conducting a transaction. Finding one another is a necessary but not sufficient condition for users to complete a transaction. What needs to be measured here is the likelihood that successful interactions occur on the platform, often referred to as match rate or **market liquidity**. Liquidity can be appreciated from the point of view of users in any group. It can be seen as a user's reasonable expectation of finding what they are looking for on the platform. Referring again to marketplaces, liquidity can be measured on the demand and the supply side. On the *supply side*, **provider liquidity** is defined as the percentage of listings that lead to transactions within a certain period. For instance, on short-term accommodation platforms, liquidity corresponds to the proportion of total available rooms that are booked each night. For food-delivery or ride-hailing platforms, liquidity should better be measured hourly: What is the percentage of available restaurants (drivers) that get an order (a ride) per hour? On the *demand side*, liquidity corresponds to the probability that a request by a buyer is met by a seller. It can be measured by the percentage of availability requests resulting in rented apartments (short-term accommodation), orders that result in a meal delivery (food delivery), or drive requests resulting in a ride (ride-hailing).

Liquidity metrics can be seen as a subset of a more general class of performance metrics that are important for platforms, namely **conversion rates**.

They are measured as the percentage of users that complete some desired action on your platform, for instance, creating an account, listing an item, downloading a picture, uploading some content, etc. Conversion rates are thus negatively correlated with the bounce rate (which, as described previously, corresponds to the percentage of visitors leaving the platform website or app without having accomplished any action).

The relevant conversion rates depend on the nature of your platform. They might also vary according to the group of users that you are considering. Note that pipelines generally do not differentiate in this way. For example, a robot advisor app in the fintech sector will consider that conversion occurs as soon as a visitor creates an account and makes their first deposit of money. As there is no platform element in the business model, there is only one definition for the conversion rate. In the same sector, a crowdfunding platform (like Kickstarter) connects entrepreneurs in search of funding with potential backers. Here, a relevant conversion rate on the backers' side would be the share of visitors who end up contributing to some project. In contrast, on the entrepreneurs' side, the conversion would take place once an entrepreneur completes the upload of an application file for review by the platform. As with the MAU, it is therefore not possible (and not desirable) to have a standardized definition of what the conversion rate actually represents. Each platform will place the cursor where it considers it most relevant to the market in which it operates.

> **An important KPI is market liquidity, which measures the likelihood that successful interaction takes place on the platform.**

As stressed previously, the metrics that you choose must be relevant *and* actionable. That is, they must tell you what your current performance is and how you can improve it. As far as liquidity is concerned, you can improve it indirectly through various techniques, such as algorithmic scheduling and feedback management. Choudary (2018, p. 5) shares some examples:

> Platforms like Deliveroo require workers to sign up for certain work schedules in advance and automatically assign work requests to workers while limiting their ability to accept or reject requests. [...] ride-hailing platforms

provide notifications and feedback to workers advising them on how to manage their schedules to earn more money on the platform.

However, other platforms that get less involved in organizing the interaction have fewer levers to act on liquidity. This is often the case for platforms that rely on advertising as their main monetization strategy. If your platform belongs to that type, your main goal is to satisfy the advertisers by maintaining high traffic. Even if monitoring the exchanges between users may seem of secondary importance, it can be useful to do so for statistical purposes, as part of your Business Intelligence (BI) strategy. You will gain a better understanding of what is really taking place on the platform, which will certainly prove useful when designing your strategy, as illustrated in Case 6.11.

Case 6.11 2ememain.be is betting on BI

2ememain.be, a peer-to-peer marketplace platform for all kinds of second-hand objects, was founded in 1999 and was then one of the first classified ad sites in Belgium. Since then, 2ememain. be has continued to grow to become the local market leader. At the time of this writing, the platform is part of the eBay group and counts more than 3 million MAUs. Selling or buying on the platform is free of charge (there are no commissions, nor service fees). Therefore, one could think that the platform has no particular interest in following the transactions, especially since these are most often finalized outside the platform (physical meeting, exchange by email, or telephone). However, when a seller decides to withdraw an item for sale before it has reached its free online duration (the platform automatically withdraws ads after one month), the platform asks the seller the reason for this withdrawal by suggesting several possible answers, among which the fact that the item has been sold through the platform. In this way, the platform collects interesting statistics on the factors that influence a sale, the highly sought-after objects, the length of time between the moment of putting an item online and the moment of sale, etc. All this information will be useful for the platform to improve its value proposition and strengthen its marketing communication. Finally, systematically eliminating ads older than 28 days helps to clean up the platform by preventing potential buyers from wasting time looking at items that are either sold or no longer available. The platform, therefore, reduces the risk of dissatisfaction on both sides of the market.

KPIs for the network effects perspective

It is the presence and the management of network effects that set platforms apart from other types of businesses. Hence, the performance of a platform cannot be properly assessed without measuring the strength and evolutions of the network effects that are at play among platform users (as identified in the Linkage Map). As network effects play out over time, metrics for the network effects perspective necessarily have a dynamic nature. To gather relevant information, you must compare successive cohorts of users and analyze the evolution of static metrics over successive periods.

The first approach consists in breaking down the MAU into two categories: The users who join the platform for the first time (*first-time users*) and those who come back following past visits (*recurrent users*). One can then build a metric known as the **loyalty ratio** by dividing the number of recurrent users by the total number of users (recurring + first-time). Distinguishing between these two types of users allows the platform to measure its performance in two related, but distinct, dimensions, namely the ability to attract new users and the ability to retain existing ones.[23] To see the importance of distinguishing between new and recurrent users, let us consider the following two hypothetical situations:

1. Imagine that the number of MAUs increases sharply over time, but essentially through the influx of new users. As a result, the loyalty ratio *decreases*. This situation should alert you, as it indicates that your efforts to attract new users are paying off, but that they are not helping to consolidate a user base for the long term. It is a bit of a flash in the pan: Network effects are either weak or short-lived. To avoid wasting resources, you would be well advised to try to understand why these users, a priori seduced by your value proposition, choose not to stay on the platform.

2. Consider now the opposite situation: The increase in the MAU is mainly driven by recurrent users, which *increases* the loyalty ratio. This may seem paradoxical because if the total number increases, one would think that the differential is necessarily composed of new users. However, this is not necessarily the case. Indeed, as the indicator is measured monthly, it could well be that registered users decide to use the platform with a higher frequency or intensity, or simply users return to the platform after having deserted it for a while. This could be due to some seasonal effect (as holidays approach, for example), a marketing campaign that targets existing users rather than new prospects, or the implementation of some loyalty program. In any case, this situation is less problematic than the first one, in that it suggests that once acquired, a user tends to come back. Network effects seem thus strong enough but entry costs may have risen over time (or the competition has developed). The recommendation would then be to focus more on acquiring new users by choosing a new channel or a new market, for instance.

In sum, if the loyalty ratio increases when you compute it for subsequent cohorts of users, then you can conclude that strong network effects are at play on your platform. It appears indeed that new cohorts of users are better retained than older cohorts.

To grow, a platform can, like any business, spend resources to attract new users (for example through a targeted advertising campaign on social networks); this can be defined as 'paid growth'. Yet, the specificity of platforms is that they can benefit from 'organic growth' by managing network effects, as it is the presence of existing users that makes the platform attractive to new users. To distinguish paid from organic growth, you can identify the channels that bring new users to the platform. New users who responded to your marketing action (paid growth) would arrive on the platform after visiting some third-party site and clicking on some ad link. In contrast, new users stimulated by the presence of existing users (organic growth) would arrive directly on the platform, without any prior visit to other websites. You can then compute what we could call the **paid-to-organic users ratio** by dividing the number of 'paid new users' by the number of 'organic new users' that arrive on the platform during a given period after some marketing action. Ideally, successive comparable marketing actions should lead to lower values of this ratio (or the same value of the ratio should be reached after less costly marketing actions). In other words, your platform should depend less on paid growth as time passes. This would be evidence that you have built strong and defensible network effects.

As we noted in Chapter 3, for network effects to confer a durable competitive advantage, they need to be defensible. One condition for this is that network effects should be specific to your platform, in the sense that they only benefit users who register with your platform. This is so if most users singlehome, that is, are only active on a single platform at a time. It is thus crucial to evaluate to which extent this is actually the case on your platform. A useful metric is the **proportion of singlehoming users** in the total population of users. A large proportion is indicative of high switching costs, a highly differentiated and unique value proposition, or both. In any case, network effects are specific and thus defensible, which is what you are aiming for. Conversely, an over-representation of multihomers will be seen as a risk factor. Indeed, this high volatility could have serious consequences if the platform were to be enveloped or if a cheaper alternative suddenly appeared on the market. Again, techniques can be put in place to gain an advantage over competitors. For example, by minimizing the number of steps and constraints to create a new account, it is possible to attract new users (and thus reduce switching costs). In this respect, one metric that may make sense is the time required to complete competitors' onboarding flows. For similar services, ease of access can be a key factor in capturing new users before competitors do. The aim here is to avoid discouraging potential users who see the available offers as relatively similar.

> To estimate the strength of network effects, you can track the evolution of the loyalty ratio, the paid-to-organic users ratio, and the proportion of singlehoming users.

KPIs for the financial perspective

Let us first stress that platforms should not be too obsessed with financial indicators in their early years of existence. Indeed, due to the economic mechanisms at work on markets with platforms, it is not abnormal for a platform to consent to heavy losses at the beginning. The road to profitability is often longer than for a conventional business. Before being profitable, the goal of a platform is often to impose itself on the market by keeping the competition at bay. As long as investors are willing to follow, all is well. As explained previously, this can be seen as a bet on the future.

This being said, it remains important for platforms to set financial objectives and monitor the evolution of their financial performance. What needs to be tracked depends on the platform's monetization strategy. A platform that relies on membership fees or advertising must monitor closely the evolution of the number of MAU, as these users are the direct or indirect source of revenue. If the platform sets transaction fees, then the volume and value of transactions matter more than the number of users. A marketplace, for instance, would follow the evolution of the **Gross Merchandise Value**, which measures the total sales value of the products or services that are exchanged on the platform during a given period of time.

It may also be useful to express some of the previous KPIs in monetary terms. For instance, we advised monitoring the evolution of the loyalty ratio across consecutive cohorts of users to estimate the strength of network effects. Additional information can be obtained by comparing the *revenues* generated by recurrent vs. first-time users instead of their numbers. If, for instance, recurrent users tend to conduct more transactions than first-time users, then the loyalty ratio will be larger in monetary than in absolute terms.

To gauge the effectiveness of your marketing efforts (or the cost of paid growth), you can also compute the **User Acquisition Cost** (UAC). Recall that we introduced this concept in Chapter 4, as part of the Lever Selector. At the time, our goal was to find out which group to attract first. Hence, we did not need to quantify the UAC (we just had to evaluate for which group the UAC was likely to be smaller). Yet, it is quite possible to quantify the UAC once the platform is in operation. The ratio 'Total budget spent over a given period to attract new users' (that is, advertising campaigns and other marketing expenses)/'Number of targeted users who joined the platform over that same period' provides you with the average UAC (see Case 4.1. for an illustration). If this ratio decreases for successive equivalent marketing campaigns, then it means that positive network effects are at play, as new users become less costly to attract over time.

> **Useful financial KPIs for platforms are the Gross Merchandise Value and the User Acquisition Cost. It is also useful to express other KPIs in monetary terms.**

In Figure 6.6, we have complemented the MBSC with a list of the main KPIs for each perspective.

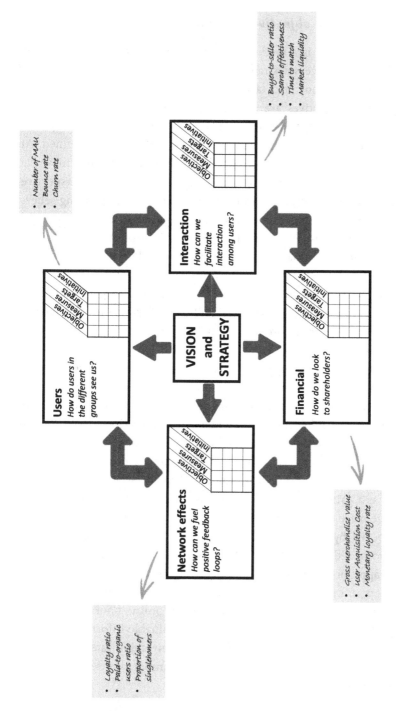

Figure 6.6 KPIs for the Multisided Balanced Scorecard.

Defining objectives, targets, and initiatives

Recall that the MBSC is a methodology to help a platform implement its vision. Once you have set strategic priorities and selected relevant and actionable metrics, your next tasks consist in defining objectives, targets, and initiatives. Objectives are broken down and quantified versions of your strategic goals; their achievement is measured by monitoring some appropriate metric for which some target level has been pre-defined. An initiative is a project or action designed to help the platform achieve the corresponding objective. For instance, in the network effects perspective, an objective for a marketplace can be to curb multihoming among sellers; the appropriate metric is the ratio of singlehoming sellers in the total population of sellers; the target can be set at 90% (that is, multihoming is limited to 10% of sellers); an initiative could be to reward sellers who demonstrate that they sell exclusively on the platform.

It would be pointless to describe generic objectives, targets, and initiatives for the four perspectives of the MBSC. Each platform will have to define its own list, in accordance with its specificities and the stage of its development. To assist you in this complex – but crucial – task, we invite you to go back to some of the canvases that you completed in the previous chapters of this book. First of all, return to the Multi-Sided Value Proposition canvas (Chapter 2) and have a close look at the Gain creators, Pain relievers, and Solutions that you identified there. Given that these are the key components of your value proposition, it makes sense to evaluate how well you are doing on each of them and to design initiatives to improve your performance. For instance, if 'Providing a cheap alternative' is known as a gain creator for travelers on Airbnb, it is crucial to monitor the average price of rooms in each location and compare it to the alternatives proposed by rivals and substitutes; if need be, actions can be taken to help hosts reduce their costs. If fears can be reduced by enhancing trust, an appropriate initiative can be to introduce a 'Super Host' status and to keep an eye on the share of Super Hosts within the total population of hosts. Finally, if 'Providing an efficient online booking system' is perceived by users as the core offering, then valuable information on the performance can be gained by tracking the conversion rate between the number of queries on the platform and the number of effective reservations confirmed.

The Lever Selector (Chapter 4) can also help you. Remember that its two dimensions are UAC and Attraction Power (AP). The lever that a group of users exerts is more efficient the lower the UAC and the larger the AP. We detailed the different elements that affect the UAC or the AP. Looking at those will give you inspiration about which initiatives to put in place to reduce the UAC or enhance the AP of a given group of users.

Go back to the Multisided Value Proposition Canvas and the Lever Selector to define relevant objectives, targets, and initiatives for monitoring and improving the performance of your platform.

To close this chapter (and this book!), we let you meditate upon this quote by Greg S. Reid:

> A dream written down with a date becomes a goal. A goal broken down into steps becomes a plan. A plan backed by action makes your dreams come true.

We sincerely hope that the tools and concepts we have developed in this book will help you make your 'platform dream' come true. And if you are looking for more inspiration, do not hesitate to pay regular visits to our website: www.platformstrategies.org.

SHORT ANSWERS TO THE KEY QUESTIONS

- *How can a platform raise the overall level of trust between users?* To avoid problems related to asymmetric information, it is the responsibility of the platform operator to build trust among the different user groups. The platform can take action to control the quality and seriousness of users and act accordingly (warnings, exclusions, warranties, guarantees, etc.). It can also delegate this function to the participants themselves through the 3Rs, namely ratings, reviews, and recommendations systems.

- *What is 'platform leakage' and how can it be curbed?* Platform leakage (a.k.a. bypass or disintermediation) occurs when users leave the platform once they have found their match and complete transactions outside the platform. Leakage undermines a platform's profitability. To reduce the risk of leakage, a platform operator can implement proactive or reactive actions. Proactive actions increase the perceived or real value of using the platform, while reactive actions make bypassing the platform more costly for users (technically or contractually).

- *Should rapid growth be an absolute goal?* Wanting to grow quickly at all costs is a very risky and expensive strategy, especially in the case of platforms. There are several reasons for this: The sums of money spent to attract users, notably by subsidizing their participation, may never be recovered; the support of investors often hangs by a thread, that of hope in hypothetical future profitability; being obsessed with growth prevents from correcting certain choices related to the business model that may not have been the most appropriate.

- *Which are the options to grow a platform?* You can grow by densifying or diversifying your value proposition. You densify your value proposition by expanding activities within your initial market (you can add features, functionalities, or geographies; onboard another group of users; sell your own products or services). You diversify your value proposition by entering adjacent markets (the idea is to leverage your existing activities to outperform your competitors, either by providing more value to users or operating at lower costs in the new market).

- *How can the performance of a platform be measured?* We recommend using an adapted version of the well-known BSC methodology, which we call the Multisided BSC. Appropriate and actionable metrics must be found to evaluate performance along four perspectives: The user and financial perspectives are shared with the BSC; the interaction and network effects perspectives are specific to the Multisided BSC. The metrics are meant to evaluate the achievement of your strategic objectives and help you design actions to improve your performance.

FURTHER READINGS

Here are some selected readings we advise you to read if you want to dig deeper into the four topics covered in this chapter. On *trust*: See Botsman (2017) for a general presentation and Belleflamme and Peitz (2018) for a description of the use of 3R systems. On *retention*: See the two 'Platform Chronicles' that Hagiu and Wright (2021a and 2021b) devote to platform leakage; see also Zhu and Iansiti (2019). On *growth*: See Belleflamme and Neysen (2017) for the full story of Take Eat Easy's failed growth – and the lessons that can be drawn from it; see also Zhu (2019) on entry by a platform into the space of its independent providers, as well as Eisenmann, Parker, and Van Alstyne (2011) on platform envelopment strategies. On *monitoring*: the seminal description of the BSC by Kaplan and Norton (1992) remains a very good read; the following blog posts provide useful insights about platform-relevant metrics: Choudary (n.a.), Jin and Coolican (2018), Jordan et al. (2020), Makkonen (2022).

Notes

1. This section closely follows Belleflamme and Peitz (2021, 4.3.1 and 4.3.2).
2. See, for example, Rachitsky (2020) or Coolican et al. (2021).
3. See www.thumbtack.com/pro-center/faq (last accessed on August 25, 2018).
4. See Rakuten.Today (2016).
5. See, for example, Resnick *et al.* (2006) or Cabral and Hortaçsu (2010).
6. See https://eva.coop/#/ (last accessed on November 16, 2021).
7. See www.airbnb.com/help/article/199/what-should-i-do-if-someone-asks-me-to-pay-outside-of-the-airbnb-website (last accessed on November 4, 2021).
8. One can say that inactive users exert negative cross-side network effects on active users in other groups on the platform.
9. See https://venturebeat.com/2011/11/15/the-making-of-the-xbox-part-2/ (last accessed on April 15, 2022).
10. We follow here Hagiu and Rothman (2016).

11. This case is taken from Belleflamme and Neysen (2017).

12. As Roth (2022) explains, one user can initiate the group order within the Uber Eats app by choosing the restaurant and then inviting group members directly from their phone contacts; this is arguably more convenient than passing one phone around.

13. See *Two-Sided: the Marketplace Podcast* (Season 2, Episode 3): Focus on a problem that you have experienced yourself – James Younger (TempStars). https://www.sharetribe.com/twosided/s2e03-focus-problem-experienced-yourself-james-younger-tempstars/.

14. See, for example, Madani (2022).

15. We follow here Zhu (2019).

16. See, in particular, the EU Commission *Google Shopping* and *Google Android* decisions (respectively, Case AT.39740, 27 June 2017, and Case AT.40099, 18 July 2018); the EU Commission also initiated proceedings against Amazon (regarding its e-commerce business practices on 20 November 2020) and Apple (regarding Apple Pay in June 2020 and the App Store in April 2021).

17. See Eisenmann, Parker and Van Alstyne (2011). In economic terms, the platform using the envelopment strategy benefits from economies of scope, either on the demand side (users are willing to pay more) or on the supply side (the unit cost of production is lower).

18. See Porter (2020).

19. See https://expandedramblings.com/index.php/meituan-stats-facts/.

20. Eisape (2020) also recommends a change of perspective for adjusting the BSC to the case of platforms. His recommendations, however, differ from ours (in particular regarding the learning and growth perspective).

21. We adapt the representation of the BSC proposed by Dudic *et al.* (2020).

22. The churn rate is the opposite of the retention rate.

23. Distinguishing new from recurrent users may also be important because the two categories play different roles on the platform. On crowdfunding platforms, for instance, empirical evidence suggests that recurrent backers exert a significant influence on new backers Belleflamme et al. (2022) argue that recurrent – more experienced – backers are better at spotting successful projects and are more likely to contribute to these projects at earlier stages of the funding campaign; new backers, who lack experience and knowledge, tend then to follow the choices of recurrent backers.

Bibliography

Belleflamme, P., Lambert, T. and Schwienbacher, A. (2022). Spillovers in crowdfunding. Mimeo. http://dx.doi.org/10.2139/ssrn.3259191.

Belleflamme, P. and Neysen, N. (2017). The rise and fall of Take Eat Easy, or why markets are not easy to take in the sharing economy. *Digiworld Economic Journal* 108, 59–76. https://en.idate.org/product/the-sharing-economy-myths-and-realities/.

Belleflamme, P. and Peitz M. (2018). Inside the engine room of digital platforms: Review, ratings, and recommendations. In Ganuza, J.J. and G. Llobet (Eds). *Economic analysis of the digital revolution.* FUNCAS Social and Economic Studies 5. Funcas: Madrid. https://blog.funcas.es/wp-content/uploads/2018/11/Economic-Analysis-of-the-Digital-Revolution.pdf.

Belleflamme, P. and Peitz M. (2021). *The economics of platforms: Concepts and strategy.* Cambridge: Cambridge University Press.

Botsman, R. (2017). *Who can you trust? How technology is rewriting the rules of human relationships.* New York: Public Affairs.

Cabral, L. and Hortaçsu, A. (2010). The dynamics of seller reputation: Evidence from eBay. *The Journal of Industrial Economics* 58, 54–78. https://doi.org/10.1111/j.1467-6451.2010.00405.x.

Choudary, S.W. (n.a.) Platform metrics: The core metric for platforms, networks and marketplaces. https://platformthinkinglabs.com/materials/platform-metrics-the-core-metric-for-platforms-networks-and-marketplaces/

Choudary, S.W. (2018) The architecture of digital labour platforms: Policy recommendations on platform design for worker well-being. *International Labour Office – Future of Work Research Paper series.* Geneva: ILO. https://www.ilo.org/wcmsp5/groups/public/---dgreports/---cabinet/documents/publication/wcms_630603.pdf.

Coolican, D'A., Barros, B., Jordan, J., Chen, A., Jin, L. and Murrow, L. (2021). *The a16z Marketplace 100–2022.* Menlo Park CA: Andreessen Horowitz. https://a16z.com/marketplace-100/.

Dudic, Z., Dudic, B., Gregus, M., Novackova, D., and Djakovic, I. (2020). The innovativeness and ssage of the Balanced Scorecard Model in SMEs. *Sustainability* 12(8): 3221. https://doi.org/10.3390/su12083221.

Eisape, D. (2020). Platform business models in sharing economy: Using a balanced scorecard approach to compare Airbnb, Marriott and Uber business model canvases. *Nordic Journal of Media Management* 3, 401–432. https://doi.org/10.5278/njmm.2597-0445.5842.

Eisenmann, T., Parker, G., and Van Alstyne, M. (2011). Platform envelopment. *Strategic Management Journal* 32, 1270–1285. https://doi.org/10.1002/smj.935.

Farronato, C., Fradkin, A., Larsen, B. and Brynjolfsson, E. (2020). Consumer protection in an online world: An analysis of occupational licensing. *National Bureau of Economic Research Working Paper Series*, No. 26601, April. https://www.nber.org/papers/w26601.

Gu, G. and Zhu, F. (2021). Trust and disintermediation: Evidence from an online freelance marketplace. *Management Science* 67, 794–807. https://doi.org/10.1287/mnsc.2020.3583.

Hagiu, A. and Rothman, S. (2006). Network effects aren't enough. *Harvard Business Review*, April, 64–71. https://hbr.org/2016/04/network-effects-arent-enough.

Hagiu, A. and J. Wright (2021a). Platform leakage I. *Platform Chronicles* (May 4). https://platformchronicles.substack.com/p/platform-leakage.

Hagiu, A. and J. Wright (2021b). Platform leakage II: The good, the bad, and the ugly. *Platform Chronicles* (May 18). https://platformchronicles.substack.com/p/platform-leakage-ii-the-good-the.

Jin, L. and Coolican, D'A. (2018). 16 ways to measure network effects. Future. https://future.com/how-to-measure-network-effects/.

Jordan, J., Jin, L., Coolican, D'A. and Chen, A. (2020). 13 metrics for marketplace companies. Future. https://future.com/marketplace-metrics/.

Joy, J. (2021). Ask an Alum. Love at first Swipe. *Columbia Magazine* (Spring/Summer), 47–48. https://magazine.columbia.edu/sites/default/files/2021-04/2021_Spring-Summer_PDF.pdf.

Kaplan, R.S. and Norton, D.P. (1992). The Balanced Scorecard. Measures that drive performance. *Harvard Business Review*, January/February, 71–79. https://hbr.org/1992/01/the-balanced-scorecard-measures-that-drive-performance-2.

Lehman, T., Terrier, C. and Lalive, R., (2022). Improving matching efficiency in two-sided markets using a mutual popularity ranking approach. Mimeo. https://drive.google.com/file/d/161wjZAyhgwZPKv3XfMrlyoiElmrTTDwu/view.

Liu, C. (2019). The platform and data strategy of Meituan. Hackernoon (February 12). https://hackernoon.com/the-platform-and-data-strategy-of-meituan-1dbo3d5cfffa.

Madani, D. (2022). Spotify removes Neil Young's music over Joe Rogan dispute. *NBC News* (January 26). https://www.nbcnews.com/pop-culture/pop-culture-news/spotify-agrees-remove-neil-youngs-music-joe-rogan-dispute-rcna13698.

Makkonen, J. (2022). 11 marketplace metrics you should be tracking to measure your success. Sharetribe. https://www.sharetribe.com/academy/measure-your-success-key-marketplace-metrics/.

Morgan, B. (2018). How Amazon has reorganized around artificial intelligence and machine learning. *Forbes* (July 16). https://www.forbes.com/sites/blakemorgan/2018/07/16/how-amazon-has-re-organized-around-artificial-intelligence-and-machine-learning/?sh=4a96db2f7361.

Porter, J. (2020). Uber to offer boat rides in London as new commuter service. *The Verge* (July 8) https://www.theverge.com/2020/7/8/21317224/uber-commuter-boat-thames-clipper-london-riverboat-service.

Rachitsky, L. (2020). Twitter tread @leenysan, 25 June 2020.

Rakuten.Today (2016). Speeding up C2C: Image recognition making e-commerce easier. (August 23). https://rakuten.today/blog/image-recognition-making-e-commerce-easier.html.

Resnick, P., Zeckhauser, R. and Swanson, J. (2006). The value of reputation on eBay: A controlled experiment. *Experimental Economics* 9, 79–101. https://doi.org/10.1007/s10683-006-4309-2.

Roth, E. (2022). Uber Eats brings bill splitting to deliveries. *The Verge* (March 9). https://www.theverge.com/2022/3/9/22969561/uber-eats-bill-splitting-deliveries-takeout.

Zhu, F. (2019). Friends or foes? Examining platform owners' entry into complementors' spaces. *Journal of Economic & Management Strategy* 28, 23–28. https://doi.org/10.1111/jems.12303.

Zhu, F. and M. Iansiti (2019). Why some platforms thrive and others don't. *Harvard Business Review* 97(1), 118–125. https://hbr.org/2019/01/why-some-platforms-thrive-and-others-dont.

INDEX

Note: Page numbers in **bold** refer to figures.

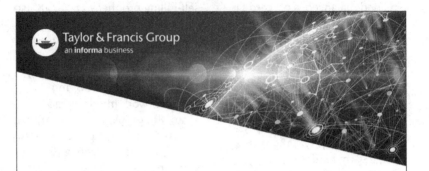

Printed in the United States
by Baker & Taylor Publisher Services